STEERING FROM THE CENTRE:
STRENGTHENING POLITICAL CONTROL IN WESTERN
DEMOCRACIES

Governments face new challenges in an era marked by globalization, shifting economic and national security policies, pervasive electronic media, and policy reform. *Steering from the Centre* details how chief executives in ten Western democracies have responded to governance challenges in the wake of reform ideas, such as the New Public Management, that stress deregulation and decentralization.

This volume analyses the extent to which the centre of government can retain political and administrative control when delivery of public services is increasingly done through networks, contacts, partnerships, and a host of other devolved arrangements. International in scope, *Steering from the Centre* covers the experiences of diverse countries, including the United States, Canada, Britain, Australia, Germany, Italy, and France, and examines how various centralization/decentralization strategies have played out in these differing national and institutional contexts.

CARL DAHLSTRÖM is an associate professor in the Department of Political Science at the University of Gothenburg.

B. GUY PETERS is the Maurice Falk Professor of American Government in the Department of Political Science at the University of Pittsburgh.

JON PIERRE is a professor in the Department of Political Science at the University of Gothenburg.

EDITED BY CARL DAHLSTRÖM,
B. GUY PETERS, AND JON PIERRE

Steering from the Centre

Strengthening Political Control in Western Democracies

UNIVERSITY OF TORONTO PRESS
Toronto Buffalo London

© University of Toronto Press 2011
Toronto Buffalo London
www.utppublishing.com
Printed in Canada

ISBN 978-1-4426-4148-8 (cloth)
ISBN 978-1-4426-1069-9 (paper)

Printed on acid-free, 100% post-consumer recycled paper with vegetable-based inks.

Library and Archives Canada Cataloguing in Publication

Steering from the centre : strengthening political control in Western democracies / edited by Carl Dahlström, B. Guy Peters, and Jon Pierre.

Includes bibliographical references.
ISBN 978-1-4426-4148-8 (bound). – ISBN 978-1-4426-1069-9 (pbk.)

1. Public administration.   I. Dahlström, Carl   II. Peters, B. Guy
III. Pierre, Jon

JF1351.S76 2011   351   C2011-904459-5

University of Toronto Press acknowledges the financial assistance to its publishing program of the Canada Council for the Arts and the Ontario Arts Council.

 Canada Council   Conseil des Arts
for the Arts   du Canada

 ONTARIO ARTS COUNCIL
CONSEIL DES ARTS DE L'ONTARIO

University of Toronto Press acknowledges the financial support of the Government of Canada through the Canada Book Fund for its publishing activities.

Contents

Figures and Tables   vii

Preface   ix

PART ONE: INTRODUCTION

1 Steering from the Centre: Strengthening Political Control in Western Democracies   3

CARL DAHLSTRÖM, B. GUY PETERS, AND JON PIERRE

PART TWO: CONTINENTAL EUROPE

2 Steering from the Centre in France in the 2000s: When Reorganizations Meet Politicization   27

PHILIPPE BEZES AND PATRICK LE LIDEC

3 Steering from the German Centre: More Policy Coordination and Fewer Policy Initiatives   54

JULIA FLEISCHER

4 The Core Executive in Italy: A More Visible Skipper, but Still Little Steering   80

FRANCESCO STOLFI

PART THREE: ANGLO-AMERICAN DEMOCRACIES

5 Central Steering in Australia   99

JOHN HALLIGAN

6 Governing from the Centre(s): Governance Challenges in the United States 123

B. GUY PETERS

7 Steering from the Centre: The Canadian Way 147

DONALD J. SAVOIE

8 The Paradoxes of Britain's Strong Centre: Delegating Decisions and Reclaiming Control 166

MARTIN SMITH

PART FOUR: SCANDINAVIA

9 Steering the Swedish State: Politicization as a Coordination Strategy 193

CARL DAHLSTRÖM AND JON PIERRE

10 Steering from the Centre in Denmark 212

LOTTE JENSEN

11 Towards Stronger Political Steering: Program Management Reform in the Finnish Government 241

SIRPA KEKKONEN AND TAPIO RAUNIO

PART FIVE: CONCLUSION

12 Steering Strategies in Western Democracies 263

CARL DAHLSTRÖM, B. GUY PETERS, AND JON PIERRE

Contributors 277

Figures and Tables

Figures

3.1 Previous position of permanent state secretaries in German Federal ministries, 1949–2009   63

8.1 The Prime Minister's Delivery Unit   177

9.1 Political appointees in the Swedish Government Offices 1981–2008, including and excluding the Ministry for Foreign Affairs   201

9.2 Political advisers in the Ministry of Finance, the Ministry of Defence, and the Prime Minister's Office, 1981–1999   207

Tables

5.1 Steering Strategies   102

7.1 Number of Staff in Central Agencies, 1970 and 2005, Government of Canada   155

8.1 Priorities of Prime Minister's Delivery Unit   176

9.1 Employees in the Swedish Government Offices, 1981–2008   195

10.1 Centrifugal and Centripetal Mechanisms   218

10.2 Trends in Central Government Strategies after 2000   222

11.1 Finnish Governments, 1983–2009   246

Preface

This book grew out of a conference organized by REKO, a research program on the Swedish central government office. The program is co-chaired by Bengt Jacobsson (Södertörn University), Jon Pierre (University of Gothenburg), and Rune Premfors (SCORE and Stockholm University). The core research question in the program is to what extent and how the central government office provides governance in a political system characterized by executive autonomy, complex international contingencies, and social complexity. Needless to say, these features are typical not just to Sweden but for most other countries as well, hence the idea to organize an international conference devoted to the question of the centrality of government in contemporary governance.

The sponsor of the research program, the Riksbankens Jubileumsfond, generously offered additional funding for the conference.

We want to thank the contributors to the volume for their involvement in this project. Also, Daniel Quinlan at the University of Toronto Press has throughout been very supportive of the book project. Two anonymous reviewers have helped the editors and contributors produce a more coherent volume.

Gothenburg and Pittsburgh,
Carl Dahlström
B. Guy Peters
Jon Pierre

PART ONE

Introduction

1 Steering from the Centre: Strengthening Political Control in Western Democracies

CARL DAHLSTRÖM, B. GUY PETERS, and JON PIERRE

Governing is one of the oldest activities of the human race but it has perhaps never been more difficult or complex. The societies have themselves become more complex, and at the same time citizens are more resistant to the potential role of the state in the economy and society in addressing the problems (Norris 2000; Wagner, Dufour, and Schneider 2003). In addition, many political elites have come to favour several sets of ideas that bring traditional forms of governing into question – most notably the New Public Management (Christensen and Laegreid 2007) that has stressed making public management more similar to private sector management, Other reformers have advocated greater use of social actors through networks (Sørenson and Torfing 2007) to supplement or replace action through public bureaucracies. Thus, despite the successes of the public sector in providing economic growth and human security in many societies, the continued efficacy of a strong public sector has become questioned by both political elites and the general public.

The public sector has responded to the changes in their environment, and changes in ideas about governing, with a variety of structural and procedural mechanisms. Many of these changes have altered the role of the centre of government in the process of governing. This decentring (Peters 2008) of the public sector has involved a wide variety of instruments designed to improve governing, although most of these have had the effect of reducing the control of political leaders, and even lessening the role of senior public servants in governing. Decentralization and devolution of powers have been the fundamental strategies of this style of governing. In particular, the responses by the public sectors of the advanced democracies have involved not only changes in their own styles of governing, but also reforms that involve a range of private sector action.

This decentring of governance is occurring at the same time that there are numerous discussions about the 'presidentialization' of parliamentary regimes, and the 'imperial' nature of many presidential systems (Poguntke and Webb 2005; Bäck 2007; Aberbach 2005). On the one hand, presidents and prime ministers appear to have become ever more powerful, at least within their own cabinets and their parliaments, but at the same time they and their ministers appear to have declining control over the actual making and implementation of public policy. The chapters in this book (see especially those by Savoie and Fleischer) examine this apparent contradiction and the dynamics of change in the centre of government.

Reforms within Government

The changes occurring within the public sector have involved a variety of means of delegating responsibility for policy-making and implementation from political officials to other actors within government. One of the most common of these 'decentring' reforms has been to devolve power to autonomous and quasi-autonomous agencies to deliver services that once would have been provided by ministerial bureaucracies (Pollitt and Talbot 2004). Although the exact nature of the governance structures of these organizations does differ, their general impact is to reduce the capacity of the centre of government to control the execution of many aspects of policy, and in some instances also policy-making.

We will be discussing the capacity of the centre of government to exercise control over the remainder of government. By capacity we mean that the officials in question have the combination of resources – including authority – to influence the behaviour of other actors. Having those resources does not mean that those in the centre will necessarily be effective in imposing their will on others, given that the other actors also have resources (see Fleischer in this volume) but it does mean that they do have some opportunity for that control.

At more of an extreme, there has also been some tendency to delegate control over important policy areas to responsible public organizations such as central banks and some highly insulated regulatory organizations. The logic of these changes has been to allow these organizations to make 'credible commitments' (North 1991) to market actors that might not be possible if these functions were retained in the control of the centre. That said, the degree of control over these autonomous institutions that can be exercised by political leaders, and therefore to some extent the degree of democracy, is also limited (Vibert 2007).

Central governments have also tended to off-load a number of responsibilities onto subnational governments. Although this decentralization is generally considered to be a political virtue, it may also reduce the steering capacity of the centre. In federal systems the decentralization of public activities is ingrained into the constitutional structure, as is true to some extent in the Nordic countries, but decentralization has become more common in regimes that had been more strictly unitary. These changes can be justified in democratic terms and in terms of improved policy performance, but they also may reduce the need of central government to attempt to control everything. That load-shedding may ease the work of central government but it may also reduce the capacity for central steering. There is a case to be made for the perspective that decentralization requires a strong centre (Pierre and Peters 2000), so that any shedding of responsibility needs to be done within the context of clear priorities and direction from the centre.

Involving Actors outside Government

The range of reforms in the public sector that involve actors outside the public sector has been more extensive. Most of these, consistent with the market ethos of NPM (Peters 2001), have involved market actors, although some have involved social actors such as non-governmental organizations (NGOs). Indeed, one of the most common responses to governance problems has been to shed them entirely and to give them to the private sector through privatization and deregulation. In all these formats for change, however, the basic idea behind the reforms has been, often quite explicitly, to allow other actors to complement or supplant the decisions of political actors. The assumptions have generally been that this will make the public sector more efficient and in some cases that these changes will make the public sector more democratic.

Contracts, partnerships, franchising, and private financial arrangements have been principal examples of using market-based mechanisms to achieve public purposes. All of these methods involve using private sector actors and the logic of the market to try to make public sector programs more like the private sector. These instruments also involve reducing the capacity of political actors to control the choices being made. Contracts and franchising that tend to involve specifying performance on the part of the private actors but even those ex ante controls are less likely to provide adequate control than the more hierarchical methods associated with conventional public management. Likewise, partnerships tend to provide the private sector actor a somewhat unfair advantage in that the values of the public sector have been transformed to be more like those of markets so that there may be fewer protections for public values (Pierre and Peters 2010).

For policy instruments that involve non-market actors there are equal, or perhaps even greater, problems in exercising political control. The 'New Governance' (Salamon 2001) in which the public sector uses a variety of negotiated means of implementing policy has been widely lauded as a means of overcoming the hierarchical nature of governing, and also as a means of involving a wider range of the public in making policy. In addition, there are some claims that networks and other social instruments can be more efficient that the conventional bureaucratic instruments of government (but see Olsen 2008). Whether efficient or not, these instruments do reduce the capacity of other public sector actors, notably the political centre, to exert control. By using these negotiated 'soft law' instruments public sector actors have in essence ceded the right to make decisions.

Thus, the reform of the public sector over the past several decades has been associated with the declining capacity of actors at the centre of government – presidents, prime ministers, ministers, and senior public servants – to control the actions of their own governments (Painter and Pierre 2005). Some of this diminution of the role of political officials has been intentional, given that much of the logic of the NPM has been that managers are more capable of running the state better than can the political leaders. But some of the erosion of the 'primacy of politics' has been unintended, and the product of simple adherence to what had become the 'flavour of the month' in reforming the public sector.

The Consequences of Decentring

Several of the more obvious consequences of decentring the public sector have already been mentioned or implied. Moving much of the activity of making and implementing public policy out of the direct control of political officials has had both political and policy effects. Further, the reduction of central control over policy and implementation has tended to lessen the sense of a common pattern of governance for societies in favor of a more segmented style of approaching public problems.

The reforms of the public sector will affect decision-making, although those effects may be difficult to predict. On the one hand, moving decisions out of the political arena can make decisions too easy, so that choices may be made without adequate deliberation. On the other hand, involving multiple actors who may have competing values and interests may create deadlock and produce some of the conditions described by Scharpf (1988) when discussing difficulties in making decisions in multiactor situations. This is not to say that the decision-making in the public sector has been ideal – far from it – but it does argue for considering the consequences of reform.

In addition to undermining the primacy of politics, there are several more specific impacts on governing. One of these is reduced coordination and coherence in the public sector. One function, among many, of cabinets and a chief executive in government is to force various policy areas together, and to require choosing priorities from among the many contending options (Bouckaert, Ormond, and Peters 2000). When much of the action of governing is moved away from these central institutions, and, further, when the actors involved are empowered to make their own decisions, then the capacity to coordinate is reduced significantly (see Verhoest, Bouckaert, and Peters 2010).

Finally, and most importantly, the decentring of government tends to reduce democratic controls and the accountability of the public sector for its actions. In the first place the connection between voting and policy choice that is central to democracy is weakened when actors who do not have that democratic legitimacy make policy decisions. Richard Rose pointed out some years ago that the link between voting and policy choice is fragile, but the various reforms already mentioned make this linkage even more tenuous.

There are a number of instruments for accountability, but the traditional focus has been on the role of prime ministers, ministers, and other political leaders in governing, and finding the means to hold them to account for their actions and the actions of their governments (Day and Klein 1987; Mulgan 2000). With much of the administrative activity of governing, and a good deal of the policy-making, farmed out to actors who are not subject to the conventional forms of accountability, the capacity of the public to control these activities is diminished. The difficult part for many politicians, however, is that the press and the public will not absolve them of responsibility even though they have few means of influencing the policy decisions.

In summary, the transformation of governing has tended to reduce the effectiveness of central actors in government, even if those actors appear to be more politically powerful. These contradictory changes have produced some benefits through increased efficiency of some forms of service delivery, but at the same time have created significant problems of accountability and control. These difficulties have, in turn, created a variety of reactions from governments and from other social actors. We will now describe three types of reactions from governments, which we call 'Letting Go,' 'Holding On,' and 'Restoring the Centre.'

Letting Go

To some extent the simplest government reaction has been to continue devolving power and control from the core of government to operative structures, partnerships, subnational governments, and transnational institutions. This strategy was related to a changing role of the state more broadly; the ideology in this respect during the 1980s ands 1990s was that the state should not be the key provider of services, nor should it exercise command and control over other societal actors. Instead, its chief role should be that of an enabler and coordinator (Pierre and Peters 2000; Page and Wright 2007). Also, as we will argue, this development was only partially a coherent strategy of institutional reform; it was also an adaptation to international integration. These reforms were believed to be adequate measures in a situation where international integration was continuously deepening, where fiscal constraints (either as result of an economic reality or as a political conviction) prevented central government from steering subnational government by tax incentives and grants, and where there was growing belief that public administration could be modernized by adopting market-like features such as separating policy from operations. The previous, centralized model was simply seen as obsolete and not geared to tackle contemporary problems. Lack of coordination was probably not seen as a potential consequence of these changes; instead, by clarifying different roles (policy-making, operations, purchaser, provider, and so on) in the system there were also believed to be clearer relationships among those roles.

The philosophy of relaxing central control as a strategy to cope with increasing international embeddedness and public service inefficiencies and rigidities has not followed a coherent reform strategy but more been an incremental and rather poorly coordinated strategy. The overall objective has been to allow for greater institutional autonomy, managerialism, and collaborative strategies of policy implementation. This reform illustrates the shift towards an enabling state. An additional aspect of the reform is that it sought to lower the threshold between the public and private sectors and to define collective interests in dialogue with policy targets. It was clearly a matter of 'letting go' – to diffuse political authority – although the advocates of reform maintained that this 'reinvention' was a way of adapting government to organizational models practised elsewhere in society in the late twentieth century. Society was becoming increasingly complex, and centralized government was no longer the appropriate organizational model to steer society. By allowing for transnational institutions such as the European Union (EU) or the World Trade Organization (WTO) to address regional and global issues; hiving off segments of public service production to the market; granting regions and local government more autonomy; and giving managers operative control, central government could focus on its core issues.

It should be noted that sometimes a strategy of relaxing central control was recognition of an already ongoing process rather than a new policy course being set. In several countries, regions and sometimes even individual cities had embarked on a strategy of exploring international networks or extracting resources from transnational institutions like the EU, partly to become more autonomous in relationship to central government. Also, in some national contexts, partnerships or 'social contracts' with strategic actors in the external environment of the state (including policy targets) had been used for a considerable time. That said, the introduction of autonomous agencies in the Anglo-American countries signaled a new direction, as did the new models of public service delivery either in concert with for-profit organizations or through contracting out or privatization.

Enabling and coordination, however, are not synonymous with a passive role for the state. The enabling state strategy includes deregulation and the restructuring of services, tasks that have proven more arduous and challenging than might have been expected. While the policy targets may applaud replacing coercive policy instruments with more subtle measures, such change does not necessarily mean less work for politicians or senior civil servants in the political centre. Also, deregulation has proven to be a complex political project, where the abolition of rules in some cases has been followed by reregulation as the downsides of deregulation surfaced.

The strategy of displacing political authority downwards, upwards, and outwards thus had a significant impact on the political centre, although less so in terms of organizational challenges than theory would predict. More importantly, however, it deprived the system of leadership and coordination. Political leadership has two components, political control and organizational leadership, and in hindsight it seems as if the reform that abolished the former also did away with the latter. Thus, although the reform initially served to depoliticize government it also created a leadership deficit, not so much in terms of partisan control over the public bureaucracy as in terms of organizational leadership and coordination exercised by the political centre. Managers could increase the efficiency of their organizations but lacked the overview to ensure coordination among organizations. Politicians initially engaged in defining long-term goals for departments and agencies and other devolved institutions but once that was done they had few levers to use to steer the system.

Partly as a result of this weakening leadership, elected politicians in several western democracies during the late 1990s and early 2000s sought to regain some of their previous control over the public administration and the civil service (Light 1995; Peters and Pierre 2001, 2004). True, we cannot assess to what extent this reassertion of political control was driven by a perceived need to increase leadership or political/ ideological control or to what extent it merely reflected a frustration among the political elite with a loss of power in the system. What does seem clear, however, is that the 'letting go' strategy coupled with NPM reform did not decrease but rather increased the need for coordination – which could only be exercised by the centre and which required some reaffirmation of leadership.

Where does all this leave the political and administrative centre of the system? We can see three sets of issues that warrant further investigation. In retrospect, it is easy to criticize the architects of reform for underestimating the problems that lie in the coordination of the state. Coordination of policy and administration is arguably the biggest challenge for any contemporary government. Recent administrative reform such as agencification, decentralization, and the inclusion of the market in public service delivery has had a centrifugal effect on the system of government. There have been distinct gains from this reform in terms of efficiency and cost reduction but it has left the political centre with insufficient levers to coordinate the system. At the end of the day, the gains generated by the reform could be lost in terms of a lack of coordination, with all that entails in terms of overlapping competencies, transaction costs within the public service, and organizational inefficiency.

Second, coordination and unitary command (if we resort to the vernacular of ancient administrative theory) are prerequisites for accountability. The multilevel model of governance, in which the modern state finds itself, is in some ways detrimental to democratic accountability because it separates authority from responsibility and contextualizes political influence. Alternative mechanisms of accountability, for example, users' boards and customer choice, may play a role but at a very different level than central government. Thus, institutional architects seem to wrestle with how to balance central political and administrative control, which is desirable from a democratic point of view, against devolution, which provides more efficiency and bang for the buck.

Third, and finally, the extent to which the letting-go strategy is appropriate depends on the overarching nature of the political projects that modern governments pursue. Much of the twentieth century saw universal political projects such as the consolidation of representative democracy and social welfare dominate the political agenda in most developed countries. Those kinds of reform require a strong political centre capable of redistributing resources and authority among different social groups, sometimes also among different regions of the country (Weaver and Rockman 1993). The political agenda of the twenty-first century provides a more mixed picture. On the one hand, there are 'big issues' like environmental protection, global warming and terrorism that call for concerted, international action; on the other there are issues closer to home which require local autonomy. Thus, despite the need for coordination there are today strong forces pulling authority upward and downward, away from the political centre.

Holding On

As noted in the previous sections it is clear that the reorganization of the public sector has had impact on the functioning of the state and on the public service (Peters and Pierre 2001; Pollitt and Bouckaert 2004). We have already described how the central government handled new challenges either by creating new agencies, or by involving other actors in so-called public-private partnerships, or other similar arrangements. This development has effects also on how the central government is organized, as involvement by new and different actors calls for more coordination from the centre. There are also signs of a move back to more control from the centre of government (Christensen and Laegreid 2007; Peters 2008). Probably most importantly, the involvement of new, often non-state, actors creates pressure on the centre to deliver a 'tight coordination,' which in turn pushes for more political control of the centre.

Paul Light has described how a need for 'tight coordination' created incentives for political control of the administration in the United States in the 1930s, and laid the ground for the subsequent 'thickening of government' (Light 1995). Politicians seemed to need a politically trustworthy core of personnel to be able to deliver the coordination. The move back to the centre might create the same need for political controls. What we have seen in the past decades might be parts of a similar process in other countries, but this time as unintended consequences of public sector reforms.

There are, of course, a number of means for strengthening the political control of the political and administrative centre of government. But one of the most powerful strategies is to take political control of important recruitments into the public sector. It is powerful because it secures loyalty among centrally placed bureaucrats, and thereby increases political control over policy and implementation (Peters and Pierre 2004). During the same period as public sector reforms have been implemented, we have also seen a growing politicization of the central political administration in many countries.

The trend towards higher numbers of political appointees in the executive has been noted by numerous observers (Peters and Pierre 2004; Poguntke and Webb 2005). The number of political advisers and other politically appointed staff in the central government seems to have grown in several mature democracies (Matheson et al. 2007; SIGMA 2007), not only in countries with the executive support organized according to what Peters (1997) calls the Germanic and the Napoleonic administrative tradition, but also in countries from the Anglo-Saxon administrative tradition, and in the Scandinavian countries, both with traditionally few political appointees (Campbell and Wilson 1995; Eichbaum and Shaw 2007; Pierre 2004).

However, there are probably important differences in how governments have acted to secure coordination from the centre, and analysing this development is an important task for this volume. To describe the landscape, we will continue by discussing the level of politicization of the centre in different administrative traditions, and then turn to the development over time. As we will point out below, these traditions do have internal variations but they also have a great deal in common across the cases; this is a useful means of understanding the cases comparatively.

We will use the four public administration traditions just mentioned – the Napoleonic, the Germanic, the Anglo-Saxon, and the Scandinavian – to give a very broad description of the politicization of the centre (Peters 1997; Painter and Peters 2010). Generally, countries with a Napoleonic administrative tradition have the highest degree of politicization of the centre, and have had for a long time (Dahlström 2009; SIGMA 2007). This is explained by an institutional difference between the Napoleonic countries and most other countries regarding the structure of government offices. In the Napoleonic countries the ministers have private offices, so-called *cabinets ministériels*, where most appointees are politically appointed (Cassese 1999; Page and Wright 1999; Rouban 1999, 2004; Suleiman 1975). This organizational characteristic of the summit provides a politically appointed core available for the ministers (Peters, Rhodes, and Wright 2000).

In most of the Germanic countries there is nothing like the 'cabinets ministériels,' but several elite positions in the core are still politically appointed. In Germany there is, for example, the institution of 'politically appointed civil servant,' which allows the ministers to influence the highest ranks in the bureaucracy, and similar arrangements can be found in Austria (Schröter 2001; Liegl and Müller 1999; Fleischer, this volume).

The Anglo-Saxon group is probably the one with the largest variation. Here we find both countries with very low levels of politicization, as the United Kingdom, and countries with very high levels of politicization, such as the United States and to some extent also Australia (see Peters, Halligan, and Savoie in this volume). Politically appointed officials are well-known parts of the Executive Branch in the United States and in the government offices in Australia. In the United States it is commonly explained by the 'spoils system' and in Australia by a system with large private staffs for the ministers (Maley 2002; Light 1995; Rockman 2000; Tiernan 2007; Weller 2000). Although there are manifestly different levels of politicization within this tradition, the concept of a neutral civil service is important in all countries; the difference is primarily in the level in the system at which that neutrality is expected to begin.

Seen as a group, the Scandinavian countries are the ones with the least politicized centre (together with some countries from the Anglo-

Saxon tradition, namely, New Zealand, the United Kingdom, and Ireland). This is especially true in Denmark, where one special adviser is the only political appointee in the ministries (Grønnegaard Christensen 2006). In contrast to Denmark, Sweden has politically appointed officials in the government offices comparable to those in the Germanic countries and is the country within the Scandinavian group with the most politicized centre (Matheson et al. 2007; Premfors and Sundström 2007; Dahlström and Pierre, this volume).

As we mentioned in the introduction to this section, there is a general expectation in the literature for increasing numbers of political appointees over time (see, e.g., SIGMA 2007). This is probably generally true, but we believe that it is important also to highlight signs of different trends in countries belonging to different administrative traditions. These differences may represent different reactions to the common pressures identified, or alternatively a different set of environmental changes impinging on the structures and actors of the public sector.

There are signs that the trend towards higher numbers of political appointees is not equally strong in all administrative regimes, and in the countries belonging to the Napoleonic tradition we find the most important exceptions from the general trend. France saw its highest numbers of political appointees in the early to mid-1980s, after the election of 1981, and after that the number has either been stable or decreased (Rouban 2004). The development in Italy was similar with a peak in the 1980s, and it seems to have decreased until the late 1990s. Since the early 2000s, however, there are signs of another increase (Cassese 1999; Matheson et al. 2007). In Belgium the trend is not clear. The number of political appointees increased early in the period. As Guido Dierickx (2004) notes, this development reached its peak in the late 1980s when 'there was a widespread feeling among both SCS [senior civil service] and many politicians that politicization had gone to far' (Dierickx 2004: 194). During the 1990s and 2000s several steps were taken in order to modernize the government, reduce the influence of political appointees, and dismantle the ministerial cabinets. The reforms – especially the Copernicus plan in the late 1990s and early 2000s – aimed at strengthening the role of the administration in producing policy advice, but as Marleen Brans, Christophe Pelgrims, and Dieter Hoet observed, 'ministers clearly reinvented ministerial cabinets,' which created a backlash (Brans, Pelgrims, and Hoet 2006: 46; Pelgrims and Brans 2006).

The countries belonging to the Anglo-Saxon, Germanic, and Scandinavian administrative traditions are generally moving towards more political appointees in the summit. But there are also differences among these three groups in how strong the trend is. The Scandinavian group is most obviously moving towards more politically appointed officials. It is, however, also important to note that the differentiation within the Scandinavian group increases over time. The four countries have drawn apart, with Sweden as the most and Denmark as the least politicized country. Among all Western countries, Denmark is one of those with the lowest proportion of political appointees, while Sweden ends up on somewhere in the middle. In the 1970s Denmark and Sweden were almost at the same levels (Dahlström 2009; Matheson et al. 2007).

We will sum up this section by considering the development over time of the politicization of the centre in Western democracies more generally. It is especially important to note one difference between the 1970s and the end of the 2000s. Today it is very uncommon to see fewer than two political appointees per minister. The only example we know of is Denmark. But three decades ago there were seven countries below this level. Besides Denmark we could also find New Zealand, Norway, Ireland, the United Kingdom, and Sweden in the 1970s. This started to change in the 1980s and continued through the 1990s. It seems to be here, in the countries that started with the lowest levels of political appointees in the 1970s that much of the increase in political appointments has happened. As we have already discussed countries with the highest levels of politicization, such as France and Italy, the trend is flat or even decreasing, while countries in the middle, such as Germany and the Netherlands, seem to be stable. What we have seen from the 1970s and onwards is therefore not so much an explosion in politicization of the centre as a qualitative shift. Governments today do not seem to be able to deliver a 'tight coordination' without a cadre of political appointees in government offices, something that governments in all Scandinavian countries and almost all Westminster countries thought unnecessary thirty years ago.

Restoring the Centre

The politicization of government associated with the 'Holding On' strategy represents one means of giving the core executive in government more control, but it is in many ways a clumsy and rather narrow approach. Politicization may permit some control over programs but does little to help the centre make and implement more comprehensive strategies for governing. The third response to the decentring of government, which will be the primary focus of the following chapters, involves building greater coordination and strategic capacity for presidents and prime ministers and using that capacity for controlling the remainder of the public sector.

The basic idea of these reforms in the centre is to restore 'the primacy of politics' in governments that may have had more policy-making devolve to other actors inside and outside of the public sector. This is not just a reflection of the megalomania of some political leaders. It also reflects the basic democratic principle that elected leaders should be the crucial force in shaping public policies. As already noted, much of the reform of democratic states has tended to violate that basic principle by giving considerable autonomy to 'managers' in the public service (Suleiman 2003), and discussion of the more recent round of reforms in the national chapters will detail the various strategies used.

The countries included in this book have undertaken a variety of programs to attempt to restore the steering capacity of the centre of government. Many of these have been related to the perception of 'presidentialization' of parliamentary systems mentioned above, given that the personal staffs of chief executives in government have been increasing in size and influence. In addition to simply adding numbers, however, presidents and prime ministers have been instituting procedures for establishing central priorities and then enforcing them throughout the political system.

The most obvious strategy for enhancing central steering capacity has been building up larger offices such as the Bundeskanzleramt in Germany or the Cabinet Office in the United Kingdom. In almost all the cases in this volume there was some growth of these offices, although this did not necessarily produce greater capacity to direct policy choices. In Germany, for example, the power of the ministries to make policy was not affected greatly although the coordinating capacity in the centre was enhanced. Further, although this strategy tends to involve enlarging the organizations serving the chief executive, these offices may perform different tasks. Some may simply be enforcers for the executive, while others may build extensive analytical capacity, or focus on a few crucial policy issues for the executive.

Presidents and prime ministers have also developed procedures for imposing their priorities on the remainder of government. The Finnish government, for example, has created a program management system to identify the cross-cutting issues most important to the current coalition and then to encourage cooperation among the existing ministries. The United Kingdom and Australia and sought to 'join-up' government to allow for both greater central control and better program coordination. These procedures may also be somewhat informal, as when the style of governing in Canada switched to 'court politics,' placing more control in the hands of the Prime Minister.

Using financial instruments represents another set of procedures for providing central steering capacity. Budgets are always useful devices for establishing government priorities, and can also be used to promote policy coordination if the implications of one set of expenditures on other expenditures and programs are considered carefully. These methods depend on the minister of finance as much as the premier, but effective governance often depends on these two officials working together. (As Donald Savoie once said, you must be able to see no light between them for the central steering capacity to work.) These mechanisms seem to have been especially evident in the Napoleonic countries, as are shown in the French and Italian chapters.

Another set of contingencies, but also opportunities, for the political executive is associated with the media. The relative lack of interest among political observers to acknowledge the role of the media in contemporary governance is puzzling, given the weight that policymakers accord the media and their role both as communicators and as actors (see Crozier 2007; Hajer 2009; Schudson 1995, 2002). Political leaders today are very much aware of the influence that the media have in framing issues and monitoring the performance of the administration. As a result, political executives make strong efforts to control the flow of information to journalists. The Blair administration in Britain excelled in 'spinning' issues, thus ensuring that the media coverage of the government was consistent with message. As the chapters in this volume testify, controlling or containing the media is a cornerstone of the political strategy of almost all governments.

In summary, many presidents and prime ministers are attempting to find ways of restoring their capacity to govern from the centre. This may involve building or enlarging institutions, establishing procedures, or cooperating more closely with other key officials to manage the remainder of the public system. None of these methods is a guarantee, and the national chapters report different levels of success. These reforms represent just one more case of one round of change in the public sector producing the perceived need for other reforms, resulting in an almost never-ending cycle of change.

Choosing Strategies

We have detailed three major alternatives for coping with the challenges of devolved and decentralized governance. The several countries discussed in the national chapters have a rich repertoire within which to select their responses. As we have already discussed, there is a range of national responses. Many of these appear to reflect the path dependence so often noted in the behaviour of governments, with countries such as the United States and Germany that had extremely well developed central agencies serving the President elaborating those institutions still further. Likewise the relatively centralized government of France appears to have developed new instruments to reinforce that pattern of governing.

The more interesting responses have been those that represent significant departures from established patterns of behaviour. The politicization noted in the Scandinavian cases, for example, demonstrates the search for a means of control that lies outside established patterns. Likewise, the continuing increases of power within the central agencies in the United Kingdom began somewhat earlier, but there have been numerous innovations during the past several decades of coping with devolution of powers. Some of these changes in the national patterns represent genuine innovations while others represent learning from other countries, but it is clear that these established political systems continue to search for, and to try, new means of coping with the continuing challenges of governing.

Plan of the Book

This book addresses a fundamental problem in contemporary governing. Presidents and prime ministers are central actors in governing, but their place was devalued in a number of settings in response to reform ideas such as the New Public Management. Their governance resources differed prior to these reforms, they were affected differently by reforms, and governments have responded very differently. The chapters in this book detail how chief executives have responded to the governance challenges, and especially how they have developed institutional structures to support them in governing.

We have identified a set of challenges to contemporary systems of administration and public governance. We have also identified three broad strategies for addressing those challenges. This conjuncture of challenges and responses then naturally raises questions about the ways in which individual countries respond. Some of the answers, for example, administrative traditions, are implied in the discussion above, but there may be other political and administrative factors that influence the choices made by countries, or by particular sitting governments within the country. More specifically, the chapters in the book will focus on three problems and research question. The first question is descriptive, and aims at unfolding what strategies are used by the central government offices to meet a decentralized environment. The same challenges may exist in different settings but be perceived differently, and therefore acted on differently. The second question is explanatory: what explains cross-national variation in governments' objectives and strategies to regain control or increase coordination? The discussion above provides a general discussion of strategies, but individual countries have developed their own approaches.

The third question, finally, is focused on the policy effects of different strategies. To what extent have joined-up government and related strategies of coordination or politicization had an effect on public policy and policy design? Have governments maintained their basic patterns of response to governance problems or have they sought to find new mechanisms for governing. And are governments performing better, in administrative and democratic terms, as result of the recentring changes discussed?

The chapters cover a range of countries and a wide variety of experiences in rebuilding the centre of government. The countries examined represent four different administrative traditions. There are marked differences but there are also a number of similarities in the manner in which executives have been seeking to restore some governance capacity. The logic of recentring that has been common in the discussion of prime ministers has been evident in building these structures, but at the same time it is not entirely clear that the strong centre will always be capable of overcoming the strong centrifugal pressures that remain within contemporary government. The swing of the pendulum between centralization and decentralization in government continues, and these changes mark one more important set of transformations.

REFERENCES

Aberbach, J.D. (2005). The Political Significance of the George W. Bush Administration. *Social Policy and Administration* 39: 130–49.
Bäck, H. (2007). *Från statsminister til president?* Stockholm: Norstedts.

Bouckaert, G., D. Ormond, and B.G. Peters. (2000). *A Potential Governance Agenda for Finland*. Helsinki: Ministry of Finance.

Brans, M., C. Pelgrims, and D. Hoet. (2006). Comparative Observations on Tensions between Professional Policy Advice and Political Control in the Low Countries. *International Review of Administrative Sciences* 72: 57–71.

Campbell, C., and G.K. Wilson. (1995). *The End of Whitehall*. Oxford: Blackwell.

Cassese, S. (1999). Italy's Senior Civil Service: An Ossified World. In E.C. Page and V. Wright (eds.), *Bureaucratic Elites in Western European States*. Oxford: Oxford University Press.

Christensen, T., and P. Lægreid (eds.). (2007). *Transcending New Public Management: The Transformation of Public Sector Reforms*. Aldershot: Ashgate.

Crozier, M. (2007). Recursive Governance: Contemporary Political Communication and Public Policy. *Political Communication* 24: 1–18.

Dahlström, C. (2009). *Political Appointments in 18 Democracies, 1975–2007*. QoG Working Paper Series 2009:18. Gothenburg: Quality of Government Institute.

Day, P., and R. Klein. (1987). *Accountabilities*. London: Tavistock.

Dierickx, G. (2004). Politicization in the Belgian Civil Service. In B.G. Peters and J. Pierre (eds.), *Politicization of the Civil service in Comparative Perspective*. London: Routledge.

Eichbaum, C., and R. Shaw. (2007). Ministerial Advisers, Politicization and the Retreat from Westminster: The Case of New Zealand. *Public Administration* 85: 609–40.

Grønnegaard Christensen, J. (2006). Ministers and Mandarins under Danish Parlamentarism. *International Journal of Public Administration* 29: 997–1019.

Hajer, M.A. (2009). *Authoritative Governance: Policy-Making in the Age of Mediatization*. Oxford: Oxford University Press.

Liegl, B. and W. Müller. (1999). Senior Officials in Austria: A First Mapping Exercise. In E.C. Page and V. Wright (eds.), *Bureaucratic Elites in Western European States*. Oxford: Oxford University Press.

Light, P. (1995). *Thickening Government: Federal Hierarchy and the Diffusion of Accountability*. Washington: Brookings Institution.

Maley, M. (2002). Australian Ministeral Advisers and the Royal Commission on Government Administration. *Australian Journal of Public Administration* 61: 103–7.

Matheson, A., B. Weber, N. Manning, and E. Arnould. (2007). *Study on the Political Involvment in Senior Staffing and on the Delineation of Responsibilities between Ministers and Senior Civil Servants*. OECD Working Paper on Public Governance 2007/6. Paris: OECD.

Mulgan, R. (2000). 'Accountability': An Ever-Expanding Concept? *Public Administration* 78: 555–73.

Norris, P. (2000). *Critical Citizens: Global Support for Democratic Government.* Oxford: Oxford University Press.

North, D. (1991). Institutions. *Journal of Economic Perspectives* 5: 97–112.

Olsen, J.P. (2008). The Ups and Downs of Bureaucratic Organizations. *Annual Review of Political Science* 11: 13–37.

Page, E.C., and V. Wright. (1999). Introduction. In E.C. Page and V. Wright (eds.), *Bureaucratic Elites in Western European States.* Oxford: Oxford University Press.

Page, E.C., and V. Wright (eds.). (2007). *The Changing Role of Senior Service in Europe.* Basingstoke: Palgrave Macmillan.

Painter, M., and B.G. Peters. (2010). *Administrative Traditions and Administrative Reforms.* Basingstoke: Palgrave.

Painter, M., and J. Pierre (eds.). (2005). *Challenges to State Policy Capacity: Global Trends and Comparative Perspectives.* Basingstoke: Palgrave.

Pelgrims, C., and M. Brans. (2006). An Institutional Perspective on Personal Advisors in Belgium: Political Actors and the Failure to Change an Institution during a Critical Juncture. Paper presented at the 14th NISPAcee Annual Conference, 11–13 May 2006, Ljubljana, Slovenia.

Peters, B.G. (1997). Policy Transfers between Governments: The Case of Administrative Reforms. *West European Politics* 20: 71–88.

– (2001). *The Future of Governing: Four Emerging Models,* 2nd ed. Lawrence: University Press of Kansas.

– (2008). The Two Futures of Public Administration. *Public Money and Management* 28: 195–6.

Peters, B.G., and J. Pierre. (2004). Introduction. In B.G. Peters and J. Pierre (eds.), *Politicization of the Civil Service in Comparative Perspective.* London: Routledge.

Peters, B.G., and J. Pierre (eds.). (2001). *Politicians, Bureaucrats and Administrative Reform.* London: Routledge.

Peters, B.G., and D. Savoie. (2000). Administering the Summit from a Canadian Perspective. In B.G. Peters, R.A.W. Rhodes, and V. Wright (eds.), *Administering the Summit: Administration of the Core Executive in Developed Countries.* London: Macmillan.

Peters, B.G., R.A.W. Rhodes, and V. Wright (eds.). (2000). *Administering the Summit: Administration of the Core Executive in Developed Countries.* London: Macmillan.

Pierre, J. (2004). Politicization of the Swedish Civil Service: A Necessary Evil – or Just Evil? In B.G. Peters and J. Pierre (eds.), *Politicization of the Civil Service in Comparative Perspective.* London: Routledge.

Pierre, J., and B.G. Peters. (2000). *Governance, Politics and the State.* Basingstoke: Palgrave.

– (2010). Public-Private Partnerships and the Democratic Deficit: Is Performance-Based Legitimacy the Answer? In Magdalena Bexell and Ulrika Mörth (eds.), *Democracy and Public-private Partnerships in Global Governance*. Basingstoke: Palgrave.

Poguntke, T., and P. Webb (eds.). (2005). *The Presidentialization of Politics: A Comparative Study of Modern Democracies*. Oxford: Oxford University Press.

Pollitt, C., and G. Bouckaert. (2004). *Public Management Reform: A Comparative Analysis*. Oxford: Oxford University Press.

Pollitt, C., and C. Talbot. (2004). *Unbundled Government: A Critical Analysis of the Global Trend to Agencies, Quangos and Contractualisation*. London: Routledge.

Premfors, R., and G. Sundström. (2007). *Regeringskansliet*. Malmo: Liber.

Rockman, B. (2000). Administering the Summit in the United States. In B.G. Peters, R.A.W. Rhodes, and V. Wright (eds.), *Administering the Summit: Administration of the Core Executive in Developed Countries*. London: Macmillan.

Rouban, L. (1999). The Senior Civil Service in France. In E.C. Page and V. Wright. (eds.), *Bureaucratic Elites in Western European States*. Oxford: Oxford University Press.

– (2004). Politicization of the Civil Service in France: From Structural to Strategic Politicization. In B.G. Peters and J. Pierre (eds.), *Politicization of the Civil Service in Comparative Perspective*. London: Routledge.

Salamon, L.M. (2001). Introduction: The New Governance. In L.M. Salamon (ed.), *Handbook of Policy Instruments*. New York: Oxford University Press.

Scharpf, F.W. (1988). The Joint Decision Trap: Lessons from German Federalism and European Integration. *Public Administration* 66: 239–78.

Schudson, M. (1995). *The Power of News*. Cambridge, MA: Harvard University Press.

– (2002). The News Media as Political Institutions. *Annual Review of Political Science* 5: 249–69.

Schröter, E. (2001). A Solid Rock in Rough Seas? Institutional Change and Continuity in the German Federal Bureaucracy. In B.G. Peters and J. Pierre (eds.), *Politicians, Bureaucrats and Administrative Reform*. London: Routledge.

SIGMA. (2007). *Political Advisors and Civil Servants in European Countries*. SIGMA Paper no. 38. Paris: OECD.

Suleiman, E.N. (1975). *Politics, Power and Bureaucracy in France*. Princeton: Princeton University Press.

– (2003). *Dismantling Democratic Government*. Princeton: Princeton University Press.

Sørenson E., and J. Torfing (eds.). (2007). *Theories of Democratic Network Governance*. Basingstoke: Palgrave.

Tiernan, A. (2007). *Power without Responsibility? Ministerial Staffers in Australian Governments from Whitlam to Howard.* Sidney: UNSW Press.

Verhoest, K., G. Bouckaert, and B.G. Peters. (2010). *The Coordination Of Public Sector Organizations.* Basingstoke: Palgrave.

Vibert, F. (2007). *The Rise of the Unelected: The New Separation of Powers.* Cambridge: Cambridge University Press.

Wagner, A.F., M. Dufour, and F. Schneider. (2003). *Satisfaction Not Guaranteed: Institutions and Satisfaction with Democracy.* CESifo Working Paper No. 910. Munich: CESifo Group.

Weaver, K.R., and B.A. Rockman (eds.). (1993). *Do Institutions Matter?* Washington, DC: Brookings Institution.

Weller, P. (2000). Administering the Summit: Australia. In B.G. Peters, R.A.W. Rhodes, and V. Wright (eds.), *Administering the Summit: Administration of the Core Executive in Developed Countries.* Basingstoke: Macmillian.

PART TWO

Continental Europe

2 Steering from the Centre in France in the 2000s: When Reorganizations Meet Politicization

PHILIPPE BEZES and PATRICK LE LIDEC

Over the past thirty years, there is no doubt that the French state has been affected by many major transformations, potentially sufficiently significant to have altered the forms of governing and specific modes of steering from the centre. Starting in the 1980s, major privatization and decentralization programs have been implemented and have generated dynamics 'decentring' government activity. As in other Western countries, new ideas drawn from New Public Management (performance management, contracts, public-private partnership, etc.) have been subjected to specific importation and interpretation processes, giving rise to administrative reform programs characterized by their gradual development (Bezes 2009). However, the content of these dynamics affecting the French administration, their extent and timescale, as well as the issues at stake and the factors that produce them remain quite specific. Issues of steering, of responsibility, of coordination, and of coherence in state activities depend on two elements. First, they depend on how reforms have affected existing processes and tools. Second, they depend on the historical structuring of the French political and administrative system and on the inherited forms of steering and coordination that have been developed over several decades. Crucial to understanding changes in steering capacities for the centre are questions about how far previous forms of regulation of the administrative system remain robust and/or effective within the new context, how they have adapted to the reforms being carried out, and how far they have been replaced by new ways of doing things. In other words, the new solutions observed in some states (massive use of politicized appointments, a more general strengthening of political control and organizational coordination mechanisms) may well not be deployed in the French context, for several reasons: because there are other 'effective' forms of coordination, because existing mechanisms 'suffice' to solve problems, because existing arrangements prevent the development of new working methods, or because those in power prefer to strengthen existing mechanisms instead of introducing new schemas. It is also possible for new solutions simply to be added, layered onto older coordination devices that are not re-evaluated or dismantled.

This chapter presents the French evolutions of steering in four stages. First, in a short historical section, it will review some characteristics of established methods of organization, steering, and coordination within the French state. Second, it will attempt to show the specific dynamics of decentring through decentralization that have affected the political and administrative system since the 1980s, by clarifying their forms and extent and their effects on steering and coordination. A third section examines the initiatives taken in France since the beginning of the 2000s to change methods of steering and coordination through managerial reforms and explicate its transformative limits. The last section considers the importance of politicization in the French context and shows how recent reorganizations under President Sarkozy have reinforced historical modes of steering through hierarchy and politicization.

Steering from the Centre in France: The Historical Legacies

The development of new forms of steering from the centre in the French context cannot be understood without briefly referring to the inherited modes of steering and coordination that have been institutionalised for several decades. As has been said above, solutions found in some states may not appear in France. Two main dynamics can be identified, referring to two contradictory forces: the first relies on the strength of the mechanisms mixing hierarchy and politicization; the second to the complexity of the mechanisms of coordination in a fragmented state.

On one hand, the steering of the French state resulted from a centuries-long process of centralization, very much strengthened during the Napoleonic period, around a very powerful national executive and powerful mechanisms for centralized steering, resting on a uniform and hierarchical administrative model, with the prefects as its cornerstone (Wright 1992; Hayward and Wright 2002). Historically, this steering mechanism has been simultaneously hierarchical (prefects had authority over central state personnel and over local government) and political (they have been appointed by the head of the executive and come under his sole authority). Although the Third (1875) and Fourth (1946) Republics considerably reduced the power of the executive, the twofold chain of command through hierarchy and politicization were still solid. Prefects remained the robust political 'driving belt' within all political regimes and the integrative force at the local level. Their role as state-appointed was crucial because they were initially the executive power in the *départements* (the geographical entities that replaced provinces after the French Revolution) and chose, directly or indirectly, the mayors in communes. The strength of this vertical organizational hierarchy constitutes the backbone of the French steering but should not, however, be exaggerated. As shown by major French scholars analysing the 1960s (Worms 1966; Grémion 1976; Crozier and Thoenig 1975) and more recently by Patrick Le Lidec for the Third and Fourth Republics (2001, 2006), the steering and coordination mechanisms also consisted of deep negotiations between the prefects and elected notables. Besides, from the 1930s onwards, an increasing number of actors pleaded for a return to a strong executive, capable of ensuring steering and coordination of ministerial activities through hierarchy and politicization. A first step was taken on 31 January 1935, with a decree to organize the administrative services of the Prime Minister's Office and grant them permanent status. However, not until 1958, with the fall of the Fourth Republic, did France again strengthen the executive structured around the President of the Republic (elected by direct universal suffrage from 1962 onwards) and the Prime Minister (François 1996; Pinon 2003). The strong executive and increasing politicization that came with it appeared as new for the period but as 'path-dependent' considered in the French historical context: not only as a way of steering and controlling administration but also of combating the centrifugal tendencies resulting from acute fragmentation of the state (see below).

The most important layer of this 'politicization' process has been found in recruitment to ministerial cabinets and in the full use of discretionary powers belonging to the President and the government to make appointments to the top positions (e.g., Rouban 2004). Appointments came to reflect both support for, and loyalty to, a minister as well as policy expertise. The development of tighter links between politicians and senior bureaucrats has been a major and growing trend since the 1970s, and brings the French administrative system closer to the Continental ideal-type of bureaucracy characterized by a 'politically involved' public service (Page 1992; Rouban 1995; Bezes and Le Lidec 2007). From this

point of view, the increasing number of political appointees in ministerial cabinets over the past forty years provides good evidence of their
permanent and growing use in steering and coordinating public policy.
The number has increased threefold: there were 262 people working
in ministerial cabinets at the beginning of the Fifth Republic, about
500 in the 1980s, reaching an approximate 700 in the 2000s. In 2001,
within the second Jospin government including 34 ministerial and state
secretaries portfolios, the number significantly rose to 584, then to 685
under the third Raffarin government (39 portfolios) in 2004, and to 664
people under the Villepin government in 2006 (for these figures, see
Duport et al. 2007), not counting unofficial appointments, which add a
further 15–25 per cent. Although the role played by ministerial cabinets
has been frequently denounced for its pernicious effects (interposing
between minister and ministerial departments, preventing ministerial
departments from maintaining direct relations with each other and rec-
onciling their points of view), they have undoubtedly fulfilled functions of control and coordination 'from the top.'

On the other hand, issues of coordination have always constituted a
long-standing structural problem linked to the political and administrative history of the French state, particularly since the Third Republic.
Since the 1875 Constitution, the supremacy of Parliament (Rousselier
1997) and the absence of a stable, hierarchical national executive in
the person of a Prime Minister reinforced centrifugal tendencies; the
office of Prime Minister was recreated only some time later, as no more
than 'a first among equals' and undertaking this coordinating function
only in addition to the ministerial functions that mostly occupied him.
This institutional legacy has given rise to a marked level of instability
of ministries, ministerial administration that has remained relatively
autonomous of political control, and a high level of fragmentation – all
of which have favoured developing deeply rooted ministerial cultures.
Thus, each ministry has its own traditions, its own entrance examina-
tions and, in cases where it employs a large number of personnel, local
units devolved across the national territory. Indeed, gradually, more
and more ministries established their own local units, without respect
to the traditional structures of the prefects' administration, which was
organized by *département*. The ministries created these new local units
of the state at different scales (interregional, regional, *département*, and
other levels), thus undermining the prefects' authority and their ability to integrate activities. That sector-based ministries chose to implant
themselves around the national territory in this way signifies their

distrust of the policy principles upheld by the prefects, as well as of a desire to short-circuit them (Le Lidec 2006). By the mid-twentieth century, the problem of compartmentalization and excessive fragmentation was already making itself felt: it was magnified by the way the French civil service was structured in a multitude of *corps* (cross-ministerial groupings of officials with the same conditions of service, each having its own particular methods of internal management and promotion), giving it the appearance of a Balkanized administration (Thoenig 1973; Dupuy and Thoenig 1985). In France, professional groups did operate within a framework of hierarchical controls and formal procedures, but these controls were never fully established. To a greater or lesser extent, many groups such as teachers, social workers, public works agents, or *grands corps* (Thoenig 1996) were able to exercise autonomy over the means and sometimes the ends of service provision. The French model is thus characterized by considerable fragmentation at the centre but by greater integration at local level through a local-level coordination mechanism, more or less activated depending on the period, in the person of the prefect. Interministerial coordination problems, then, were shaped by the long-term history of the French state. Although several 'soft' attempts to remedy them were implemented from the 1940s to the 1960s, these issues remained sharp.

To put it simply, the French administrative system historically combines two different and contradictory modes of steering and coordination, at the levels of policy formulation and implementation. At the policy formulation level, hierarchical steering mechanisms have proved quite efficient within ministries, while networks and political mechanisms have been ways of solving interministerial games. At the implementation level, purpose-based local units of ministries have been ruled through hierarchical modes of regulation within the ministry, challenging the geographically arranged and politically sensitive cross-ministry institution of the prefect. This means that local units of ministries have been constantly caught up in a double-bind relationship, in which they are subordinate both to their ministries and to the prefects.

The Dynamics of Decentralization and Its Effects on Steering

Issues of governance and steering from the centre were first strongly redefined in France in the 1980s and 1990s due to an ongoing process of decentralization. However, one has to distinguish two phases of decentralization, each of which had different effects on steering. The first wave in the early 1980s strongly challenged the historical and hierarchical mode of governance and resulted in the fragmentation of public policies and the weakening of the centre. By contrast, the second reform of the early 2000s came with simultaneous efforts to reshape the administrative state and reinforce its steering capacities.

Decentralization policies initiated in the early 1980s profoundly affected the centre's capacities for controlling public policy. From 1982 onwards, the principle of unfettered administration of local government – already enshrined in the 1958 Constitution – became a widespread reality, and devolution of power to local governments appeared as a rational strategy of the socialist party to maximize electoral support. The launching of the 1982 decentralization primarily resulted from the fact that the socialist party was mainly structured as a party of local representatives, due to its numerous successes at local elections and its repeated failures at presidential and legislative ballots in the 1960s and 1970s. This political change resulted in an institutional change, and where it did not disappear, the control of central administration and the prefects over local government became a great deal looser. The state's field services at the local level lost influence, functions, and financial resources, although they survived alongside stronger local and regional authorities. This profound, long-lasting weakening of the centre was especially visible for methods of financing local public policy (Le Lidec 2011). Until the end of the 1970s, the state had used standard-setting, tight control over local government borrowing, and massive subsidies to direct local government investment policies, but it then lost the financial instruments that had enabled it to direct local government policy. Specific-purpose subsidies from multiple ministries were abolished and earmarked grants practically disappeared; they were replaced by block grants, and this considerably weakened ministers and central administrations, significantly increasing local government autonomy. At the same time, the volume of local government spending increased as a share of overall public spending in France; and central government has yet been unable to counter this trend through norms and minimum quality standards for local public services. Local authority spending was 8 per cent of gross domestic product (GDP) in 1980, and rose to 11.3 per cent of GDP in 2008. Local authorities in 1978 were already responsible for 63 per cent of public investment, and increased their share to 70 per cent in 2005. The share of the state in public investment went down from 26 per cent in 1993 to 15 per cent in 2006, while the proportion of social security spending went up in parallel. These developments considerably diminished the central government's steering capacity, because local government expenditure (195.2 billion euros in 2008) represented two-thirds of the expenditure of the state.

Four levels of local government concurrently deliver state services in all areas of public policy, which results in a disordered, highly complex, fragmented picture. Since the early 1990s, the distribution of tasks between the state and the various organs of local government – which, from 1982 onwards was supposed to have been organized according to a logic of (relative) specialization through grouped areas of competence – has become a fiction. In fact, the provisions of the 'general clause' governing territorial competence authorize each level of local government to intervene in all areas, with a consequent proliferation of partnerships and co-financing arrangements, an absence of accountability and transparency, and very high coordination costs: multilevel action has become the rule and single-authority action, the exception (Le Lidec 2005). Nevertheless, in investment policy the centre has invented new forms of coordination allowing long-term (five-year) commitments between various partners: long-term agreements (state-region contracts, *contrats de Plan Etat-région*, which became project contracts, *contrats de projets*, in 2007) cover financing of large investment projects (Le Galès 2008). The negotiation of these contracts and the management of the European structural funds have helped the central state to regain some influence over regional policies.

The second wave of decentralization reforms, implemented in 2003–2004, did not result in the same weakening of state steering capacity. The recent decentralization laws transferred new management responsibilities to local authorities in several public policies (social aid, education). However, they did not transfer new financial capacities and did not decentralize new decision powers: the state maintained its regulatory competences. This reform was defended as part of a more general program strengthening the strategic functions of the French state (decision-making, design, and steering – as well as monitoring and evaluating public policies) while decentralizing tasks and responsibility for implementation to local authorities (Bezes 2007). This decentralization gave an opportunity for the state to devolve some competencies with increasing costs, without transferring equivalent fiscal power and resources. In the 2000s, central government has increased its control over the amount of local resources. This has generated a recentralization of fiscal power in 2010 (Le Lidec 2011) and introduced a 'negative' steering that consists in limiting the resources of local authorities.

By contrast, central government has recently made efforts to reassert performance control over local authorities and their public policies but has mostly failed to steer at a distance. Central government has attempted to introduce controls over the nature and object of local government expenditure and to create an incentive system intended to improve local authority performance. In 2004, central government tried to create a National Council for the Evaluation of Local Public Policy, which would publish public audit reports, following a model partially – and timidly – inspired by the Audit Commission. This National Council, which was to have been chaired by an elected local councillor and made up mainly of local politicians, was presented as something much less constraining than the Audit Commission, since it lacked the power to impose financial sanctions on local authorities. However, all attempts by central government to institute central political control over the aims, effectiveness, or efficiency of local government activities were met by the veto of local elected councillors, supported vigorously by the Senate. The Senate got the National Council abolished even before it was established (Le Lidec 2005). Since this setback, central government has wanted to introduce and publish standard cost benchmarks for the main local government services, to encourage local authorities to pay more attention to improving performance. This approach, however, simply highlights the major political and constitutional obstacles to central government control over local authorities in France. Relying on the constitutional principle of local government freedom of administration and on their own members' presence in Parliament (senatorial electoral college, *cumul des mandats*), local authorities continue to refuse any form of central control, and accept only the verdict of the ballot box. This clearly demonstrates the gap that separates practices of central control over local authorities in France from those in the United Kingdom (James and John 2007).

Although decentralization policies did weaken the capacities of the centre for monitoring and steering public policies, the steering capacities of the centre vis-à-vis local governments remain ambiguous. While the centre did manage in 2009 to impose fiscal constraints over local governments in the context of the financial crisis, it did not succeed in imposing performance control over local authorities.

Neo-managerial Reforms in France before the Sarkozy Era and Their Effects on Steering

France has not remained aloof from the wave of New Public Management-inspired reforms of structures and modes of functioning of state administration, whether of central administrations or the very sizable local government units (Bezes 2008). However, the introduction of managerial instruments or new organizational forms has been filtered and constrained by the robustness of existing institutions and the strength of the mechanisms of centralization.

On one hand, no policy has systematically challenged the inherited 'Napoleonic' structures of ministries in a way comparable to the 'agencification' programs seen in countries such as the United Kingdom, with its Next Steps Programme (James 2003), or New Zealand (Boston et al. 1991). The creation of agencies stemmed neither from an overall administrative logic or strategy nor from a transformation of existing ministerial structures into delivery agencies on the U.K. model. For the most part the agencies set up were new organizational creations, put in place to respond to the economic demands of the moment, often in times of crisis, and tasked with implementing new public policies (taking control of energy, marketing medicines, etc.) or intended to regulate certain sectors (e.g.. the Financial Markets Authority, set up on the model of the U.K. Financial Services Authority). The number of agencies increased considerably, but those created throughout the 1980s and, even more so, in the 1990s acquired the classic French status of a public body with a legal personality. Many agencies have been created in agriculture (where there is a central coordinating agency), social security, social affairs, culture, and research. The health sector over the past few years has been the privileged site for the creation of agencies designed to ensure that they would be independent of political control. Generally speaking, the creation of agencies and comparable bodies has made the already fragmented organization of the state even more complex. Prefects regularly protest against this fragmentation, as it further undermines their powers of coordination. In the area of health and safety, an enormous profusion of agencies has been created 'on the hoof' in order to react to problems in the public sector, without thought to questions of overall structure, resulting in overlapping responsibilities and poor cooperation between agencies, as well as between agencies and traditional state services (Bricq 2007).

In the same vein, organizational and managerial change in the French state at territorial level was an ongoing dynamic throughout the 1990s, but its scope and effects were rather limited, not only in terms of redesign, mergers, and fragmentation but also in terms of management devolution. Of course, all ministerial units faced a real crisis, engendered by major and increasing pressures resulting from the decentralization measures initiated in the early years of the decade. Local authorities considerably strengthened their administrative capacities, while the field services of government departments at territorial level saw the number and scope of their functions and tasks significantly reduced. Decentralization also initially considerably weakened the prefects' and the Interior Ministry's capacities for coordination and control of the state's territorial policies. Between 1992 and 2003, several strategic plans were put forward to reorganize ministries (on a vertical line) and local units of the state and prefects' activities (on a horizontal line). They all expressed a desire to implement structural devolution, with responsibilities clearly rationalized and specialized. In 2003, the conclusion was reached that the reorganization and/or reduction of central administrations, establishing a steering structure for local units of the state, and the creation of focal areas had been unequally and insufficiently implemented (Cour des Comptes 2003). It had not brought significant changes in the relationships between actors at the local level within the state. In the early 2000s, steering from the centre at the territorial level remained a highly complex and multitiered governing design reflecting the tight networks of interdependencies in the French state and involving many actors such as representatives of central ministries and state field services, prefects, local authorities, and the political executive, each defending distinct interests and strategies and each capable of becoming a veto player.

Although the idea of a 'steering state model' was developed and diffused within the 1990s (Bezes 2007), the absence of systematic and drastic program of separation between central and territorial organizations has not overthrown the existing mechanisms of steering through hierarchy, politicization, and networking at the territorial level. However, the strength of the enduring dynamics of decentralization and the complexity of incremental reform designs has made them less efficient because of the increasing costs of cooperation and negotiations.

This resilient organizational context is crucial to understand the way and the extent to which the 2001 reform of the French budget procedure, on the other hand, has transformed the capacities of steering from the centre in the French context. The reform was passed in the Institutional Act on Budget Legislation (*Loi organique relative aux lois de finances*, or LOLF), adopted on 1 August 2001 and implemented in January 2006. It was originally marked by the adoption of several internationally dominant instruments of performance management articulated as a significant attempt to strengthen the role of Parliament in budgeting. The reform was based on a major change in the format and contents of the budget, moving away from line-item budgeting towards public policy and performance-sensitive frames ('frame-budgeting'). The reform drew up a program budget based on 34 task forces, corresponding (supposedly) to the French state's major public policies, further broken down into 132 programs to which appropriations are allocated. The first aim of the 2001 act was not to solve problems of steering and coordination by strengthening the political executive. Indeed, the Budget Act resulted from the disruptive power of 'external' actors outside the administrative system but inside Parliament, in the shape of cross-party National Assembly and Senate working groups operating from 1998 to 2000 (Bezes 2010a). By modifying the way in which Parliament votes on the budget, the first intention was to foster more awareness of issues, priority objectives and the results achieved by the spending ministries. This change in budget format has been accompanied by a performance management structure. Every year, ministers and program managers have been asked to make commitments to meet specific objectives and performance targets through an Annual Performance Plan (APP) appended to the Budget Act. When the budget is executed, spending ministries have to give deputies and senators (French MPs) an Annual Performance Report (APR), with explanations for the levels of performance they have achieved relative to the resources they have been allocated. The primary aim was to restore the balance of power between government and Parliament by giving MPs more stringent control over budgetary processes and by shaping a new form of accountability to Parliament. The constitutional by-law to the Budget Act also entails greater access to information, more investigative and audit powers (for the Finance Committees of both chambers) and extended powers of amendment.

By establishing new forms of management control based on objectives, performance measurement within the entire administrative system, 'real cost' approaches to policies, and a new chain of accountability to Parliament, the new rules have, however, challenged many embedded relationships. These include those between MPs and the French bureaucracy as well as those inside French administration – between ministers, senior bureaucrats in central administrations, and public servants in local units of the state. Indeed, the new budget formats have been used to create new forms of managerial steering and control by the Budget Directorate and by central administrations within ministries over territorial units. Whereas the 'external' dimension of the Budget Act was publicly endorsed, this 'internal' one, creating a new framework for managerial steering inside the bureaucracy and reinforcing the Budget Directorate's control over spending ministries, has been a more low-profile, negotiated change because of its high political costs and the concern to avoid social conflict and blame. The various programs and their 2,300 sub-programs (known as Operational Budget Programmes, or OBPs) have allowed the use of 'frame budgeting' and performance management for a new 'managerial chain' of command. It is based on management by objectives and performance indicators that connect the Budget Directorate, central administration, program managers (in central administrations), and sub-program managers (in state local units). This new chain of command and accountability has been designed to save money and reduce staff but has also been increasingly viewed as a tool for new forms of managerial coordination and steering by central departments over state territorial units within ministries. On the one hand, aggregated headings are supposed to offer much more flexible management by strengthening the autonomy of program and OBP managers through greater responsibility since they 'manage funds' and manage public policies. On the other hand, however, performance management tools (objectives, targets, indicators, performance information) also provide stronger forms of 'steering from the centre.' Have these new tools structured new forms of steering from the centre or merely reinforced inherited ones?

Without parallel or previous reorganizations of structures, limits in managerial steering at a distance have been observed while traditional centralization mechanisms have been strengthened. Indeed, no state field unit or ministerial department was placed 'at a distance' through organizational reforms so that two hierarchies have had to coexist: a budgetary potentially devolving hierarchy, structured around programs and aimed at giving more autonomy to managers while requiring more accountability through performance management; and the traditional hierarchy linked to organizational structures and the authority of law. The French administration has then faced a decoupling of its modes of steering but also experienced the dominance of the oldest dimension on the most recent managerial trend. The principle of managerial autonomy of program and OBP directors, enshrined in the LOLF and at the heart of New Public Management, clashes directly with the power games that structure ministerial organizations. Central administrations – sometimes with the approval of the Budget Directorate attempting to exercise control over public accounts – have limited the use of frame-budgeting by the managers of state field services through a multiplicity of tactics: late release of funds, keeping OBPs at the centre in order to manage devolved policies, and 'earmarking' funds in order to hem in and limit the powers of financial discretion that local managers are supposed to enjoy (Lambert and Migaud 2006). Another weak link in the new managerial chain is that there are an excessive number of sub-OBPs, known as Operational Units (OUs). There are some 18,000 OUs, which indicates the extent of fragmentation in budgetary powers, dispersing responsibilities across a large number of administrative actors rather than concentrating them. Besides, as observed in other European countries (Hood et al. 2004), performance management has allowed central administrations to monitor the activities of state local units against their objectives and targets and to exert more bureaucratic control over them. The absence of any real, systematic devolution of management activity, the resilience of the ministerial organization, and the strategic retention by the Ministry of Finance of control over devolved financial controllers have finally reinforced the permanent nature of hierarchical organization embedded in vertical and integrated structures. Rather than eliminating this, the LOLF has simply been superimposed on it and has more reinforced the existing means of steering than created radically new ones. Of course, the new formats have also generated new managerial information (in terms of objectives, targets, costs, and results). However, there is no evidence yet that these data have been used by the political executive either to improve the coordination of priority setting or to give the Budget Directorate even greater influence over the already centralized process of allocation of resources. There is, though, no doubt that the reform has strengthened the Ministry of Finance, which by 2001 had moved to the heart of the whole process of state reform (Bezes 2008).

When Reorganizations Meet Politicization via a Renewal of Presidential Leadership

More generally, since the early 2000s, and associated with a constitutional reform and an increasing budgetary constraints on French public finances, there has been a visible process of rebuilding a hierarchical structure designed to ensure greater unity of command, tighter steering, and better accountability of administrative actors to the central executive. A structural cause of this dynamics has been the alignment of the cycles of presidential and parliamentary elections as a result of the 2000 constitutional reform. The shortening of the presidential mandate from seven years to five years and the fact that the presidential election is now scheduled just before the parliamentary elections has strengthened the presidency. This move has changed the balance of power by reinforcing the presidency relative to the Prime Minister and the parliamentary majority. Although not directly linked to the 2000 constitutional reform, there also has been real strategic thinking about the effectiveness, tasks, and organization of the state, leading to reforms of ministerial structures in order to reassert unity of command over organizations that had become too fragmented and scattered. This trend has been accentuated by the new Sarkozy presidency but has also led to a new step in politicization, and thus been conducive to reinforcing a historical French mechanism of steering.

An Increasing Dynamics of Tightening the Central Steering of Ministries through Organizational Changes

A re-examination of state structures initiated by 2001 through the LOLF asked each administration to systematically re-examine its tasks, to redefine them formally in relation to the over-arching task forces, and to relinquish certain jobs that could be eliminated, delegated, or outsourced. The Prime Minister's Circular of 25 June 2003 on ministerial reform strategies charged each minister with recentring each ministry on its core tasks and with implementing changed structures, organization, and methods. Each ministry was to devise a ministerial reform strategy based on three common principles: clarification of the ministry's responsibilities in order to make arbitration decisions easier; establishing shared services and procedures in order to increase the ministry's efficiency; and concentration of resources on practical core tasks.

A second expression at the ministry level of this desire to strengthen steering powers and combat centrifugal tendencies was the creation of general secretariats by 2004. The model of the ministry general secretariat, going back to the early nineteenth century, was rediscovered and systematized. Although general secretariats no longer existed except within the offices of the President of the Republic and the Prime Minister, new general secretariats were created in the principal ministries (Chevallier 2005). A Prime Minister's Circular of 2 June 2004 called for the appointment within each major ministry of a secretary general directly responsible to the minister, with management authority over all departments and responsible for modernization. Using secretaries general to exercise tighter steering in the nine principal ministries is indicative of a marked change from the scattered approach that had prevailed until then. It is true that the extent of this move differed between ministries, with the secretary general's prerogatives varying from one ministry to another and their remit being markedly less extensive than those of permanent secretaries in the United Kingdom but their role is, however, significant. At the Ministry of the Interior, for example, the secretary general's remit is extensive. In that ministry, the secretary general directs and coordinates implementation of the minister's decisions on matters of modernization of the ministry or local and regional policy; in consultation with directors general and directors, he proposes all measures he deems necessary to the minister. He manages administrative resources shared between the central and territorial levels, and coordinates (where necessary) the management and use of resources by other general directorates and directorates within the ministry. The creation of nine secretaries general within the major ministries constitutes a powerful new coordination tool. Meetings between secretaries general ensure quicker and more effective interministerial coordination than did the traditional interministerial meetings, at which often no decisions were made (Duport et al. 2007). It thus becomes possible to overcome a classic blocking strategy of ministries afraid of losing out in arbitration decisions. In this classic interministerial obstruction manoeuvre, a ministry would delegate attendance at meetings to officials with no political authority, preventing any decisions.

In 2007, with the election of President Nicolas Sarkozy, this move to tighten intra- and then interministerial control, which had begun with the creation of general secretariats, was extended by redrawing boundaries between ministries and significantly reducing the number of full ministers, in the explicit aim of strengthening the integration and coherence of public policy via hierarchy. This redrawing of ministerial boundaries and organization should strengthen arbitration power and coordination capabilities and combat centrifugal logics. For example, a large Ministry of Ecology, Energy and Sustainable Development, and Territorial Planning (*Ministère de l'Ecologie, de l'Energie, du Développement Durable et de l'Aménagement du Territoire* – MEEDDAT) was created, subsuming the ministries of Infrastructure, Transport, Ecology, Maritime Affairs, and Regional Planning. The thirty-five central administrative directorates that made up these ministries were merged into a more integrated structure based on six major directorates and a general secretariat with extended powers. The number of senior managerial civil servants appointed by the Cabinet was thus significantly reduced, from forty-one directors general to just seven. In all ministries, processes of reorganization and mergers of directorates have begun, even if they are not always as clear-cut as this one. A large Ministry for the Budget, Public Accounts, the Civil Service, and State Reform has also been created, in order to subordinate recruitment and HRM policy more directly to the imperative to reduce public spending.

Finally, a General Review of Public Policies (*révision générale des politiques publiques* labelled RGPP) was launched by the President Sarkozy in July 2007 (Bezes 2010b) with explicit references to the Canadian Program Review initiated by the Liberal *Chrétien* government in 1995–1996 and to the 'spending reviews' carried out in the United Kingdom since 2002. Systematizing and refocusing the 'modernization audits' developed in 2006–2007 by targeting public policies, the RGPP claims to engage in 'rethinking the state' in ways that are tied directly to the fiscal imperatives of the debt and the deficit. This resulted in the adoption of a new organization of the state at territorial level by 2008 (Bezes and Le Lidec 2010) developing new mechanisms for coordinating and steering devolved state services and systematizing a framework which has been gradually designed since 2004. A hierarchy between local state levels (*régions, départements*) has been introduced, combined with a functional specialization of state field services and related to a repositioning of the prefects. The regional level is now the main level for the steering and the implementation of public policies; the *départemental* level is said to be the locus 'where the state adapts to the needs of citizens on a geographical basis.' As a consequence, the regional prefect is now considered as the pilot, guarantor of cohesion, coordinator, and arbitrator in state interministerial action in the context of a reorganized regional level (Decree of 16 February 2010 systematizing a move initiated by the Decree of 29 April 2004). The regional level has been reorganized in accordance with a top-down ministerial logic, merging the twenty-three ministerial regional directorates into eight regional directorates whose boundaries broadly mirrored the new design of 'big ministries.' The reduction of the number of regional directorates is aimed at strengthening the capacities of control of regional prefects over these regional directorates. A new hierarchy has been introduced.

Regional prefects have gained stronger formal powers over the eight regional units but also over other ministerial services such as the French gendarmerie (a military police force), fire and first aid *départemental* services, territorial delegates of French public corporations, etc. A new hierarchy was also introduced within the prefectoral corps: the regional prefect has now formal authority over the prefects of *départements*, except on specified affairs (mainly to do with public order). Prefects of *départements* have reinforced their interministerial powers and therefore are said to command directly a tightened organization of state services at the departmental level. At this level, three or four interministerial directorates (the Directorate for the Territories, the Directorate for Public Finances, the Directorate for Protection of the Population, and, in some cases – in the most heavily populated *départements* – the Directorate for Social Cohesion) were created, thus merging the dozen of pre-existing ministerial directorates at the *départemental* level. This reshaped framework should strengthen the prerogatives directly exercised by prefects, reaffirming the historical vertical and political chain of command within the French administration. However, the new logic of interministeriality should not be oversimplified. Four of the eight regional merged ministerial services have conserved their own territorial units (UTs) at the *départemental* level. Some ministerial services have a strong autonomy vis-à-vis the prefects (the inspections of primary and secondary education or the units in charge of public finances called '*directions départementales des finances publiques*,' both at the *départemental* level). Besides, the real nature of these new hierarchical lines and their corresponding relationships will have to be further explored at the implementation stage. Whatever the uncertainty of its implementation may be, this new organizational form is reinforcing the steering capacity of the centre. From now on, the President, the Prime Minister, or the ministers can rely on a team of twenty-six regional prefects that they can call together frequently and who they know personally and trust as loyal and responsive partners. This new hierarchical linkage, from the ministers to the *régional* and *départemental* prefects, has been desired by the political executive for the past seventy years (Le Lidec 2006) and is now in place. This linkage contributes considerably towards a strengthening of the centre's steering capacity.

A New Style of Presidential Leadership

This series of organizational measures has been amplified by the way the new President of the Republic has built his political leadership. By stressing the need for radical reforms and for disruptive actions, Nicolas Sarkozy has enhanced the steering role of the President as a leader of the government and has claimed direct and personal responsibility for reforms. This presidential commitment has introduced a clear change in the traditional game between the President and the Prime Minister under the Fifth Republic where the former was often not accountable for governmental decisions while the latter took responsibility for failure and acted as a blame-magnet. Changes in political leadership have relied on several main dynamics: personalization of the executive, intense use of media and opinion polls, and a disruptive political style. The main feature of the new presidential style is the systematic claim of personal responsibility for policy successes and failures. The media have coined new terms – 'hyper-President,' 'omni-President' – to describe the way Nicolas Sarkozy has constructed his political authority (Levy and Skach 2008), justified his actions in the name of systematic commitments and responsibility, and secured the legitimacy of changes he promotes. Sarkozy has developed a new disruptive leadership based on a negative diagnosis of the past, systematic criticisms of the inertia of previous presidents and governments, denunciations of previous retreats when confronting difficulties, and the strategic use of the popular idea of the French economic decline. In this context, political hierarchies have been rebuilt so that the President has gained ground over the Prime Minister. In 2007–2009, the latter frequently appeared devalued. However, he has regained legitimacy since 2009, when presidential popularity dropped in opinion polls.

The shift in power towards the presidency has been particularly visible in the media and displayed in abundance through an associated public relations policy. Since 2007, the secretary general to the Elysée Palace and the special adviser to the President have never hesitated to appear on television or radio in direct defence of the President's choices, thus pushing the Prime Minister just a little further into the background. The presidential entourage, which since the early days of the Fifth Republic had exercised arbitration functions as unobtrusive as they were extensive, no longer hesitates to give official status to this power of arbitration and to publicly disown the position of ministers, including the Prime Minister himself. The new presidential leadership has then made more visible the increasing role and influence played by spin doctors: either experts in opinion polls and communication whose numbers have increased significantly in ministerial cabinets since the 1990s (Sawicki and Mathiot 1999) or new staff in cabinets who are ·

not any longer civil servants but 'professionals or political party and association activists' supporting the government's action and called 'political advisers' (Rouban 2007). To some extent, the governmental communication seems to be centralized in the hand of the President so that ministers now have to adhere closely to the presidential guidelines. Besides, Sarkozy's governing style can be described as reflecting 'tremendous government activism' (Levy and Skach 2008) with continuous announcements of new reforms and initiatives. As a consequence, and although this trend would most probably need to be contextualized over a longer time, the political agenda has established a strong grip on the media agenda by inundating the front pages and the headlines with announcements of reforms. Ordering opinion polls is also part of the 'new' governing style as shown by the 3.3 million euros dedicated to this activity in the 2008 presidential budget, now reduced to a projected 1.4 million in 2010 after 'opinion gate,' a scandal revealing the ambiguous relationships between the presidency, pollsters, and some newspapers. Media management and control of political communication have increasingly been an obsession for political executives and their staff in a context of increased competition with new media (Internet, blogs, etc.) challenging the old. But this evolution should be carefully examined in relation to the changing structures of political parties in a digital era characterized by new forms of electioneering with permanent campaigns, personalization, and the emphasis on marketing of image and campaign issues (Farrel, Kolodny, and Medvic 2001). This extreme attention to media also needs to be examined in relation to a changing economic model characterized by weak profitability and huge fragmentation of the media market. In France, this situation may explain not only the media's 'deliberate' alignment with the political agenda and its short-term focus but also the increasing funding of press media by state subsidies, creating ambiguous relationships between public authorities and newspapers. In return, French political leaders have been increasingly exposed to strong public pressures which are all the more difficult to contain as they originate from specialized and fragmented audiences. A related effect of this activist leadership is the exposure to blame when results and situations are not positive and do not allow an engagement in credit-claiming strategies. Significantly, opinion polls revealed a rather low popularity for the French President since 2009, especially compared to François Fillon's as Prime Minister, in a context of economic and budget crisis and high pressure for reform. Governing through the media and insisting on accountability and results strongly increase the risk of being blamed in case of failures.

Third, these changes in leadership style have led to new organizational forms of steering. The increased frequency of interministerial council meetings chaired by the head of state shows that the President of the Republic intends to manage all issues directly from now on. This recentralization of authority to the President of the Republic has recently found many expressions. Several new organizations have been put under the supervision of the office of the presidency of the Republic and therefore made accountable to the President: the Council for Defence and National Security, chaired directly by the head of state; the appointment of a national intelligence coordinator, reporting directly to the President, a Council for Art Creation chaired by Nicolas Sarkozy, etc. Other ad hoc bodies have been created and appointed directly by the President to prepare reforms: the Committee for Review and Proposals on the Modernization and Rebalancing of the Institutions of the Fifth Republic, the Commission for Liberating French Economic Growth, the Committee for the Reform of Local Government (Le Lidec 2009), etc. Information-based instruments have also been more systematically organized through public debates, forums or consultations between government officials, experts, members of the public and representatives of the policy sector. From October 2007 to March 2008, a major conference on the values, missions, and jobs of the future French civil service took place. Bringing together experts, civil service trade unions, ministries, and representatives of the Ministry for Budgeting, Public Accounts, and the Civil Service, the conference produced a white paper on the future of the French civil service (Silicani 2008) aimed at framing the possible reforms and at giving legitimacy to the new political goals. In January 2009, a forum of all stakeholders of the print media was organized while a conference on public deficits was directly set up by the presidency in January 2010. Such forms of government by public debates have been simultaneously a way to test reforms, efforts to change interest groups' preferences, and strategies to build consensus. In these initiatives, both the Prime Minister and Parliament have frequently had their prerogatives taken away from them because the presidency has claimed to be the main organizer. Changes in sources of advice and expertise have also taken place. Legitimate expert positions in promoting reforms have been increasingly recruited from other categories than the *grands corps* in order to provide new competences and skills that generalist top civil servants might not be able to offer. Consultancy firms have played a growing and increasingly publicized role within the 'General Directorate for Modernising the State' (*Direction générale de la modernisation de l'Etat*, the DGME) created in 2005 and in the general public policy review (RGPP) launched in 2007. On one hand, in 2008, the staff of the DGME was about 143 people, among them 115 top executives. Within the 115 executives, however, there were only 47 senior civil servants but also 68 people under contract, including a significant number of previous consultants recruited for short terms. On the other hand, the audits of public policies and administrative organizations within the RGPP were conducted by several small 'teams,' mixing members of ministerial and interministerial inspectorates with private consultants – the first time that the use of private consultancy firms has been publicly endorsed. The upper-level civil service may not longer be the government's unique source of advice.

Reinforcing a Historical French Mechanism of Steering: Politicization Renewed

Both changes in the political style of the new President elected in 2007 and the reforms conducted since then have reinforced the historical French politicization and led to a re-differentiation process between higher civil servants and politicians. This evolution does not rely on an increase in the number of political appointees as observed in Scandinavian countries, for instance, but is based on the redesign of hierarchies and on a reduction in the number of administrative positions of command at both the central and territorial levels. In July 2010, members of ministerial cabinets reached an official total of 616 people under the Fillon government (*Projet de Loi de Finances* 2011, 40 portfolios) to whom forty-five members of the presidential cabinet should be added, these figures revealing no significant rise. In the recent French context, the renewed forms of politicization have two dimensions.

On one hand, the new presidential style has accentuated the process of restraining top bureaucrats' autonomy in policy-making. The strong political leadership has impacted the trade-off between bureaucratic professional autonomy and political control in favour of the later. The differentiation between political and bureaucratic elites and spheres has been strengthened, as a small number of members of the Fillon governments are previous top bureaucrats trained within the *Ecole nationale d'administration* (ENA), the French national school for top civil servants. This new situation helped reassert the steering capacities of the executive. Willing to restore 'political will' against 'technocrats,' the presidency implemented a tighter political control over top nominations and obtained a clearer subordination by quickly dismissing senior civil servants who were considered as responsible for policy or political failures. Clear political signals were sent to the higher civil service by removing and sidelining several top bureaucrats who were considered to have failed. Also a gradual development of job-based recruitments and the idea of private contracts have been suggested in a recent 'white paper' on the future of the French civil service (Silicani 2008), specifically for specialized positions within the top bureaucracy. A recent Prime Minister's Circular in February 2010 has taken a step towards this direction while a new interministerial position has been created within the General Secretariat of the Government (*secrétariat général du gouvernement*, SGG). This position's responsibilities include an overall regulatory role in regard to the French higher civil service in terms of staff mobility, the detection of 'high flyers,' and redeployments. This challenges the idea of a strongly self-regulated and autonomous civil service. The model of the local civil service (*fonction publique territoriale*), with rules organizing the recruitment, promotion, and mobility of people working for local authorities, has been increasingly promoted for the human resource management policy of top state bureaucrats (Jeannot 2008; Gally 2009): significantly, the local civil service is characterized by a weaker professional autonomy for civil servants and by a stronger subordination to political power.

On the other hand, the logic of organizational reforms aimed at increasing the steering and coordination of public policies between and within ministries has also strongly tightened control over ministry activities through a small number of 'super senior civil servants' at the central level (secretaries general, the tight circle of directors general from central administrative departments, etc.) and at the territorial level (prefects, regional, and departmental state units directors) thus reinforcing politicization. Indeed, the reduction in the number of central administrative directorates has helped strengthen the bonds of trust that the heads of the executive may have with each of them. These 'super senior civil servants' enjoy more direct relationships not only with their own ministers but also with the head of state. In short, fewer full ministers, fewer senior civil servants at the centre, but more politicized civil servants who have more authority, are more loyal, and report more directly to the head of government or even the head of state: this seems to be the consequence of the reorganization process in the 2000s. The role played by these more politicized 'super senior civil servants' is well emphasized by the current reform process that affects the territorial state: new devices of coordination and arbitration have been set up such as the 'committee of the forty' (*Comité des quarante*) which gathers general secretariats of ministries and regional prefects under the leadership of the general secretary of the presidency, the closest collaborator of the President.

Implementation of this reorganization also relates to a gradual process in which the political masters are reasserting control over ministerial administration and where the influence of the *grand corps* in defining public policy and their obstructive roles have been weakened. The situation described by Ezra Suleiman in the 1970s (Suleiman 1974), where ministers were 'held captive' by their advisers, who came from the ministries' *grand corps*, no longer prevails. In trying to push through state reform policies, ministers are less and less likely to form their entourages exclusively from the in-house *grand corps* or technical *corps*, and have not hesitated to appoint collaborators from elsewhere as secretaries general of ministries. In an unprecedented move, some prefects have been appointed to the general secretariat of the new super-ministry, MEEDDAT, created in 2007. The recruitment of senior civil servants on a less corporatist basis has come to be seen by their political masters as vital to promoting new directions. Secretaries general who have recently been appointed fit the profile of highly politicized senior civil servants. Some of them have been directly involved in electoral politics by running for elections. Here, as often observed, administrative reforms both *produce* and *reveal* the shifts in relationships between politicians and public servants (Peters and Pierre 2001).

Conclusion

The first concluding observation is that recent reforms have strongly mobilized steering mechanisms of hierarchical and political types at several levels. At the level of the political executive, the French system – characterized by a diarchy at the top – has been clarified in favour of the President. This has been achieved partly through reduction of the President's term in office and through a reversal in the electoral calendar, practically excluding the possibility of *cohabitation* between a President and a Prime Minister. Nicolas Sarkozy is the first President to fully benefit from these constitutional reforms and to infer all the possible conclusions for the exercise and 'presidentialization' of political leadership. The effects of a French organizational dynamic distinct from those seen in many other Western countries have made the government team itself more hierarchical. Running counter to the movement towards a proliferation of 'single-purpose organizations' with strengthened autonomy, the recent French approach consists of creating very large ministries, with a consequent strengthening of political steering from the presidency. There are fewer full ministers, and more deputy ministers and junior ministers. Within the large, reshaped ministries, new hierarchical arbitration functions have been created with the secretaries general. At territorial level, the hierarchical authority of regional prefects over *département* prefects has been asserted for the first time, as has the authority of *département* prefects over the new *département* directorates, whose number has been drastically reduced. All in all, the form of the French state resembles a pyramid at whose apex sits the head of state – although as yet no one can know, in the absence of empirical study, how this structure will be implemented and what kind of effects it will have on concrete modes of steering over practices.

The second major remark concerns the massive introduction of managerial-type steering instruments via the LOLF. The effects of these remain difficult to evaluate, since they are superimposed on organizational structures that have not been designed to take account of the new division of responsibilities and budget arbitration powers. This decoupling between the organizational forms introduced in the 2007–2008 reforms and the new managerial steering mechanisms, linked to the 2001 LOLF, has somehow complicated and blurred the governance system. However, evidence suggests that the new opportunities opened by these two dynamics of reform (organizational and managerial) will not disrupt what still makes the French state a 'Napoleonic' system: vertical hierarchy, politicization, and highly complex and often contested forms of coordination between ministries and at local level.

REFERENCES

Bezes, P. (2001). Defensive vs Offensive Approaches to Administrative Reform in France (1988–1997): The Leadership Dilemmas of French Prime Ministers. *Governance* 14: 99–132.
– (2007). The 'Steering State' Model: The Emergence of a New Organizational Form in the French Public Administration. *Sociologie du Travail* (in English) 49: 67–89.

– (2008). The Reform of the State: The French Bureaucracy in the Age of New Public Management. In A. Cole, P. Le Galès, and J. Levy (eds.), *Developments in French Politics 4*. New York: Palgrave Macmillan.

– (2009). *Réinventer l'Etat: Les réformes de l'administration française (1962–2008)*. Coll. Le Lien Social. Paris: PUF.

– (2010a). Path-Dependent and Path-Breaking Changes in the French Administrative System: The Weight of Legacy Explanations. In M. Painter and B.G. Peters (eds.), *Tradition and Public Administration*. New York: Palgrave Macmillan.

– (2010b). Morphologie de la Révision générale des politiques publiques. Une mise en perspective historique et comparative. *Revue française d'administration publique* 4: 769–96.

Bezes, P., and P. Le Lidec. (2007). French Top Civil Servants within Changing Configurations: From Monopolisation to Challenged Places and Roles? In E.C. Page and V. Wright (eds.), *From the Active to the Enabling State: The Changing Roles of Top Officials in European Nations*. London: Palgrave Macmillan.

– (2010). L'hybridation du modèle territorial français. La réorganisation de l'administration territoriale de l'Etat et la Révision générale des politiques publiques. *Revue française d'administration publique*, 4: 881–904.

Boston, J., J. Martin, J. Palliot, and P. Walsh (eds.). (1991). *Reshaping the State: New Zealand's Bureaucratic Revolution*. Auckland: Oxford University Press.

Bricq, N. (2007). *Rapport d'information no. 355 sur le dispositif des agences en matière de sécurité sanitaire*. Paris: Sénat, commission des Finances.

Chevallier, J. (2005). La reconfiguration de l'administration centrale. *Revue française d'administration publique* 116: 715–25.

Cour des Comptes. (2003). *La déconcentration des administrations et la réforme de l'État*. Paris: Direction des Journaux Officiels.

Crozier, M., and J.-C. Thoenig. (1975). La régulation des systèmes organisés complexes: Le cas du système de décision politico-administratif local en France. *Revue Française de Sociologie* 16/1: 3–32.

Duport, J.-P., et al. (2007). *Rapport sur la coordination du travail interministériel*. Paris: Mission d'audit de modernisation.

Dupuy, F., and J.-C. Thoenig. (1985). *L'administration en miettes*. Paris: Fayard.

Farrel, D.M., R. Kolodny, and S. Medvic. (2001). Parties and Campaign Professionals in a Digital Age: Political Consultants in the United States and Their Counterparts Overseas. *Politics* 6: 11–30.

François, B. (1996). *Naissance d'une constitution: la Vème République (1958–1962)*. Paris: Presses de Sciences-Po.

Gally, N. (2009). Former ensemble les cadres supérieurs de l'État et des collectivités territoriales? Les enjeux du difficile rapprochement de l'ÉNA et de l'INET. *Revue française d'administration publique* 131: 497–512.

Grèmion, C. (1979). *Profession: décideurs – pouvoir des hauts fonctionnaires et réforme de l'Etat.* Paris: Gauthier-Villars.

Grèmion, P. (1976). *Le pouvoir périphérique: Bureaucrates et notables dans le système politico-administratif français.* Paris: Le Seuil.

Hayward, J., and V. Wright. (2002). *Governing from the Centre: Core Executive Coordination in France.* Oxford: Oxford University Press.

Hood, C., O. James, G. Peters, and C. Scott. (2004). *Controlling Modern Government: Variety, Commonality and Change.* Cheltenham: Edward Elgar.

James, O. (2003). *The Executive Agency Revolution in Whitehall.* Basingstoke: Palgrave.

James, O., and P. John. (2007). Public Management at the Ballot Box: Performance Information and Electoral Support for Incumbent English Local Governments. *Journal of Public Administration Research and Theory* 17: 567–80.

Jeannot, G. (2008). Réforme de la fonction publique et réorganisation de l'Etat. *Esprit* (Dec.): 94–109.

Lambert, A., and D. Migaud. (2006). *La mise en œuvre de la loi organique relative aux lois de finances: A l'épreuve de la pratique, insuffler une nouvelle dynamique à la réforme.* Rapport au Gouvernement. Paris: Assemblée nationale.

Le Galès, P. (2008). Territorial Politics in France: Le calme avant la tempête. In A. Cole, P. Le Galès, and J. Levy (eds.), *Developments in French Politics* 4. New York: Palgrave Macmillan.

Le Lidec, P. (2001). *Les maires dans la République: L'Association des Maires de France, élément constitutif des régimes politiques français depuis 1907.* Doctoral dissertation in political science, l'Université Paris-I.

– (2005). La relance de la décentralisation en France: De la rhétorique managériale aux réalités politiques. *Politiques et Management Public* 3: 101–25.

– (2006). L'impossible renouveau du modèle préfectoral sous la IVème République. *Revue française d'administration publique* 120: 695–710.

– (2009). Réformer sous contrainte d'inonctions contradictories: L'exemple du Comité Baladur sur la réforme des collectivités locales. *Revue française d'administration publique* 131: 477–93.

– (2011). Décentralisation, structure du financement et jeux de transferts de l'impopularité en France. In P. Bezes and A. Siné (eds.), *Gouverner (par) les finances publiques.* Paris: Presses de Sciences-Po.

Levy, J., and C. Skach. (2008). The Return to a Strong Presidency. In A. Cole, P. Le Galès, and J. Levy (eds.), *Developments in French Politics* 4. New York: Palgrave Macmillan.

Page, E.C. (1992). *Political Authority and Bureaucratic Power: A Comparative Analysis.* Hemel Hempstead: Harvester Wheatsheaf.

Peters, B.G., and J Pierre (eds.). (2001). *Bureaucrats, Politicians and Institutional Change*. London: Routledge.

Pinon, S. (2003). *Les réformistes constitutionnels des années trente: Aux origines de la Ve République*. Paris: LGDJ.

Rouban, L. (1995). Public Administration at the Crossroads: The End of the French Specificity? In J. Pierre (ed.), *Bureaucracy in the Modern State: An Introduction to Comparative Public Administration*. Aldershot: Edward Elgar.

– (2004). Politicization of the Civil Service in France: From Structural to Strategic Politicization. In B.G. Peters and J. Pierre (eds.), *Politicization of the Civil Service in Comparative Perspective: The Quest for Control*. London: Routledge.

– (2007). Public Management and Politics: Senior Bureaucrats in France. *Public Administration* 85: 473–501.

Rousselier, N. (1997). *Le parlement de l'éloquence: La souveraineté de la délibération au lendemain de la Grande Guerre*. Paris: Presses de Sciences-Po.

Sawicki, F., and P. Mathiot. (1999). Les membres des cabinets ministériels socialistes en France (1981) et London (1993). *Revue française de science politique* 1–2: 3–29, 231–64.

Silicani, J.-L. (2008). *Livre blanc sur l'avenir de la fonction publique: Faire des services publics et de la fonction publique des atouts pour la France*. Paris: La Documentation française.

Suleiman, E.N. (1974). *Politics, Power and Bureaucracy in France*. Princeton: Princeton University Press.

Thoenig, J.-C. (1973). *L'Ere des technocrats: Le cas des Ponts et chaussées*. Paris: Editions d'Organisation.

– (1996). Les grands corps. *Pouvoirs* 79: 107–20.

Worms, J.-P. (1966). Le préfet et ses notables. *Sociologie du Travail* 3: 249–75.

Wright, V. (1992). *The Government and Politics of France*. London: Routledge.

3 Steering from the German Centre: More Policy Coordination and Fewer Policy Initiatives

JULIA FLEISCHER

It is almost a truism in contemporary research on executives that government policy-making has become increasingly complex, with apparent effects on the steering role of the centre of government (e.g., Peters, Rhodes, and Wright, 2000). The steering role of the centre covers various aspects, but this chapter focuses on its capacities to ensure coherent government policies and to formulate and enforce policy priorities across central government (see Dahlström, Peters, and Pierre, this volume). Two different scholarly debates address the effects of a growing complexity in executive politics on the centre. On the one hand, authors refer to *internal* changes of central government organizations and argue that administrative reforms may cause an increasing fragmentation of the state which, in turn, encourages central government offices to centralize government policy-making in order to regain control (Peters and Pierre 1998; see also Bezes and Le Lidec, Kekkonen and Raunio, as well as Smith, this volume). On the other hand, particularly for European parliamentary systems, scholars note that *external* dynamics such as the role of the media in politics, the personalization of election campaigns, and the political and economic integration of European Union (EU) member states result in a 'presidentialization of politics' (Poguntke and Webb 2005; see also Jensen, as well as Stolfi, this volume).

Although these dynamics in executive politics are observed for many countries, Germany seems to be a deviant case. Internally, German central government organization has not been reformed as radically as others over the past decades, for example, regarding the devolution of functions from central to regional level or the delegation of tasks from ministries to non-majoritarian semi-autonomous agencies (Pollitt and Bouckaert 2004; Goetz 2005). Hence, it is very unlikely that government policy-making in Germany centralizes as a response to unintended side-effects of public sector reforms. Externally, Germany is widely acknowledged to face various environmental pressures, due to the export dependency of its national economy, its founding membership of the EU, and its Bismarckian welfare state (Green and Paterson 2005). However, it has been portrayed as a 'chancellor democracy' (Niclauß 1988) ever since – to emphasize the pivotal role of the German chancellor within the politico-administrative system. This notion may be regarded as an 'early version of presidentialization' (Poguntke 2005: 65), although it refers among other features to the chancellor's tight control over her party whereas the recent debate on presidentialization stresses the opposite – the growing distance between the head of government as party leader and her party (Poguntke and Webb 2005). Yet, the chancellor's strong position can be assumed as a constant feature of German government policy-making. Despite that, or because of it, it is comparatively difficult for the office holder to substantially strengthen her steering role in executive politics (Poguntke 2005: 81). Accordingly, both academic debates argue that the German centre of government has been less strengthened than others.

This chapter seeks to explain how such a less strengthened centre of government steers executive politics. Here, the centre refers to both the German chancellor as head of government as well as the Federal chancellery as central government office at her disposal which also serves the entire cabinet (Behrendt 1967; Müller-Rommel 2000; Busse 2005). It argues that the German politico-administrative system affects the steering role of the centre and refers its remit towards coordinating departmental interests rather than formulating and enforcing policy priorities across the central government. Moreover, the Federal chancellery responds to myriad constraints from its institutional environment with an organizational structure that provides high coordination but comparatively low policy initiation and enforcement capacities.

A New Institutionalist Explanation for the Steering Role of the Centre

To examine the steering role of the centre of government, this chapter follows the new institutionalist turn in organization theory which addresses causal interactions between institutions and organizations (see Scott 2008; Christensen et al. 2007). From this perspective, the steering role of the centre is influenced by institutional features at the macro-level of politico-administrative systems as well as its own organizational characteristics that correspond to this institutional context. In turn, the steering role of the centre becomes 'institutionalized,' that is, entrenched into the institutional underpinning of executive politics.

A recent overview of new institutionalism provides a rather broad definition of institutions: 'Institutions are comprised of regulative, normative, and cultural-cognitive elements that, together with associated activities and resources, provide stability and meaning to social life' (Scott 2008: 48). These three ideal types of pillars are present in any institutional system and interact to promote and sustain orderly behaviour (Scott and Davis 2003: 258; Scott 2008: 50–9). The three commonly distinguished new institutionalist subsets – rational choice institutionalism, historical institutionalism, and sociological institutionalism (Hall and Taylor 1996) – are not uniquely associated with one of these three institutional pillars (Scott 2008: 70, 89). Instead, new institutionalists vary in their attention to the three institutional elements.

First, scholars emphasizing *regulative* features of institutions view institutions as systems of rules which constrain, but also permit actors' behaviour (North 1990: 4; Scott and Davis 2003: 259; Christensen et al. 2007: 20–3; Williamson 1985, 1996). For government policy-making, regulative institutions include constitutions, laws, or formal enforcement procedures that are assumed to affect government actors' behaviour (Alexander and Scott 1984; Scott 2008: 52). Second, scholars concentrating on *normative* institutional features define institutions as the moral framework for actors' preferences in social life (Scott and Davis 2003: 260). Normative institutions define goals and objectives but also designate appropriate behaviour to pursue them (Christensen et al. 2007: 37–43). They are internalized by actors, and range from generalized societal norms to occupational and professional standards (March and Olsen 1989: 308; Ruef and Scott 1998: 878). For executive politics, scholars refer to normative expectations and values of government actors that are transmitted, for example, in relational structures such as networks (Scott 2008: 97). Finally, many organization theorists focus on *cognitive* features, defined as frames through which meaning is constructed (Scott 2008: 56–9). These shared meanings are taken for granted by actors and construct 'cognitive maps' (Tolman 1948) as interpretation schemes that guide government actors' behaviour (Rein and Schon 1996: 89). Such cognitive frames construct policy paradigms underlying policy controversies (Hall 1989; Ziegler 1997; Hay 2001) or are summarized as administrative culture or departmental philosophies (Jann 1983, 2002; Rhodes, Wanna, and Weller 2008). Following this threefold definition of institutions, central government organizations can be characterized as 'institutional structures' (Campbell and Lindberg 1990; Scott and Davis 2003: 266–8), composed of *regulative* elements instructing governmental actors how to formulate government policies in a formally correct manner, *normative* elements suggesting appropriate practices of policy formulation, and *cognitive* elements specifying how the developed practice of policy formulation helps to accomplish predefined goals (see also Jann 2008).

New institutionalist organization theorists also assume that actors respond to these institutional constraints and emphasize the explanatory relevance of organizational structure (Scott 2008: 164). Because new institutionalism takes a more 'totalistic or monolithic view of organizational and societal structures' (Scott 2008: 211), however, no comprehensive theoretical approach has been formulated yet to explain how organizational attributes of actors affect their responses to institutional requirements. Instead, scholars still contest the explanatory relevance of organizational features (Fligstein 1985, 1990; Keck and Tushman 1993; Greening and Gray 1994). Likewise, new institutionalist organization theory lacks indicators to measure organizational characteristics. Therefore, this chapter uses primarily indicators for organizational attributes suggested by earlier contingency theorists, but rejects their theoretical argument and uses them only as heuristics (see Pugh et al. 1963, 1968; Hood and Dunsire 1981). In addition, it analyses an organizational feature that is stressed by recent empirical research on central government offices (Bakvis 1997; Peters and Barker 1993; Peters, Rhodes, and Wright 2000; James and Ben-Gera 2004; James 2007; Dahlström, Peters, and Pierre, this volume).

The Institutional Context of Executive Politics in Germany

This chapter focuses on five institutional characteristics of the German politico-administrative system that address the inner workings of the executive 'from above' and 'from below' (Goetz 2003: 74): The state structure, the type of party government, and the key principles structuring cabinet decisions emphasize a *governmental* perspective on executives and stress political aspects of policy-making. In contrast, the administrative tradition and the partisan politicization of the civil service, that is, partisan appointments, follow an *administrative* perspective on policy-making and highlight the bureaucratic foundations of executive power. Although these 'institutional underpinnings to govern' (Manning et al. 1999) are located at two different analytical levels, they interact in practice. Hence, party government affects principles that structure cabinet decision-making, as evidenced by coalition governments which establish more mechanisms to ensure the involvement of all coalition parties in cabinet decisions than do single-party governments (Blondel and Müller-Rommel 1993; Saalfeld 1999: 145). Likewise, the administrative tradition of the civil service is related to party patronage in civil service positions; for example, in countries with a *Rechtsstaat* tradition such partisan appointments are more often legally regulated than in countries with a public interest tradition (Rouban 2003: 317–19). Similarly, coalition governments typically allow broader partisan politicization of civil servants whereas single-party governments more often restrict such appointments (Page and Wright 1999: 275–6). In the following, though, these institutional underpinnings to govern are discussed separately, emphasizing their distinct hypothesized effects on the steering role of the centre of government.

A Governmental Perspective on the Institutional Underpinnings to Govern in Germany

First, according to the German Basic Law (Grundgesetz, GG), Germany is a federal state with sixteen states (Länder; Art. 20 GG) and a strong local self-government (Art. 28.2 GG) – allocating decision-making competencies at different state levels. Whereas the federal government is mostly responsible for policy formulation, the Länder are strongly engaged in policy implementation, but participate in federal policy formulation via the upper chamber (Bundesrat). In 2006, a comprehensive reform of the German federalism aimed to simplify these fragmented responsibilities, but resulted in rather minor advancements (Burkhart, Manow, and Ziblatt 2008; Scharpf, 2007, 2008). This German 'executive federalism' (Lehmbruch 1979) is characterized by negotiations, bargaining, and compromise among actors, which result frequently in 'joint-decision traps' (Scharpf 1988). The German chancellor becomes the 'chief negotiator' (Poguntke 2005: 68), particularly as the relevance of the Bundesrat has increased over time (Mayntz 1980; Scharpf 1988; Smith 1991). The Federal chancellery supports her in this role, and most often the chancellery's chief of staff (ChefBK), who is traditionally one of the chancellor's closest personal aides (Walter and Müller 2002), acts as intermediary. In addition, the chancellery provides administrative support, for example, for preparing meetings of the mediation committee (*Vermittlungsausschuss*) established in distinct legislative procedures to solve conflicts between the two legislative chambers (Lehnert and Linhart 2009; for the U.S. experience see Peters, this volume).

Second, the personalized proportional representation in Germany traditionally causes 'minimal winning coalitions' between a catch-all party and a smaller party. (In both the late 1960s and the late 2000s, Germany has been governed by a grand coalition of the two catch-all parties.) In these coalition governments, policy initiatives are most often developed incrementally to accommodate divergent interests (Smith 1991). In turn, government actors become accustomed to policy compromise by 'negative coordination,' that is, by compromises based on the least common denominator (Scharpf 1997). Moreover, German coalition governments traditionally establish bodies which include executive and legislative actors to support coordination between coalition partners (Rudzio 2006; Miller 2009). These bodies are rather informal. The most important one is the 'coalition steering committee' (*Koalitionsausschuss*) which typically comprises the chancellor, the vice-chancellor, the chairmen of the parliamentary parties, and, if they are not among the aforementioned, the party chairmen (Coalition Agreement, 2009: 131); occasionally, also other cabinet ministers or Members of Parliament may attend. This committee also provides wide-ranging policy influence for the chancellor, because a policy consensus accomplished in this body is conventionally binding for the legislature (Saalfeld 2003). Because of these dynamics in German coalition governments, policy initiatives by the centre are difficult to prepare, but also regarded as unnecessary. Instead, government actors favor incremental policymaking without strong central policy direction and solve conflicts in bodies that intertwine executive and legislative actors. These allow some policy influence by the centre, but simultaneously safeguard the involvement of all relevant coalition actors.

Finally, a constitutional provision frames cabinet decision-making in Germany: 'The Federal Chancellor shall determine and be responsible for the general guidelines of policy. Within these limits each Federal Minister shall conduct the affairs of his department independently and on his own responsibility. The Federal Government shall resolve differences of opinion between Federal Ministers' (Art. 65 GG).

Although this triangle of leadership by the chancellor (*Kanzlerprinzip*), the cabinet (*Kabinettsprinzip*), and the cabinet ministers (*Ressort-*

prinzip) is continually changing, over time the third became the most recognized and protected (Mayntz 1984). Accordingly, the focus of cabinet ministers in cabinet on their own policy proposals and government policy-making in general is dominated by departmental initiatives (Mayntz 1980: 156; König 1987; Benzner 1989: 112–22; Smeddinck and Tils 2002: 314–20). The cabinet principle, though, is assumed to be the least relevant principle in practice and developed over time into a conflict-management scheme. That is, since the early 1970s it is a common normative expectation among cabinet members to avoid conflicts in cabinet and solve them before meetings. Therefore, both principles assign a significant coordinating and arbitrating authority to the chancellery as cabinet secretariat and simultaneously reduce its engagement in formulating policy (Mayntz 1980: 146–7).

The third constitutional principle of leadership by the chancellor is exercised in different forms. First, the chancellor issues her policy guidelines regularly in government declarations in parliament, traditionally at the beginning of a new legislative term or to announce major policy initiatives or changes. In practice, though, these declarations are often prepared jointly by the chancellery and the affected ministries and thus either summarize departmental policy initiatives or declare and explain changes of previous departmental policies (Korte 2002a; Stüwe 2005). Second, the chancellor principle is applied in foreign and EU policy, which is assumed to be the office holder's traditional prerogative (Niclauß 1988; Beichelt 2007).

Although 'summitry' (King 1994: 161) increased over time, and thus the German chancellor is more often engaged in decision-making at the international and EU level, these policies are most often prepared ex ante between the chancellery and affected ministries. For example, traditionally the chancellor appoints a permanent state secretary inside the Ministry for Economic Affairs as her sherpa for preparing G-8 summits (Fleischer 2011). Finally, the chancellor may use her constitutional prerogative on selected policy issues, commonly known as '*Chefsachen*,' that is, as the chancellor's personal projects. On the one hand, chancellors announce a policy issue as a *Chefsache* to prioritize it, for example, supporting a particular departmental policy initiative or strengthening the German position at international level, overlapping with her engagement in foreign and EU affairs noted above. On the other hand, chancellors declare a *Chefsache* to symbolize their personal commitment and involvement in the decision-making process, often acting as mediator in interdepartmental conflicts (Korte 2002b; Holtmann

2008; Schuett-Wetschky 2008). Thus, the constitutionally safeguarded chancellor principle allows the German head of government explicitly to issue policy guidelines, but these are often exercised to support or coordinate departmental policy initiatives rather than to issue direct orders.

An Administrative Perspective on the Institutional Underpinnings to Govern in Germany

First, the Rechtsstaat tradition imposes two different constraints on German executive politics and the steering role of the centre. On the one hand, parliamentary legislation is subject to judicial review by the Federal Constitutional Court, creating an important possibility to modify or block governmental policies even after they have been accepted by parliament. The simple prospect of court action often induces the legislator to modify or drop government initiatives (von Beyme 1996: 375; Knill 1999: 119). As a consequence, government policy-making in Germany is not only confined by compliance with the constitution, but also restricted by a potentially far-reaching ruling of the court that co-defines the political feasibility of policy initiatives. This comparatively strong and policy-active role of the court restricts the centre's steering role, not only by limiting available policy options, but also by increasing the need for consensus among all actors in many policy initiatives to avoid a legal case (Benz 2008).

On the other hand, the Rechtsstaat tradition strongly frames the processes of government policy-making. The two most important legally binding 'rule-books' are the 'Rules of Procedure of the Federal Government' (*Geschäftsordnung der Bundesregierung*, GOBReg) and the 'Joint Rules of Procedure of the Federal Ministries' (*Gemeinsame Geschäftsordnung der Bundesministerien*, GGO). The GOBReg define the chancellor's prerogative to issue policy guidelines in stating that they are 'binding' upon cabinet ministers (§ 1.1 GOBReg 2002). Moreover, they require that 'issues of controversy between Federal ministers have to be submitted to the Federal government only if an attempt to compromise between the Federal ministers or, in case of absence, between their deputies has failed. The Federal chancellor may chair a meeting of affected Federal ministers on issues of controversy prior to cabinet meetings' (s. 17 GOBReg 2002).

Thus, these formal rules assign to the chancellor the role as principal mediator in conflicts among ministers. In practice, however, such conflicts are often settled by a formal expansion of the issue to increase the number of affected ministries and enable package deals, or by transferring it either to the coalition steering committee when the involved ministers are from different parties or to party bodies when conflicts occur between ministers from the same party (König 1991: 210–1).

The GGO stipulate particular requirements on departmental policy-making, for example, that the ministry leading a policy initiative (*Federführung*) is also responsible for ensuring that other ministries with an interest in the issue participate via co-signature (*Mitzeichnung*; s. 15 GGO 2009; Benzner 1989: 112–22; Smeddinck and Tils 2002: 314–20). Also, the GGO allocate privileges to distinct ministries, for example, to the Ministries of Finance, of the Interior, and of Justice (ss. 44, 45, 46, Annex 6, GGO 2009); currently, almost every ministry enjoys particular consultation privileges for distinct issues (Annex 6, GGO 2009). The GGO also emphasize the pivotal role of the chancellery: 'The Federal ministries will inform the Federal chancellery in good time of all matters of fundamental political importance' (s. 24.1 GGO 2009).

Hence, these rules allocate privileges of consultation to various ministries in interdepartmental policy-making, but likewise stress the central role of the chancellery in executive politics, again referring to coordination responsibilities rather than a general obligation for initiation of policy.

Second, party-political appointees in Germany are commonly known as 'political civil servants' (*politische Beamte*). The members of this group of around 150 civil servants can be temporarily retired at any time with no reason because they hold high-ranking positions where full agreement with the government's goals is required (s. 30.1 *Beamtenstatusgesetz* 2009; Kugele 1976). In practice, about half of all political civil servants remain in office after government turnovers (Derlien 2003: 410). Since 1953, this group is defined by the Federal Civil Service Law (*Bundesbeamtengesetz*, BBG) enumerating their positions, which include all permanent state secretaries and division heads of the federal bureaucracy (s. 54 BBG 2009). These civil servants are not appointed as such, but rather enter this special category by being promoted or recruited to the pay grade and rank (Mayntz 1984: 183-4; s. 15.2 GOBReg 2002).

This comparatively strong partisan politicization of the German civil service may generally constrain a steering from the centre because cabinet ministers benefit from politically skilled civil servants at their disposal. In practice, however, the two top layers of the federal bureaucracy are also responsible for the continuous scrutiny of departmental proposals for political feasibility and thus partly unburden the central

Figure 3.1: Previous position of permanent state secretaries in
German federal ministries, 1949–2009

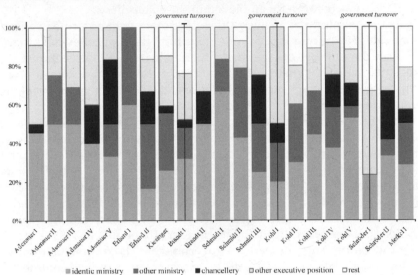

Source: Own dataset, information compiled from Schindler, 2000; Kempf and
Merz, 2001, 2008; Hoffmann, 2003; Syad Ali, 2003; Knoll, 2004; Feldkamp,
2005; Munzinger-Archive Online and press releases from the Federal
chancellery and Federal ministries.

Note: The figure includes all permanent state secretaries appointed during
each cabinet (for definition, see Schindler 2000; 1030). The methodological
problem of the different lengths of cabinets and numbers of permanent state
secretary posts is partly reduced by presenting and discussing the data in
percentages.

government office. To access these capabilities, the chancellery directs
formalized networks with these actors: Under the chairmanship of the
ChefBK, a weekly meeting of all permanent state secretaries prepares
cabinet meetings and enables the centre of government to benefit from
their 'political pre-screening.' The meeting also serves as additional
mediation arena for interdepartmental conflicts (Busse 2005: 92).

Most permanent state secretaries at the federal level are promoted
from executive positions and thus possess comprehensive administrative skills. Of approximately 350 post holders since 1949, around 91 per
cent held executive offices before appointment (see Figure 3.1). The

chancellery seeks to influence such promotions (Rudzio 2006: 244) and keeps intensive contacts particularly with those permanent state secretaries who were formerly employed in the chancellery.

As the longitudinal analysis shows, for more than a third of all German cabinets the number of promotions from the chancellery was higher than the number of candidates recruited from all other ministries together. Thus, it is plausible to assume that cabinet ministers appoint candidates from the chancellery because of their competencies and skills gained in the chancellery. These promotions occur most often during the second cabinet after a government turnover, illustrating that candidates become well known for their capabilities during the first cabinet of the new government. These dynamics were particularly apparent for the government turnovers in 1969 and 1998, but not in 1982 – which points to the relevance of party-political considerations in such recruitments (Manow 1996; Manow and Zorn 2004; see also Thies 2001).

In sum, institutional features of the German politico-administrative system impose several constraints on executive politics and the steering role of the centre of German governments. The fragmented multi-actor system entails various regulative requirements which confine the centre's scope of action to policy coordination rather than policy initiation. Likewise, the Rechtsstaat tradition and the strong position of the Constitutional Court, the various formal rules for executive politics, as well as the partisan politicization of the civil service enforce regulative controls on the centre – and limit its possibilities of policy initiation while emphasizing its role in interdepartmental coordination. Correspondingly, normative elements support this narrow steering role of the centre; for example, government actors expect and respect the centre of government as key mediator. Similarly, political civil servants are normatively accepted as appropriate 'transmission belts' (Hesse and Ellwein 1992: 316) inside ministries as well as between the centre and ministries. These emerging networks are again strongly oriented towards coordination and mediation of interdepartmental conflicts rather than towards formulating and enforcing policy initiatives of the centre. Likewise, the dominant cognitive worldview among government actors assigns ministries the prerogative to formulate government policies and rejects a strong interference from the centre.

The 'Complying' Organization of the Federal Chancellery

Most studies addressing the chancellery's organization explain these characteristics by the leadership style of the chancellor or ChefBK rather than the institutional features of the German politico-administrative system (e.g., Müller-Rommel 1994; Knoll 2004). In contrast, this chapter argues that political leadership might be relevant, but the organization of a central government office reflects also its institutional environment. Following contingency theorists and subsequent debates on the application of their measures on government organizations (Pugh et al. 1963, 1968; Hood and Dunsire 1981), this chapter focuses particularly on three organizational characteristics, namely the chancellery's size, configuration, and expertise.

First, the size of an organization defines *how* an organization conducts its tasks by delineating the number of personnel and *what* the tasks of an organization are by limiting the budget encroachments by other organizations (Ragsdale and Theis III 1997: 1297). Organizational size can be assessed differently (see Kimberly 1976); the size of the Federal chancellery is measured here by the number of full-time equivalent personnel. Second, an organizational configuration maps the 'system of relationships between positions or jobs described in terms of the authority of superiors and the responsibility of subordinates' (Pugh et al. 1963: 305). Here, configuration is described as 'authority configuration,' which refers to the vertical 'span of control,' that is, the number of authority levels, and as 'status configuration,' describing the number of ranks and grades within an organization (Pugh et al. 1963: 306). Finally, organizational expertise is defined as the degree to which an organization possesses formal expertise among its members (Hood and Dunsire 1981: 62–4). This chapter assesses the chancellery's expertise by analysing the professional background of its personnel. This indicator may interact with the status configuration, because in many government organizations grades and ranks serve also as signals for distinct professional or educational backgrounds and careers. Furthermore, this organizational analysis of the German central government office includes internal advisory arrangements as a fourth organizational feature which has been emphasized in recent empirical studies on central government offices (Bakvis 1997; Peters and Barker 1993; Peters, Rhodes, and Wright 2000; James and Ben-Gera 2004; James 2007; Fleischer 2011).

The Contingent Chancellery: Size, Configuration, and Expertise

First, in its early years the Federal chancellery comprised around 100 officials, and its personnel increased only moderately during the first two decades. After the general election in 1969 resulted in the first government turnover since 1949, the size of the Federal chancellery increased sharply from nearly 250 to around 450 members (Knoll 2004: 178). Since then, the chancellery's size remained rather stable with approximately 500 officials today (Federal Budget 2009). Compared with ministries that vary between some 420 officials in the Ministry for Family Affairs, Senior Citizens, Women and Youth and about 1,900 officials in the Ministry of Finance (Federal Budget 2009), the chancellery's size is rather small.

Second, the authority configuration of the chancellery reveals a hierarchical organization differentiated into a political leadership level and an administrative line structure. At the political leadership level, the ChefBK is the most pivotal actor in the chancellery. The holder of this office is ranked either as permanent state secretary or minister without portfolio – with the latter formalizing the informal perception that the ChefBK enjoys the same status as cabinet ministers (Knoll 2004: 421–3); for two short periods, a dual leadership was established at the top level with a ChefBK and an additional parliamentary state secretary as well as an additional permanent state secretary, but this structure failed both times and was soon abolished (Murswieck 2003: 128). In practice, the ChefBK performs various roles because of the chancellery's dual function as the chancellor's office and the cabinet secretariat (Walter and Müller 2002). Moreover, a small number of 'Federal commissioners' (*Bundesbeauftragte*) has been formally associated with the chancellery's leadership since the 1970s. These commissioners are either appointed on a legal basis, for example, the commissioner for migration policy (s. 92 *Aufenthaltsgesetz* 2008), or by an organizational decree of the chancellor, for example, the ChefBK as commissioner for the intelligence services (Knoll 2004: 230). Recently, agency heads have also been appointed as commissioners, for example, the commissioner for the Stasi records (s. 35.1 *Stasi-Unterlagen-Gesetz* 1991). However, the number of these commissioners remained very small and although their influential position within their policy field results partly from their formal affiliation to the chancellery, they are less perceived as elements of the centre of government – but offer the chancellor opportunities to get involved in policy (Clemens 2009: 133). Moreover, both the chancellor and the ChefBK are often supported by small staffs at the top organizational level, which provide administrative support but may also engage in policy formulation. The most prominent recent example for a policy initiative strongly directed by such a staff was the 'Agenda 2010,' a government reform program for social and labour market policy issued in 2003 which was mainly prepared by the so-called ChefBK's staff, although it was also coordinated with affected ministries (Korte 2007: 175).

At the operational level, the chancellery is organized into line divisions whose heads are often portrayed as the chancellor's personal advisers for their particular policy area (*FAZ* 2007). These division heads benefit from a rather exceptional normative convention: They are widely perceived as equal to permanent state secretaries in ministries and thus communicate with these formally higher-ranked senior civil servants on an equal basis (private information).[1] The line divisions are organized into sections, partly arranged into groups that exist since the early 1970s. These groups allow placing policy issues into context and simultaneously assign group heads as managers of issues addressed by different sections (Busse 1998: 140–1). In general, the line sections are either responsible for cross-cutting issues such as EU affairs or the relations between the Federal and Länder levels, or they are mirror sections which monitor ministries. Some mirror sections are responsible for one ministry, others for a major policy area associated with a particular ministry. These responsibilities of the chancellery's line structure changed only gradually since its most radical change after the government turnover in 1969, when three line divisions were expanded to five line divisions. Later changes were rather minor adjustments, for example, when in 1975 after the 'Guillaume affair' a sixth line division for the intelligence services was created (Knoll 2004: 230) or when in 2002 the existing planning division was substituted with a division for EU affairs (Beichelt 2007).

Finally, the professional background of chancellery personnel is strongly related to the 'rotation principle,' a cabinet decision which stipulates that all higher civil servants inside the chancellery are seconded from Federal ministries for a distinct period of time; there are now approximately 120 such officials (Federal Budget 2009). These secondees are generally regarded as highly talented and many are offered a promotion when they return to their parent ministry. This continuous influx of departmental secondees affects strongly the expertise of the chancellery: These officials are specialists in the policy areas of their parent ministries and add a generalist perspective on policy-making (*Die Zeit* 2006: 4). The number of seconded officials varies and reflects the ministries' different size and available positions for rotation, but also the chancellery's requirements for expertise. Officials from the Foreign Office are continuously seconded to the chancellery because of provisions of the diplomatic service, but the other ministries differ over time: During the 1980s, most officials were rotated from the Ministries for Labour and for Education, whereas during the 1990s and 2000s the Ministries of Finance, Economic Affairs, and Defence became more dominant. These dynamics may be partly explained by the increasing relevance of financial and economic policies as a result of European integration as well as the stronger military engagement of Germany. Also, the increasing number of officials from the Ministry for Economic Affairs is related to the chancellor's agenda in privatization policy since the late 1980s, whereas officials from the Ministry of Finance are also seconded because they are generally perceived as having a valuable overview on other ministries (Fleischer 2011).

In sum, except the radical changes in the aftermath of the government turnover in 1969, the chancellery's organization developed rather gradually and resulted in a size, configuration, and expertise which provide substantial capacities for coordinating government policy-making as well as initiating and enforcing policies. The authority configuration of the chancellery is characterized by comparatively flat hierarchies, whereas the status configuration is rather complex because it comprises various grades and ranks, including diplomatic ranks. Besides, some officials inside the chancellery enjoy often a higher informal status than their formal rank. Although the rotation principle enables the centre to adjust its expertise according to its own policy priorities, these recruitment patterns simultaneously limit its formulation and enforcement of policy initiatives across central government. Such activities are very likely to counteract departmental interests and thus are prone to fail given the dual loyalty of departmental secondees. Instead, this underlying principle facilitates networks of experts between the central government office and ministries that ultimately sustain the coordination role of the centre in government policy-making.

The Chancellery as Strategic Apex of the Chancellor

Despite the strategic capacities within line sections, various organizational arrangements have been created at the chancellery for policy and strategy advice which contribute to its capacities to formulate and enforce its own policy initiatives. First, several staffs have been established at the chancellery's organizational top level on a temporary basis to support the ChefBK and the chancellor on particular policy issues, for example, after 1992 for German reunification and after 1998 for the reconstruction of Eastern Germany as well as the German-French relations (Knoll 2004: 391–4). These staffs provide capacity for the centre to influence government policy-making, often in policy areas that cut across ministries. Therefore, their responsibilities are not only oriented towards policy initiation but also towards enhancing the coordination between affected ministries. Occasionally, such staffs symbolize the chancellor's attention to particular issues, as in the case of German-French relations, but offer less significant influence on policy.

Second, the chancellery's line structure was repeatedly equipped with extra strategy capacities (see Fleischer 2009). After the general election in 1969, the first full-fledged line division for planning was created and gained considerable influence as a hub for a newly introduced government-wide planning and coordination system (Süß 2005). This new planning system referred explicitly to prioritizing policies and thus provided capacity for the centre to affect departmental policy initiatives. However, the system was soon successfully rejected by ministries, which feared excessive central influence (Müller-Rommel and Pieper 1991: 9). As a consequence, the formal ex ante coordination of the cabinet timetable remained, but the planning system lost its proactive impetus and turned soon into a 'policy-unrelated bookkeeping' (Ronge 1977: 81). After the government turnover in 1982, the planning division was re-oriented towards press and media relations for the chancellor with very low influence on government policy (Knoll 2004: chapter H.II). When the next government turnover took place in 1998, the planning division was re-launched, but addressed rather exceptional policy issues such as the compensation scheme for Nazi-forced labourers or the conferences of left/centre governments on 'progressive governance' (Schröder, Kocka, and Neidhardt, 2002). Thus, it was not strongly interested in affecting interdepartmental coordination, or promoting and enforcing its own policy ideas across the central government. After the general election in 2002, the line division was abolished and partly integrated into a staff for the ChefBK which was comparatively more involved in formulating new government policies (e.g., Agenda 2010, see above), albeit still rather weak in enforcing these policies vis-à-vis the ministries. In 2005, the new chancellor created a small planning staff at the chancellor's direct disposal which seems to support her more strongly in party-political conflicts than in executive politics (FAZ 2006: 4).

Finally, the chancellery experiences temporary organizational changes of its line structure linked to the work of external expert councils or commissions. These expert bodies are primarily designated to advise on major government policies such as migration, the labor market, pensions, health, or biotechnology (Rudzio 2006: 259–60). Moreover, they provide an additional negotiation arena between divergent policy interests (Siefken 2007). Here, the chancellery hosts temporary liaison offices, for example, for the expert commission that scrutinized the labour market in 2002 and provided several policy recommendations that were also incorporated into the Agenda 2010 noted above (Siefken 2006). Currently, the chancellery provides a liaison office for the National Regulatory Control Council that is engaged in de-bureaucratization policies (Beus 2007). The liaison offices offer the centre direct access to these external expert councils or commissions that perform a similar 'feasibility role' as permanent state secretaries in the ministries. Simultaneously, the centre may use its close access for influencing the experts (Siefken 2007).

In sum, various organizational arrangements inside the Federal chancellery provide some capabilities for formulating policy initiatives. However, advisory arrangements in the line structure were only initially oriented towards priority setting and soon turned towards a synchronization of proposals by the ministries. Occasionally, these weak line capabilities to promote own policy initiatives are compensated for by temporary staffs at the top level for particular policy issues or by line support for external expert councils and commissions that offer possibilities to influence distinct policy areas.

Conclusion

This chapter examines the steering role of the German centre of government in executive politics. It reveals that this steering role is strongly affected by contextual regulative, normative, and cognitive elements which confine its remit to coherent government policy-making and limit its capability to formulate and enforce its own policy initiatives. From a regulative perspective, several governmental and administrative features put checks on the steering role of the centre, ranging from a multiactor constellation in executive federalism and coalition government, a powerful Constitutional Court, to various formal procedural requirements on executive politics and a cadre of political civil servants at the disposal of ministers. From a normative perspective, government actors expect an arbitrating centre and assign the prerogative of policy initiation to ministries. Likewise, political civil servants are perceived as an appropriate resource to support ministers, while the centre is not privileged to be equipped with additional political appointees. From a cognitive perspective, the dominant world-view in German executive politics is ministry-oriented, and thus the centre of government is primarily seen as a policy coordinator rather than as a policy initiator.

The chancellery's organization complies with this 'institutional definition' of the steering role of the German chancellery in executive politics which subordinates policy initiatives to policy coordination. In accordance with the departmental principle, the chancellery is composed of rotating departmental secondees and mirror sections considering departmental interests. Similar to ministries, political civil servants are appointed only at the two top organizational levels, and the chancellery hosts no additional political appointees to formulate and enforce policy initiatives. Instead, such policy capacities are provided by staffs at the top organizational level or temporary organizational units supporting external expert councils or commissions.

A new institutionalist organization theory perspective informs us that these interactions between institutional constraints and organizational actors are recursive and thus argues that the centre of government also affects the institutional underpinnings of executive politics in order to institutionalize its own steering role. For the German chancellery, particular administrative elements have been affected. On the one hand, the chancellery deploys the existing procedural mechanisms and developed a normative status as final arbiter which is accepted by conflicting ministries. On the other hand, the network of political civil servants directed by the centre not only imposes regulative requirements on ministries, but also disseminates normative expectations about appropriate behaviour for interactions with the centre and ultimately ensures that the centre can unburden itself from political feasibility analyses – and improve its coordination capacities.

To conclude, the German centre of government has not been strengthened like many others, but steers executive politics by focusing on its institutionalized role as the 'hub of executive coordination.' Here, both aspects of steering interact: The comparatively modest capacities of the German centre of government to formulate and enforce its own policy initiatives are partly compensated for by a strong coordination role – which deploys the institutional opportunities of the politico-administrative system and the organizational characteristics of the central government office.

NOTE

1 To provide a recent example (see Fleischer and Parrado 2010), the interministerial committees to manage two special funds established to cope
   with the global financial and economic crisis in Germany comprise four
   permanent state secretaries from affected ministries as well as one division
   head from the chancellery, on an equal basis.

REFERENCES

Bakvis, H. (1997). Advising the Executive: Think Tanks, Consultants, Political
   Staff and Kitchen Cabinets. In P.M. Weller and H. Bakvis (eds.), *The Hollow
   Crown*. Houndmills: Macmillan.
Behrendt, G. (1967). *Das Bundeskanzleramt*. Bonn: Athenäum.
Beichelt, T. (2007). Over-efficiency in German EU Policy Coordination. *German
   Politics* 16: 421–33.
Benz, A. (2008). From Joint Decision Traps to Over-regulated Federalism:
   Adverse Effects of a Successful Constitutional Reform. *German Politics* 17:
   440–56.
Benzner, B. (1989). *Ministerialbürokratie und Interessengruppen: Eine empirische
   Analyse der personellen Verflechtung zwischen bundesstaatlicher Ministerialorga-
   nisation und gesellschaftlichen Gruppeninteressen in der Bundesrepublik Deutsch-
   land im Zeitraum 1949–1984*. Baden-Baden: Nomos.
Beus, H.B. (2007). Der Abbau von Bürokratie als politisches Ziel: Die Maßnah-
   men der Bundesregierung. *Zeitschrift für Staats- und Europawissenschaften* 5:
   68–77.
Beyme, K. von. (1996). *Das politische System der Bundesrepublik Deutschland nach
   der Vereinigung*. Munich: Piper.
Blondel, J., and F. Müller-Rommel (eds.). (1993). *Governing Together*. Hound-
   mills: St Martin's Press.
Burkhart, S., P. Manow, and D. Ziblatt. (2008). A More Efficient and Account-
   able Federalism? An Analysis of the Consequences of Germany's 2006
   Constitutional Reform. *German Politics* 17: 522–40.
Busse, V. (1998). Hierarchieebenen und Gruppenstruktur am Beispiel des
   Bundeskanzleramtes. *Verwaltungsarchiv* 89: 137–43.
– (2005). *Bundeskanzleramt und Bundesregierung: Aufgaben, Organisation,
   Arbeitsweise*, 4th ed. Heidelberg: Hüthig.
Campbell, J.L., and L.N. Lindberg. (1990). Property Rights and the Organi-
   zation of Economic Activity by the State. *American Sociological Review* 55:
   634–47.

Christensen, T., P. Lægreid, P.G. Roness, and K.A. Røvik. (2007). *Organization Theory for the Public Sector: Instrument, Culture and Myth*. London: Routledge.

Clemens, C. (2009). Modernisation or Disorientation? Policy Change in Merkel's CDU. *German Politics* 18: 121–39.

Coalition Agreement. (2009). *Growth. Education. Solidarity*, Oct. Berlin.

Derlien, H.-U. (2003). Mandarins or Managers? The Bureaucratic Elite in Bonn, 1970 to 1987 and Beyond. *Governance* 16: 401–28.

Die Zeit. (2006). Die leise Machtmaschine: Vom Lagezentrum bis zur Skylobby – Wo und wie in Angela Merkels Kanzleramt Politik gemacht wird. *Die Zeit* (8 June): 3–5.

Feldkamp, M.F. (2005). *Datenhandbuch zur Geschichte des Deutschen Bundestages 1994 bis 2003*. Baden-Baden: Nomos.

Fleischer, J. (2009). Power Resources of Parliamentary Executives: The Institutionalization of Policy Advice in Western Europe. *West European Politics* 32: 196–214.

– (2011). Das Primat der Richtlinienkompetenz in politischen Prozessen: Zur Bedeutung der Organisation des Bundeskanzleramtes. In M. Florack and T. Grunden (eds.), *Regierungszentralen: Führung, Steuerung und Koordination zwischen Formalität und Informalität*. Wiesbaden: VS Verlag für Sozialwissenschaften.

Fleischer, J., and S. Parrado. (2010). Power Distribution in Ambiguous Times: How the Financial Crisis Affects Executive Coordination in Germany and Spain. *Der moderne staat* 3: 361–76.

Fligstein, N. (1985). The Spread of the Multidivisional Form among Large Firms. *American Sociological Review* 50: 377–91.

– (1990). *The Transformation of Corporate Control*. Cambridge, MA: Harvard University Press.

Frankfurter Allgemeine Zeitung (FAZ). (2006). Wenn es auf Gesichtswahrung ankommt. *FAZ* (13 March): 4.

– (2007). Redigierer. *FAZ* (24 March): 8.

Goetz, K.H. (2003). Executives in a Comparative Context. In J. Hayward and A. Menon (eds.), *Governing Europe*. Oxford: Oxford University Press.

– (2005). Administrative Reform. In S. Green and W.E. Paterson (eds.), *Governance in Contemporary Germany: The Semisovereign State Revisited*. Cambridge: Cambridge University Press.

– (2007). German Officials and the Federal Policy Process: The Decline of Sectional Leadership. In E.C. Page and V. Wright (eds.), *From the Active to the Enabling State: The Changing Role of Top Officials in European Nations*. Basingstoke: Palgrave.

Green, S., and W.E. Paterson (eds.). (2005). *Governance in Contemporary Germany: The Semisovereign State Revisited*. Cambridge: Cambridge University Press.

Greening, D. W., and B. Gray. (1994). Testing a Model of Organizational Response to Social and Political Issues. *Academy of Management Journal* 37: 467–98.

Hall, P.A. (1989). *The Political Power of Economic Ideas*. Princeton: Princeton University Press.

Hall, P.A., and R.C.R. Taylor. (1996). Political Science and the Three New Institutionalisms. *Political Studies* 44: 936–57.

Hay, C. (2001). The 'Crisis' of Keynesianism and the Rise of Neoliberalism in Britain. In J.L. Campbell and O.K. Pedersen (eds.), *The Rise of Neoliberalism and Institutional Analysis*. Princeton: Princeton University Press.

Hesse, J.J., and T. Ellwein. (1992). *Das Regierungssystem der Bundesrepublik Deutschland*, 7th ed. Opladen: Westdeutscher Verlag.

Hoffmann, H. (2003). *Die Bundesministerien 1949–1999: Bezeichnungen, amtliche Abkürzungen, Zuständigkeiten, Aufbauorganisation, Leitungspersonen*. Koblenz: Bundesarchiv.

Holtmann, E. (2008). Die Richtlinienkompetenz des Bundeskanzlers: Kein Phantom? In E. Holtmann and W.J. Patzelt (eds.), *Führen Regierungen tatsächlich? Zur Praxis gouvernementalen Handelns*. Wiesbaden: VS Verlag für Sozialwissenschaften.

Hood, C., and A. Dunsire. (1981). *Bureaumetrics: The Quantitative Comparison of British Central Government Agencies*. Alabama: University of Alabama Press.

James, S. (ed.). (2007). *Political Advisers and Civil Servants in European Countries*. SIGMA Paper No. 38. Paris: OECD.

James, S., and M. Ben-Gera. (2004). *A Comparative Analysis of Government Offices in OECD Countries: Meeting of Senior Officials from Centres of Government on Using New Tools for Decision-Making – Impacts on Information, Communication and Organization*. Paris: OECD.

Jann, W. (1983). *Staatliche Programme und 'Verwaltungskultur': Bekämpfung des Drogenmißbrauchs und der Jugendarbeitslosigkeit in Schweden, Großbritannien und der Bundesrepublik Deutschland im Vergleich*. Opladen: Westdeutscher Verlag.

– (2002). Verwaltungskultur: Ein Überblick über den Stand der empirisch und international vergleichenden Forschung. *Die Verwaltung* 33: 325–49.

– (2008). Regieren als Governance Problem: Bedeutung und Möglichkeiten institutioneller Steuerung. In W. Jann and K. König (eds.), *Regieren zu Beginn des 21. Jahrhunderts*. Tubingen: Mohr Siebeck.

Keck, S.L., and M.L. Tushman. (1993). Environmental and Organizational Context and Executive Team Structure. *Academy of Management Journal* 36: 1314–44.

Kempf, U., and H.-G. Merz. (2001). *Kanzler und Minister 1949–1998: Biografi-*

sches Lexikon der deutschen Bundesregierungen. Wiesbaden: Westdeutscher Verlag.

— (2008). *Kanzler und Minister 1998–2005: Biografisches Lexikon der deutschen Bundesregierungen*. Wiesbaden: VS Verlag für Sozialwissenschaften.

Kimberly, J.R. (1976). Organizational Size and the Structuralist Perspective: A Review, Critique, and Proposal. *Administrative Science Quarterly* 21: 571–97.

King, A.S. (1994). Chief Executives in Western Europe. In I. Budge and D. McKay (eds.), *Developing Democracy*. London: Sage.

Knill, C. (1999). Explaining Cross-National Variance in Administrative Reform: Autonomous versus Instrumental Bureaucracies. *Journal of Public Policy* 19: 113–39.

Knoll, T. (2004). *Das Bonner Bundeskanzleramt: Organization und Funktionen von 1949–1999*. Wiesbaden: VS Verlag für Sozialwissenschaften.

König, K. (1987). Gesetzgebungsvorhaben im Verfahren der Ministerialverwaltung. In W. Blümel, D. Merten, and H. Quaritsch (eds.), *Verwaltung im Rechtsstaat*. Cologne: Heymanns.

— (1991). Formalisierung und Informalisierung im Regierungszentrum. In H.-H. Hartwich and G. Wewer (eds.), *Regieren in der Bundesrepublik: Formale und informale Komponenten des Regierens*. Opladen: Leske and Budrich.

Korte, K.R. (2002a). The Effects of German Unification on the Federal Chancellor's Decision-Making. *German Politics* 11: 83–98.

— (2007). Der Pragmatiker des Augenblicks: Das Politikmanagement von Bundeskanzler Gerhard Schröder 2002–2005. In C. Egle and R. Zohlnhöfer (eds.), *Ende des rot-grünen Projektes*. Wiesbaden: VS Verlag für Sozialwissenschaften.

Korte, K.R. (ed.). (2002b). 'Das Wort hat der Herr Bundeskanzler': Eine Analyse der Großen Regierungserklärungen von Adenauer bis Schröder. Wiesbaden: Westdeutscher Verlag.

Kugele, D. (1976). *Der politische Beamte: Eine Studie über Genesis, Motiv, Bewährung und Reform einer politisch-administrativen Institution*. Munich: Tuduv.

Lehmbruch, G. (1979). Ein später Sieg Bismarcks: Exekutivföderalismus und Parlamentarische Parteiregierung. *Der Bürger im Staat* 29: 34–7.

Lehnert, M., and E. Linhart. (2009). Der Einfluss der Mehrheitsverhältnisse im Vermittlungsausschuss auf den deutschen Gesetzgebungsprozess. In S. Susumu, J. Behnke, and T. Bräuninger (eds.), *Jahrbuch für Handlungs- und Entscheidungstheorie*, vol. 5. Wiesbaden: VS Verlag für Sozialwissenschaften.

Manning, N., N. Barma, J. Blondel, E. Pilichowski, and V. Wright. (1999). *Strategic Decisionmaking in Cabinet Government: Institutional Underpinnings and Obstacles*. Washington, DC: World Bank.

Manow, P. (1996). Informalisierung und Parteipolitisierung: Zum Wandel exekutiver Entscheidungsprozesse in der Bundesrepublik. *Zeitschrift für Parlamentsfragen* 27: 96–107.

Manow, P., and H. Zorn. (2004). *Office versus Policy Motives in Portfolio Allocation: The Case of Junior Ministers.* MPIfG Discussion Paper 04/9. Cologne: Max Planck Institute for the Study of Societies.

March, J.G., and J.P. Olsen. (1989). *Rediscovering Institutions.* New York: Free Press.

Mayntz, R. (1980). Executive Leadership in Germany: Dispersion of Power or 'Kanzlerdemokratie'? In R. Rose and E.N. Suleiman (eds.), *Presidents and Prime Ministers.* Washington, DC: American Enterprise Institute for Public Policy Research.

– (1984). German Federal Bureaucrats: A Functional Elite between Politics and Administration. In E.N. Suleiman (ed.), *Bureaucrats and Policy-Making: A Comparative Overview.* New York: Holmes and Meier.

Miller, B. (2009). Informelle Einflussnahme? Parlamentarier im Koalitionsausschuss. In H. Schöne and J. von Blumenthal (eds.), *Parlamentarismusforschung in Deutschland: Ergebnisse und Perspektiven 40 Jahre nach Erscheinen von Gerhard Loewenbergs Standardwerk zum Deutschen Bundestag.* Baden-Baden: Nomos.

Müller-Rommel, F. (1994). The Chancellor and His Staff. In S. Padgett (ed.), *Adenauer to Kohl: The Development of the German Chancellorship.* London: Hurst.

– (2000). Management of Politics in the German Chancellor's Office. In B.G. Peters, R.A.W. Rhodes, and V. Wright (eds.), *Administering the Summit: Administration of the Core Executive in Developed Countries.* Houndmills: Macmillan.

Müller-Rommel, F., and G. Pieper. (1991). Das Bundeskanzleramt als Regierungszentrale. *Aus Politik und Zeitgeschichte* 21–2: 3–13.

Murswieck, A. (2003). Des Kanzlers Macht: Zum Regierungsstil Gerhard Schröders. In C. Egle, T. Ostheim, and R. Zohlnhöfer (eds.), *Das rot-grüne Projekt: Eine Bilanz der Regierung Schröder 1998–2002.* Opladen: Westdeutscher Verlag.

Niclauß, K. (1988). *Kanzlerdemokratie: Bonner Regierungspraxis von Konrad Adenauer bis Helmut Kohl.* Stuttgart: Kohlhammer.

North, D.C. (1990). *Institutions, Institutional Change and Economic Performance.* Cambridge: Cambridge University Press.

Page, E., and V. Wright. (1999). Conclusion: Senior Officials in Western Europe. In E. Page and V. Wright (eds.), *Bureaucratic Elites in Western European States: A Comparative Analysis of Top Officials.* Oxford: Oxford University Press.

Peters, B.G., and J. Pierre. (1998). Governance without Government? Rethinking Public Administration. *Journal of Public Administration Research and Theory* 8: 223–43.

Peters, B.G., and A. Barker (eds.). (1993). *Advising West European Governments: Inquiries, Expertise and Public Policy*. Edinburgh: Edinburgh University Press.

Peters, B.G., R.A.W. Rhodes, and V. Wright (eds.). (2000). *Administering the Summit. Administration of the Core Executive in Developed Countries*. Houndmills: Macmillan.

Poguntke, T. (2005). A Presidentializing Party State? The Federal Republic of Germany. In T. Poguntke and P. Webb (eds.), *The Presidentialization of Politics: A Comparative Study of Modern Democracies*. Oxford: Oxford University Press.

Poguntke, T., and P. Webb (eds.). (2005). *The Presidentialization of Politics: A Comparative Study of Modern Democracies*. Oxford: Oxford University Press.

Pollitt, C., and G. Bouckaert. (2004). *Public Management Reform: An International Comparison*, 2nd ed. Oxford: Oxford University Press.

Pugh, D.S., D.J. Hickson, C.R. Hinings, K.M. Macdonald, C. Turner, and T. Lupton. (1963). A Conceptual Scheme for Organizational Analysis. *Administrative Science Quarterly* 8: 289–315.

Pugh, D.S., D.J. Hickson, C.R. Hinings, and C. Turner. (1968). Dimensions of Organization Structure. *Administrative Science Quarterly* 13: 33–47.

Ragsdale, L., and J.J. Theis III. (1997). The Institutionalization of the American Presidency, 1924–92. *American Journal of Political Science* 41: 1280–1318.

Rein, M., and D. Schon. (1996). Frame Critical Policy Analysis and Frame Reflective Policy Practice. *Knowledge and Policy: The International Journal of Knowledge Transfer and Utilization* 9: 85–104.

Rhodes, R.A.W., J. Wanna, and P.M. Weller. (2008). Reinventing Westminster: How Public Executives Reframe Their World. *Policy and Politics* 36: 461–79.

Ronge, V. (1977). Bundeskanzleramt. In K. Sontheimer and H.H. Röhring (eds.), *Handbuch des politischen Systems der Bundesrepublik Deutschland*. Munich: Piper.

Rouban, L. (2003). Politicization of the Civil Service. In B.G. Peters and J. Pierre (eds.), *Handbook of Public Administration*. London: Sage.

Rudzio, W. (2006). *Das politische System der Bundesrepublik Deutschland*, 7th ed. Wiesbaden: VS Verlag für Sozialwissenschaften.

Ruef, M., and W.R. Scott. (1998). A Multidimensional Model of Organizational Legitimacy: Hospital Survival in Changing Institutional Environments. *Administrative Science Quarterly* 43: 877–904.

Saalfeld, T. (1999). Coalition Politics and Management in the Kohl Era, 1982–98. *German Politics* 8: 141–73.

– (2003). Germany: Multiple Veto Points, Informal Co-ordination and Problems of Hidden Action. In K. Strøm, W.C. Müller, and T. Bergman (eds.), *Delegation and Accountability in Parliamentary Democracies*. Oxford: Oxford University Press.

Scharpf, F.W. (1988). The Joint-Decision Trap: Lessons From German Federalism and European Integration. *Public Administration* 66: 239–78.

– (1997). *Games Real Actors Play: Actor-Centred Institutionalism in Policy Research*. Oxford: Westview.

– (2007). Nicht genutzte Chancen der Föderalismusreform. In C. Egle and R. Zohlnhöfer (eds.), *Ende des rot-grünen Projektes: Eine Bilanz der Regierung Schröder 2002–2005*. Wiesbaden: VS Verlag für Sozialwissenschaften.

– (2008). Community, Diversity and Autonomy: The Challenges of Reforming German Federalism. *German Politics* 17: 509–21.

Schindler, P. (2000). *Datenhandbuch zur Geschichte des Deutschen Bundestages 1949 bis 1999*. Baden-Baden: Nomos.

Schröder, G., J. Kocka, and F. Neidhardt. (2002). *Progressive Governance for the XXI Century: Contribution to the Berlin Conference 02–03 June 2000*. Munich: Beck.

Schuett-Wetschky, E. (2008). Richtlinienkompetenz (hierarchische Führung) oder demokratische politische Führung? Antwort an Everhard Holtmann. In E. Holtmann and W.J. Patzelt (eds.), *Führen Regierungen tatsächlich? Zur Praxis gouvernementalen Handelns*. Wiesbaden: VS Verlag für Sozialwissenschaften.

Scott, W.R. (2008). *Institutions and Organizations*, 3rd ed. London: Sage.

Scott, W.R., and G.F. Davis. (2003). *Organizations: Rational, Natural and Open Systems*, 5th ed. Englewood Cliffs: Prentice-Hall.

Scott, W.R., M. Ruef, P.J. Mendel, and C.A. Caronna. (2000). *Institutional Change and Healthcare Organizations: From Professional Dominance to Managed Care*. Chicago: University of Chicago Press.

Siefken, S.T. (2006). Regierten die Kommissionen? Eine Bilanz der rot-grünen Bundesregierungen 1998 bis 2005. *Zeitschrift für Parlamentsfragen* 37: 559–81.

– (2007). *Expertenkommissionen im politischen Prozess: Eine Bilanz zur rot-grünen Bundesregierung 1998–2005*. Wiesbaden: VS Verlag für Sozialwissenschaften.

Smeddinck, U., and R. Tils. (2002). *Normgenese und Handlungslogiken in der Ministerialverwaltung: Die Entstehung des Bundes-Bodenschutzgesetzes – Eine politik- und rechtswissenschaftliche Analyse*. Baden-Baden: Nomos.

Smith, G. (1991). The Resources of a German Chancellor. *West European Politics* 14: 48–61.

Stüwe, K. (2005). *Die Rede des Kanzlers: Regierungserklärungen von Adenauer bis Schröder*. Wiesbaden: VS Verlag für Sozialwissenschaften.

Süß, W. (2005). 'Wer aber denkt für das Ganze?' Aufstieg und Fall der ressortübergreifenden Planung im Bundeskanzleramt. In M. Frese, J. Paulus, and K. Teppe (eds.), *Demokratisierung und gesellschaftlicher Aufbruch*. Paderborn: Ferdinand Schöningh.

Syed Ali, A. (2003). *Karrierewege und Rekrutierungsmuster bei Regierungsmitgliedern auf Bundesebene von 1949–2002*. Doctoral dissertation, Martin-Luther-Universität, Halle-Wittenberg.

Thies, M.F. (2001). Keeping Tabs on Partners: The Logic of Delegation in Coalition Governments. *American Journal of Political Science* 45: 580–98.

Tolman, E.C. (1948). Cognitive Maps in Rats and Men. *Psychological Review* 55: 189–208.

Walter, F., and K. Müller. (2002). Die Chefs des Kanzleramtes: Stille Elite in der Schaltzentrale des parlamentarischen Systems. *Zeitschrift für Parlamentsfragen* 33: 474–501.

Williamson, O.E. (1985). *The Economic Institutions of Capitalism*. New York: Free Press.

– (1996). *The Mechanisms of Governance*. New York: Oxford University Press.

Ziegler, J.N. (1997). *Governing Ideas: Strategies for Innovation in France and Germany*. Ithaca: Cornell University Press.

4 The Core Executive in Italy: A More Visible Skipper, but Still Little Steering

FRANCESCO STOLFI

This chapter charts the evolution of the power of the Italian core executive since the early 1990s in three key dimensions: political and institutional power within the cabinet, administrative power (i.e., the power to steer the administration), and scope, namely the area of political decision-making falling within the remit of the central government.

The first dimension, which refers to the horizontal coordination powers within the executive, has been influenced by three factors: the change in electoral rules, the personalization of politics connected to the peculiar patterns of media ownership in the country, and fiscal pressure. Overall, the upshot has been a significant change in the role and position of the core executive (the prime minister and finance minister in particular). From their relative weakness vis-à-vis the rest of the cabinet until the early 1990s, prime ministers and finance ministers now tend to stand above it, although some prime ministers, for reasons that have to do with coalitional dynamics, their personalities, and differential access to personal power bases in the media, have been more able than others to secure their leadership.

The second dimension refers to the vertical coordination powers that transmit the policy impulses from the political to the administrative levels. The fundamental development in this area has been the increasing politicization of the administration. As in other countries, this phenomenon was set off by a drive to improve the coordination capabilities of the centre of government. However, it has evolved in ways that were not intended by the reformers, and that are more in keeping with the long-term nature of policy-making in Italy. Politicians have used politicization for clientelistic purposes and to reassert their control over everyday decisions with distributive implications.

Finally, no treatment of the evolution of core executive power in Italy would be complete without mention of the process of regionalization that has taken place since the 1990s. However, its impact on the authority of the core executive remains unclear, both because the central government retains instruments to influence policy at the regional level, and because the process itself has not concluded yet.

In sum, the picture that we get from the Italian case is one of change. The impact of this change on policy-making, however, is not necessarily positive. Governments and particularly prime ministers are more accountable to voters than in the past, but the policy capacity of governments has not kept up with this greater accountability. The upshot is a style of policy-making that risks emphasizing spectacularization over substantive policies.

The Strengthening of the Political and Institutional Position of the Italian Core Executive

From the admittedly very low levels in the period after the Second World War the political and institutional position of the Italian core executive has significantly improved in the past fifteen years. Until the early 1990s Italy was a typical case of 'government by ministry' (Andeweg 1993). Ministers and the party (or party factions) they represented would have control of their ministries, from which they would serve their constituencies, while little attention was given to the implementation of a common government program. This was the result of the combined effect of an extremely proportional electoral law, which favoured party fragmentation, and the fact that the main opposition party, the Italian Communist Party, was unable to be part of a coalition in the context of Cold War, which effectively ruled out government alternation.

In these conditions common government programs had little or no weight in the eyes of the coalition partners and of the voters. As a result the prime minister, the supposed guardian of the government program (Weller 1991), had little political weight within the cabinet. Prime ministers would be selected by the coalition partners after the elections, and, lacking direct electoral legitimacy, would be at the mercy of the shifting power relations among the parties in the coalition and, if coming from the relative majority party (the Christian Democrats), they would also have to contend with the power of the party's secretary general. That the coalitions were also rather large (five parties in the 1980s) further reduced the prime minister's ability to coordinate policy.

Responsibility for fiscal policy was distributed among three different ministers, thus making its coordination difficult. Furthermore, in particular in the 1970s and 1980s, the weakening of a shared sense of fiscal discipline within the cabinet meant that the minister responsible for the control of government spending (the treasury minister) found it increasingly hard to resist the demands of his colleagues, with disastrous results for Italian public finances.

Repeated attempts were made to strengthen the prime minister and to improve the coordination of fiscal policy by concentrating responsibility in a single minister. However, the political constraints of coalition government made reform impossible. In fact, even though the Constitution of 1948 called for a law organizing the cabinet and regulating the role of the prime minister, for forty years no such law was passed.

In the 1990s, however, a series of reforms raised the institutional position of both the prime minister and the treasury minister to the levels that still obtain today. In 1993 the rules for the organization of the cabinet were finally introduced. These rules gave the prime minister sole responsibility over the government agenda in parliament and formalized the 'pre-council' meeting, namely a preparatory meeting chaired by a fiduciary of the prime minister where representatives of each ministry and of the legislative office come together to coordinate their positions on the agenda to be discussed in the upcoming Council of Ministers.

The institutional position of the prime minister was further strengthened in 1999. Legislative decree 303/1999 gave the Prime Minister's Office budgetary autonomy and the operational flexibility that comes with it, thus allowing the prime minister the ability to shape the bureaucratic machinery that serves him according to his policy priorities. Furthermore, the decree finally shed the administrative functions that had accumulated in the office over time and that were under the direct control of the ministers without portfolio. Moreover, the prime minister was given the power to propose to the cabinet the dismissal of undersecretaries, non-cabinet ministers in charge of specific policy areas within ministries. A similar concentration of power occurred with regard to fiscal policy. Over the course of the 1990s responsibility for it was gradually concentrated, with the process eventually leading in 2001 to the creation of a single finance ministry.

However, the institutionalization of policy coordination powers under the control of the prime minister stopped and even reversed after 2001, in particular with Silvio Berlusconi's return to power. In keeping with his expertise in and emphasis on the media (Seisselberg 1996), when Berlusconi became prime minister again (2001–2006) he used the new flexibility of the Prime Minister's Office to strengthen its media and communication structures (Calise 2005). At the same time, some of the prime minister's policy coordination powers receded. For instance, in 2006 the Prime Minister's Office reacquired some of the direct operational tasks that the 1999 reform had eliminated precisely because they were an obstacle to the prime minister's coordination function (Alesse 2007).

The evolution of the coordination powers of the prime minister, increasing in the 1990s and decreasing in the 2000s, can be explained by the combination of structural changes in the electoral and party systems with the peculiar effects of the personalization of politics.

As regards the first factor, the 1990s saw a significant change in electoral rules, from proportional representation to a mostly majoritarian system. As a result, the party system has coalesced around two, centre-right and centre-left, coalitions. These are relatively stable coalitions bound by a common program and the support for a common candidate premier. Before the elections, the coalition leaders embody the coalition's program. If the coalition wins the elections, they are responsible before the voters for the implementation of the program. This has given the prime minister new political relief and electoral legitimacy that is independent from the parties in the government coalition (Vassallo 2007).

The bipolarization of the Italian party system was able to resist the reintroduction of a proportional representation electoral system in 2005. The system is in any case rather majoritarian, as it provides for a significant seat premium for the winning coalition, thus providing an incentive for the formation of pre-electoral coalitions. Moreover, in the past few years the two coalitions have begun to coalesce around two main parties, the Partito Democratico on the left and Popolo della Libertà on the right.

In turn, the requirements of the new bipolar electoral competition, and in particular of the new political relevance of the government coalitions' program, have called for a prime minister able to coordinate its implementation, and were indeed the explicit reason for the reforms that strengthened the prime minister in the late 1990s (Pajno 2000). The concentration of power in a strong finance minister also owes a great deal to the bipolarization of political competition and the greater cohesiveness of the government coalitions, which have reduced the need to distribute the control of fiscal policy among different coalition partners (Stolfi 2008). Furthermore, first the need to fulfil the fiscal requirements for participation in the Economic and Monetary Union, and later the acceptance by successive cabinets of the need for greater fiscal responsibility than in the past have also contributed to raising the standing of the finance minister (De Ioanna and Goretti 2008; Fabbrini 2000). Consistently with the overall majoritarian shift in Italian politics that has followed the majoritarian electoral reform of the 1990s, the executive has also tightened its control over parliament through changes in the standing orders and through ample use of legislative instruments that limit the role of parliament.

Furthermore, we suggested above that the personalization of politics might have had a perverse effect in Italy, effectively reducing the incentive for the prime minister to invest in policy coordination and the implementation of the government program, or at least for a prime minister that had a good understanding of the mass media and controls most of them (Hibberd 2007).

Specifically, Berlusconi's rise and the deployment of media for and against him have contributed to personalize politics (Diamanti and Lello 2005), turning elections into periodical referenda on Berlusconi. He has been especially adept at making direct appeals and commitments to the voters through public and private television channels (Pasquino 2007). The media orientation of the Berlusconi government has had institutional implications. As we saw above the Prime Minister's Office has been reorganized to emphasize its media activities, while the structure tasked to monitor the implementation of the government program has been refocused on managing the external image of the government rather than on maintaining the coherence of government policies (Natalini 2006).

The main conclusion that can be drawn from this brief excursus is that while both bipolarization and personalization have concentrated political power into the centre of government, personalization, coupled with the ability to manage the government's image presented to the media, has also had the perverse effect of reducing the prime minister's incentive to actually coordinate government policy.

Moving beyond this overall assessment, one should, however, note that the ebb and flow of coalition dynamics has also affected the political power of the core executive vis-à-vis the rest of the cabinet. First, the political power of the prime minister has varied with the number of parties in the coalition, more fragmented coalitions tending to increase the bargaining power of individual parties at the expense of the prime minister. Hence, prime ministerial autonomy has in general been lower with the centre-left governments, which have been based on more fragmented coalitions than the centre-right governments.

Second, the autonomy of the prime minister has depended on expectations on his political future and on the future electoral performance of the coalition. Thus, Berlusconi's power to control his allies, very high at the beginning of his 2001–2006 government, was progressively reduced as the electoral chances of the centre-right worsened, while Romano Prodi's tenuous hold on the fragmented centre-left coalition in 2006–2008 was further weakened when it became clear that he was not going to be the coalition leader in the next elections. Similarly, although finance ministers have overall become much more powerful within the cabinet than they were in the 1970s and 1980s, their ability to enforce their will over their colleagues also depends on their individual circumstances, purely 'technical' ministers being weaker than ministers who have the support of important coalition partners.

The Politicization of Public Administration: From Organizational Strategy to Clientelistic Tool

This section briefly sketches the trajectory of administrative reforms that began in the 1990s. Their goal was to improve the vertical coordination in policy-making, and one of the planks of the reform program was the introduction of politicization in the appointment of public managers. However, as we will see, the whole structure of reform, conscientiously designed though it was, largely failed at the implementation stage. As for politicization, it was indeed implemented, but it took on features that were not intended by the reformers. Rather than a strategy to facilitate coordination, it became a way to foster clientelism and to reassert political control over the administration through the back door.

The reforms that strengthened the institutional resources of the prime minister within the cabinet were part of a broader reform program that, after decades of immobility, swept through the public administration in the 1990s. Given the notorious inefficiency of the Italian public administration, its reform had been debated for decades. Until the early 1990s, however, actual reforms were rare, as changes to the organization of the public administration tended to be limited to personnel matters. Things changed dramatically in the 1990s, leading observers to speak of a shift from 'improbable to permanent reform' (Capano 2000).

The inspiration for change came from both domestic reflection, in particular by administrative lawyers, and international theories and experiences. On the domestic side, in 1979 the famous Giannini report set the blueprint for many of the innovations of the 1990s. The domestic tradition was complemented in the mid-1990s by the influence of New Public Management, whose prescriptions were spread by some of the few non-lawyers interested in public administration (Dente 1995a) and later adopted by the reformist centre-left governments of 1996–2001 (Bassanini 2000).

The opportunity for reform arose from the same context outlined in the previous section. The government parties' loss of control in the wake of the corruption scandals of 1992–1993 gave reformers a first window of opportunity. Later in the decade, the shift to a bipolarized party system gave governments with a reform program (in particular the centre-left governments of 1996–2001) the relatively stable majorities needed to introduce the reforms.

The core of the reforms was the separation of politics and administration, a perennial concern of public administration reformers in Italy as elsewhere, made more acute in the early 1990s by the scandals that had exposed the most pernicious effects that the mingling of politics and administration could cause. Throughout the postwar period the relationship between civil servants and politicians had been based on a bargain, whereby the former traded off any real decision-making power in exchange for job security (Cassese 1983). This was also consistent with a legalistic attitude, rooted in the law background of most civil servants, which emphasized adherence to detailed procedures rather than achieving policy results. As for the politicians, they gained full control of discretional decision-making within the administration, with all the distributive, and worse, opportunities it afforded.

Therefore, by the early 1990s, breaking the hierarchical dependence of top civil servants on the politicians was considered fundamental, not only in light of the *Tangentopoli* scandals that brought down the postwar party system in 1992–1994 when a vast web of political corruption became public, but also because it was felt that establishing two separate spheres, politics for the definition of goals, broad strategies and policy coordination, and administration for actual policy-making, was necessary to give coherence to government policy-making as a whole.

The objective of the reforms that unfolded throughout the 1990s was to have a coherent policy-making system, with at its head a prime minister able to coordinate the cabinet on the one hand, and control the implementation of policies on the other. The first leg was to be achieved through the reforms described in the previous section. The second leg was based on a system whereby the Prime Minister's Office issues yearly policy directives (*direttive madri* or 'mother directives') which are reflected in the yearly budget decisions, while individual ministers issue directives for their own ministries according to the broad lines of the mother directive. The line administrations are given managerial and financial autonomy to pursue the goals outlined in the ministerial directives, and the public managers are made responsible for achieving these goals. Controls and incentives close the circle, linking the line administrations to the ministers and the ministerial cabinets, and the latter to the Prime Minister's Office.

Politicization of the public administration was part and parcel of this reform design, as it was supposed to give administrators a stake in the results of policy in the context of a clear separation of tasks, with politicians setting the broad policy goals of the government and civil servants taking charge of the technical design and implementation of policy.

Thus, the same piece of legislation (legislative decree 80/98) that completed the separation between politics and administration also introduced the spoils system into the Italian administrative system, making all top civil servants subject to political confirmation by the incoming government. It also introduced what detractors have called the 'temporization' of public management (Natalini 2006: 70), making all managerial contracts temporary (between a minimum of two and a maximum of seven years). Finally, it set a quota (5%) of managers who could be appointed from outside the public administration.

After the opening to politicization in 1998, the process has gained speed. The centre-right government that succeeded the centre-left in 2001 continued on the road of politicization and temporization of public management. In 2002, law 145/02 extended de facto the mechanism of political appointment from the top civil servants to all directors, with a one-off cancellation of all existing managerial appointments. The law also further temporized managerial contracts, eliminating minimum lengths and cutting maximum lengths to three (for the top civil servants) or five years (for all other directors). The law also increased the quota of public management positions open to administration outsiders (to 10% of top positions and 8% of director positions). The centre-left, which briefly returned to power in 2006–2008, also appeared to continue further along the same path, extending the time available to incoming governments to change the top civil servants and extending the spoil system to the directors of agencies (law 286/06).

Politicization (for the top civil servants) and temporization (for all other public managers) were respectively meant to create a fiduciary relationship between politicians and top administrators and to give all other administrators a stake in the policies assigned to them. However, the end result has been to reassert the politicians' control of day-to-day distributive decision-making and to give them an opportunity for cliental hiring.

As one of the key architects of the reform himself admitted (Bassanini 2008), the reform of public management depended too much on the functioning of other elements of the administrative reform, and in particular on the actual implementation of strategic planning and internal auditing. Temporization in particular has been especially problematic. The renewal of the managers' contracts, as well as their bonuses, was to depend on a system of performance assessment whereby managers would be evaluated against the achievement of the policy objectives assigned to them. In turn, the policy objectives would derive from the ministerial directives, which would present the strategic plans elaborated by the ministerial cabinets. In reality, little of this system works.

Politicians have not invested in strategic planning. Strategic plans are drafted after the approval of the government budget, namely after resources have already been allocated (Bevilacqua and Notamurzi 2007: 129). Absent properly working strategic planning, the directives are too vague to provide the benchmarks for the evaluation of the managers (Natalini 2006: 61). In fact, in many ministries the internal and strategic auditing service has only a marginal role in setting the objectives, and no capacity to assess whether they have been reached. In sum, it is the administration that sets the objectives and it is the administration that then certifies that they have been met (Battini et al. 2007: 9). Managers themselves have fought tooth and nail to prevent all but the most perfunctory performance assessments, and to make sure that all managers receive their bonuses; in recent years, 99 per cent of managers have achieved 'praiseworthy results' (Della Cananea 2008).

In fairness, it has also been difficult to hold managers accountable for results when their managerial autonomy has been significantly curtailed in practice. The financial administration has continued to keep control of the financial flows to the line administrations, in contradiction to the intentions of the budget reform of 1997 (Stolfi, Goretti, and Rizzuto 2008). The scope of managers' autonomy has been further reduced in favour of control on the part of the Finance Ministry in recent years. The Berlusconi government has made it mandatory for all central government administrations to make use of a single purchasing organization, *Concessionaria Servizi Informativi Pubblici* (CONSIP), a company which negotiates all contracts for the provision of all factors of production (both goods and services) to the public administration and which is entirely owned by the Finance Ministry.

Under these conditions, the selection and retention of managers can only depend on their political affiliation and their willingness to accept instructions from the political authorities. With law 145/02, the dependence of managers on politicians was pushed further. With the elimination of minimum contract lengths, after this law the average contract would last between two and three years, and in some cases as little as five months (Natalini 2006: 73–4), placing managers at the beck and call of politicians. The end result is quite ironic. In the old hierarchical system, politicians controlled all discretionary decision-making, and the civil servants would 'hide behind the politicians' signature.' Now, under a system of supposed separation between politics and administration, politicians again control discretionary decision-making. Through their control of contracts, they can easily get what they want from the managers. It is now the politicians that can 'hide behind the signature of the civil servants' (Battini 2009): As the reformers had originally advocated (Dente 1995b: 82), the appointment of the top civil servants should have been made by the government, but subject to the approval of parliament or of an independent authority, precisely to avoid that the power of appointment and removal might encroach upon the autonomy of the public managers. As the system has been implemented, however, politicians do not need to give any explanation for their choices of appointments or removals, which magnifies their power over the top civil servants.

Furthermore, the rapid increase in salaries that has accompanied the temporization of public managers, combined with the lack of effective managerial control, has facilitated the use of politicization as a tool for clientelistic hiring, benefitting personnel coming from the 'underbrush of politics' rather than attracting professionals from the private sector (Salvemini 2006).

The very extension of political control over managerial hiring below the higher echelons of the administration has deprived the top managers of a tool to achieve the policy goals assigned to them and signals a greater concern with the use of personnel for clientelistic purposes. Another indicator of the clientelist use of the political selection of personnel is the continuous rise in the size of ministerial cabinets, even as the qualifications of the personnel employed in the cabinets remain low; as of 2008, the ministerial cabinets have a combined staff of 2,300, up from approximately 120 in the 1980s (Torchia 2009).

In the Finance Ministry, less than 50 per cent of cabinet staff has a university degree (Fiorentino and Milani 2007: 93). Ironically, in the cabinet of the Ministry for Education, University and Research, only 15 per cent of staff has a university degree, although most of the staff is in the highest bureaucratic ranks (Battini et al. 2007: 10–11).

Compared with other countries in this collection, then, in the Italian case the pendulum of politicization has swung along a somewhat eccentric trajectory; while politicization was originally introduced as an organizational instrument to ensure political leadership over the broad contours of policy, it has not been used to achieve this goal or even to inject ideology into the policy process. Rather, it has evolved into a tool for clientelistic hiring and as a way to reassert political control over discretionary administrative decision-making, thus breaking down the very separation of politics and administration that the reforms of the 1990s were supposed to ensure.

Regionalization: An Unfinished Project

In the past two decades Italy has embarked on a process of regionalization that has not been concluded yet. Although regional governments had been created as early as 1970 (and those of some autonomous regions even before), until the 1990s Italy was a centralized country, with regions entirely depending on earmarked transfers from the centre to manage the administrative functions assigned to them (chief among them health services). Regional elections were minor affairs, and most voters would not even know who the president of their region's government was.

The combined pressure of an ascendant regional political movement, the Northern League, and of the collapse of the post–Second World War party system following the *Tangentopoli* scandals opened the door for dramatic changes. Not only the centre-right governments with which the Northern League has generally allied itself, but also the centre-left moved to increase the autonomy of the regions from the mid-1990s on. Earmarks were eliminated, and regions were given some modest autonomy in setting tax rates. In 1997, under a centre-left government, a large area of administrative functions was devolved to the regions and the local governments, and in 2001 a constitutional amendment, also passed by a centre-left majority, transferred to the regions legislative powers in a number of policy areas.

In parallel to these developments, after the scandals of the early 1990s popular opinion turned in favour of more direct expressions of voters' will from the old parliamentary regime that prevailed at all levels of government. Since 1993 mayors are directly elected, and direct election has been extended to the presidents of the regional governments in 2000, which has given 'governors' (as they are known in the media, which has adopted the U.S. terminology) local democratic legitimacy (Diamanti and Lello 2005). In turn, this has allowed local politicians to assert political autonomy from the national parties (Tronconi and Rioux 2009), thus weakening the party channels that had traditionally been an informal way in which the centre had been able to control the regions (Tarrow 1977).

The institutionalized forum in which regions and the national government meet is the State-Region Conference (*Conferenza Stato-Regioni*). Originally set up in 1983, the conference saw the scope of its activities greatly increased by the 1997 reforms. It brings together representatives of the central government (the prime minister or another minister delegated by him or her) and the presidents of the regions and of the two autonomous provinces that make up the Trentino Alto-Adige region. The law stipulates that the regions must be consulted on all central government decisions that affect them. Even though the national government can eventually decide against the opinion of the conference, it must justify why it did not take into account the position of the regions.

Overall, regionalization is still a work in progress. On the one hand, different governments have had different positions on the issue, with the current Berlusconi government (2008–), which includes the Northern League, introducing in May 2009 framework legislation that is supposed to be the legal foundation for a planned increase in the regions' legislative and fiscal autonomy. On the other hand, regional autonomy has suffered a number of setbacks, in particular during the previous (2001–2006) Berlusconi government, which froze the regions' limited ability to set their tax rates. As for the devolution of legislative authority as per the 2001 constitutional revision, its implementation has been fraught with difficulties, in particular in relation to the exact definition of the boundary between regional and central powers in areas where both levels of government are supposed to be competent.

Furthermore, the greater autonomy of regional governments has been tempered by the use of central funds (beyond the general funds assigned based on the current framework of state-regions fiscal relations) as incentives to promote specific policies on the part of the regions. Moreover, the central government retains the ability to sidestep regional and local governments if local emergencies arise. Sometimes these emergencies become entrenched, involving the central government in activities that are not supposed to be part of its purview. An example is the garbage crisis that has enveloped Naples for the past fifteen years. Successive governments have tried to address it with emergency measures that derogate to normal procedures and often derogate to the derogation of previous measures. Between 1994 and 2008, 113 such measures have been passed, which have ended up creating a parallel administrative system (Gnes 2008; Leonardi and Nanetti 2008).

Conclusion

This chapter has provided a brief overview of the developments in the position of the core executive in Italy along three dimensions: the core executive's political and institutional resources to guide policy within the cabinet (horizontal coordination), the ability of the political actors to transmit policy impulses to the bureaucracy (vertical coordination), and finally the scope of the government's authority, with reference to the balance between national and regional levels of government.

In all three dimensions the past two decades have seen significant change. Significant legislative powers, administrative functions and fiscal resources have been devolved to the regions, although all three aspects are still far from settled. Moreover, regional presidents have risen in public stature, thanks to their direct election. However, the process of regionalization has proceeded in fits and starts and is not over yet, so that it is unclear where the balance between central and regional governments will come to rest.

The political position of the core executive and in particular of the prime minister has gained strength since the early 1990s, and this has in turn increased its institutional resources. The stronger political role of the core executive is because of the bipolarization of the party system, the personalization of politics and, as regards the finance minister, the fact that Italian politics has come to accept the constraints imposed by the country's difficult financial situation, by the criteria to join the European Monetary Union (EMU) and by the current Growth and Stability Pact.

Bipolarization has favored the creation of relatively stable coalitions, and their leaders are viewed by voters as candidates to the prime minister position. Even though this expectation is only based on the political dynamics of a bipolar party system and not on any legal requirement, this de facto electoral investiture gives the prime minister a measure of direct democratic legitimacy and thus of political autonomy from the parties in the government coalition.

The prime minister's political autonomy has been further augmented by the personalization of politics that has taken place since the early 1990s. The main beneficiary of personalization has been Silvio Berlusconi, who can count on his own political party and his own media, and whose entry into the political fray in 1994 indeed greatly increased the voters' attention to individual political leaders.

The paradox is that while bipolar political competition has brought forward a clearer programmatic alternative between opposing coalitions, thus raising the political relevance of government programs and of their implementation, for which the premier is indeed responsible before the voters, the machinery of government has largely failed to follow suit. As we have seen, the reforms that were supposed to improve the ability of the public administration to plan policies and to assess their implementation and the performance of its personnel vis-à-vis the achievement of the government's programmatic goals have mostly remained on paper.

As in the past, vertical coordination continues to rely on the informal network of 'gabinettisti,' the chefs de cabinet who have developed personal connections in the long years they have worked in various cabinets, often swapping positions among each other from one ministry to the next. Beside the gabinettisti network, which operates in particular at the technical stage before the presentation of measures in the Council of Ministers, downstream in the policy process the most effective type of coordination remains the use of the 'golden reins' of finance, as the Finance Ministry's control of the purse's strings allows it to decide which policies are effectively implemented. Quite apart from the problematic implications for democratic governance, as spending decisions authorized by parliament can be frozen by an executive decision, this type of coordination fails to address the issue of the quality of policies, because its terms of reference and the instruments used are solely financial.

As for the development of politicization in the Italian public administration, it was originally thought as a way to improve vertical coordination, to facilitate the transmission of programmatic guidelines from the politicians to the administrators. However, it has turned into a tool for clientelistic hiring and a way to reassert political control over the discretionary decision-making of the public administration, thus doing nothing to reduce the fragmentation of policy-making.

The overall impact on policy-making of the changes described in this chapter has been complex. Much more than in the first forty years the postwar period, voters focus on the prime minister and expect him to deliver on his coalition's promises. Indeed, governments do seem to deliver by implementing most of their programs (Moury and Marangoni 2008). However, program implementation in the Italian context tends to be confined to the passing of legislation, with actual policy implementation still lagging behind.

Furthermore, even when policies are actually implemented, they largely continue to be made in a fragmented manner. The reforms of the public administration, including politicization, aimed to create a system producing strategies at the centre, with a feedback system that through the ministerial cabinets would connect back to the centre again in a continuous process of evaluation, adjustment, and recalibration of policies. However, the failure of the reforms and the drift of politicization towards clientelism have effectively perpetuated the fragmentation of policy-making along ministerial lines. Even centrepieces of government programs, such as the policy of investment in infrastructure emphasized by the Berlusconi government of 2001–2006, have been implemented in a fragmented fashion that has reduced their impact (Camera dei Deputati – Servizio Studi 2004).

The combination of heightened voter expectations and persisting lack of strategic and implementation capabilities risks creating incentives for governments to emphasize a politics of ambitious declarations that are not followed up or to pursue initiatives with immediate high media impact rather than coherent policy programs, whose effect is necessarily deferred. Scholars have in fact observed a tendency to permanent campaigning and the spectacularization of policy-making, particularly by the Berlusconi governments (Pasquino 2007). As the reorientation of the Berlusconi government towards media management rather than actual policy coordination intimates, the combination of personalization of politics and media control can have perverse effects on the quality of policy-making.

ACKNOWLEDGMENT

I would like to thank Carl Dahlström, Guy Peters, Jon Pierre, the participants in the Conference 'Steering from the Centre,' Gothenburg, 14–16 January 2009, and an anonymous referee for their comments on a previous draft. Responsibility for errors and omissions is mine.

REFERENCES

Alesse, R. (2007). La riorganizzazione dei ministeri. *Quaderni Costituzionali* 27/1: 141–7.

Andeweg, R.B. (1993). A Model of the Cabinet System. In J. Blondel and F. Müller-Rommel (eds.), *Governing Together*, 23–42. Houndsmills: Macmillan.

Bassanini, F. (2000). Overview of Administrative Reform and Implementation in Italy: Organization, Personnel, Procedures and Delivery of Public Services. *International Journal of Public Administration* 23/2–3: 229–52.

– (2008). I principi costituzionali e il quadro istituzionale. In G. D'Alessio (ed.), *L'amministrazione come professione*, 31–61. Bologna: Il Mulino.

Battini, S. (2009). Il Personale. In L. Torchia (ed.), *Il sistema amministrativo italiano*. Bologna: Il Mulino.

Battini, S., G. Vesperini, C. Franchini, G. Della Cananea, and B.G. Mattarella. (2007). Introduzione. In S. Cassese and B.G. Mattarella (eds.), *Gli uffici di staff nelle pubbliche amministrazioni italiane e straniere*, 7–19. Rome: IRPA.

Bevilacqua, D., and C. Notamurzi. (2007). Il Ministero dell'Interno. In S. Cassese and B.G. Mattarella (eds.), *Gli uffici di staff nelle pubbliche amministrazioni italiane e straniere*, 103–79. Rome: IRPA.

Calise, M. (2005). Presidentialization, Italian Style. In T. Poguntke and P. Webb (eds.), *The Presidentialization of Politics*, 88–106. Oxford: Oxford University Press.

Camera dei Deputati – Servizio Studi. (2004). *Le infrastrutture strategiche in Italia: L'attuazione della 'legge obiettivo.'* Rome: Camera dei Deputati.

Capano, G. (2000). Le politiche amministrative: Dall'improbabile riforma alla riforma permanente? In G.D. Palma, S. Fabbrini, and G. Freddi (eds.), *Condannata al successo?* 153–98. Bologna: Il Mulino.

Cassese, S. (1983). *Il sistema amministrativo italiano*. Bologna: Il Mulino.

De Ioanna, P., and C. Goretti. (2008). *La decisione di bilancio in Italia*. Bologna: Il Mulino.

Della Cananea, G. (2008). Un'amministrazione che costa di più e funziona peggio? In M. P. Chiti and R. Ursi (eds.), *La dirigenza pubblica*, 137–48. Turin: Giappichelli.

Dente, B. (1995a). I caratteri generali del processo di riforma. In B. Dente (ed.), *Riformare la pubblica amministrazione*, 3–28. Turin: Edizioni della Fondazione Agnelli.

– (1995b). *In un diverso Stato*. Bologna: Il Mulino.

Diamanti, I., and E. Lello, E. (2005). La Casa delle Libertà. *Modern Italy* 10/1: 9–35.

Fabbrini, S. (2000). *Tra pressioni e veti: Il cambiamento politico in Italia*. Rome: Laterza.

Fiorentino, L., and V. Milani. (2007). Il Ministero dell'Economia e Finanze. In S. Cassese and B.G. Mattarella (eds.), *Gli uffici di staff nelle pubbliche amministrazioni italiane e straniere*, 79–101. Rome: IRPA.

Gnes, M. (2008). Le ordinanze di protezione civile per fronteggiare l'emergenza nel settore dello smaltimento dei rifiuti nella Regione Campania. *Rivista giuridica del Mezzogiorno* 22/2: 433–68.

Hibberd, M. (2007). Conflict of Interest and Media Pluralism in Italian Broacasting. *West European Politics* 30/4: 881–902.

Leonardi, R., and R.Y. Nanetti. (2008). *La sfida di Napoli*. Milan: Angelo Guarini.

Moury, C., and F. Marangoni. (2008). *Goverment Law-Making in Italy*. CIES Working Paper 52/2008.

Natalini, A. (2006). *Il tempo delle riforme amministrative*. Bologna: Il Mulino.

Pajno, A. (2000). La Presidenza del Consiglio dei Ministri dal vecchio al nuovo ordinamento. In A. Pajno and L. Torchia (eds.), *La riforma del governo*, 35–106. Bologna: Il Mulino.

Pasquino, G. (2007). The Five Faces of Silvio Berlusconi. *Modern Italy* 12/1: 39–54.

Salvemini, M.T. (2006). La paga del dirigente pubblico. *La Voce* (2 May).

Seisselberg, J. (1996). Conditions of Success and Political Problems of a 'Media-Mediated Personality-Party': The Case of Forza Italia. *West European Politics* 19/4: 715–43.

Stolfi, F. (2008). The Europeanization of Italy's Budget Institutions in the 1990s. *Journal of European Public Policy* 15/4: 550–66.

Stolfi, F., C. Goretti, and L. Rizzuto. (2008). Italy. Paper presented at the Workshop on the Impact and Consequences of Budget Reform in OECD Nations, The Hague, 12–13 June.

Tarrow, S. (1977). *Between Centre and Periphery: Grassroots Politicians in Italy and France*. New Haven: Yale University Press.

Torchia, L. (2009). Sistema amministrativo e Costituzioni. In L. Torchia (ed.), *Il sistema amministrativo italiano*. Bologna: Il Mulino.

Tronconi, F., and C. Rioux. (2009). The Political Systems of Italian Regions between State-Wide Logics and Increasing Differentiation. *Modern Italy* 14/2: 151–66.

Vassallo, S. (2007). Government under Berlusconi: The Functioning of the Core Institutions in Italy. *West European Politics* 30/4: 692–710.

Weller, P. (1991). Support for Prime Ministers. In C. Campbell and M.J. Wyszomirski (eds.), *Executive Leadership in Anglo-American Systems*, 361–79. Pittsburgh: University of Pittsburgh Press.

PART THREE

Anglo-American Democracies

5 Central Steering in Australia

JOHN HALLIGAN

As governing has become more complex and challenging, and subject to higher aspirations, central steering has come to the fore. Central steering covers several functions and mechanisms, the choice of roles being shaped by context (e.g., system of government and administrative tradition), leadership style, and environmental challenges. Coordination, a major element of steering, has become prominent again internationally, where movement away from disaggregation has been pronounced and governments have been seeking to reassert central direction and oversight in order to improve performance. The tension between the decentring and recentring of governance is a perennial issue, but what type of contradiction emerges from the changing dynamics at the centre (Dahlström, Peters, and Pierre 2011) depends on the mix and the country context.

Of the Anglo-Saxon countries, Australia has emphasized a strong prime minister's department and enhancing the resources of the political executive. Although several models have been evident during the reform era, the long-term trend has been towards strengthening central steering, and that system is being pushed to a new level under political leadership that is more strategic, intergovernmental, and performance focused.

This chapter first seeks to clarify central steering and the administrative and political machinery available. It then addresses questions about challenges to governance and strategies for coping with problems. The chapter concludes with a consideration of how to interpret these responses over time, and the implications of changes in administration for the effectiveness of public governance.

Steering from the Centre

The main dimensions of central steering are generally strategic direction, priority setting, coordination, and driving implementation of change and policy, although in practice they are not all necessarily significant at the one time. Steering within a governance perspective may be primarily a question of 'setting priorities and defining goals,' whereas under New Public Management (NPM) it may primarily be 'an interorganizational strategy aimed at unleashing productive elements of the public service' (Peters and Pierre 1998: 231). A broader view is that the state is not in charge having become a societal player, albeit an important one, for example, the 'serving not steering' of Denhardt and Denhardt (2003), but a more state-centric position is relevant to national government like Australia's.

There is an assumption that coordination falls within steering (Dahlström, Peters and Pierre, this volume). Following one scheme for analysing levels of 'coordination' generically (Metcalfe, 1994), steering might cover activities like government strategy and establishing central priorities whereas coordination within steering would include the search for agreement and avoidance of divergences among departments.

Coordination has been a perennial consideration in system design, but has been featuring more in reform agendas (Peters 2006; Verhoest and Bouckaert 2005; Verhoest, Bouckaert, and Peters 2007), and has acquired some fresh characteristics. A traditional conception of coordination envisages parties taking each other into account in a process of linking activities and decisions harmoniously or reciprocally (Kernaghan and Siegel 1987). Coordination may be represented as 'remedial activity,' implying a reactive focus, such as responding to disasters and to communications problems. It would be an overstatement to depict traditional approaches as solely retrospective, but the recent emphasis has moved more to the prospective. Another definition addresses procedural and policy/functional coordination centred on central agencies (Painter 1987). Horizontal government approaches developed in the past decade to promote interagency collaboration and cooperation reflect both old and new forms of organization for connecting distinct parts of the public sector. Such approaches represent a break with conventional approaches for dealing with complex policy problems in Anglo-Saxon countries (Perri 6 2005). Within these concepts and applications there is a range of meanings from managing horizontal relationships (operating more at the interagency level) to broader formulations that envisage integration of government operations (Perri 6 2005; Verhoest and Bouckaert 2005).

The several approaches to studying the centre have different emphases. The 'executive leadership' or 'core executive' approaches emphasizes the role of the political executive (e.g., Campbell 1988; Campbell and Halligan 1993). The literature on the 'steering state' covers a range of positions that have in common a division between steering functions and implementation, although how this separation occurs varies widely in practice (e.g., Bezes 2007). A variation on this theme, the hollowing out of the state (Frederickson and Frederickson 2006) is focused on delivery beyond the centre. Moving closer to the core, the question of the state's capacity has been examined (Painter and Pierre 2005) including the relationship with coordination (Verhoest and Bouckaert 2005). The interest in coordination, long a staple of public administration (Painter 1987), re-emerged as the vacuum at the centre widened (e.g., Peters 2006). The specialized field of central agencies is under-researched, but Lindquist (2001; see also Smith, this volume) has distinguished the strong centre in Anglo-Saxon countries, based on central institutions and high capacity for coordination, from the smaller and less influential centres of European systems.

Five models are differentiated (see Halligan 2006) for considering central strategies, based (1) on whether relationships are concentrated in the core of government, central government or encompass third parties (such as state governments and nongovernment providers); and (2) the mix of political and administrative machinery that is used. Each steering strategy has different implications for the effectiveness of governance (see Table 5.1).

The *integrated hierarchical* model is grounded in traditional public administration that steered through laws and regulations, hierarchy, and control over the details of financial and personnel transactions. The *prototype steering model* departs from this transactional basis by differentiating strategic policy from operational and delivery matters. The emphasis is on the redefinition of the centre to enhance directive capacity and political focusing, with decentralization being a secondary consideration. A balanced steering and rowing arrangement is one possible outcome, but it may also be a stepping stone to a stronger 'steering state' conception, as discussed next.

The *devolved model* is assumed to be a product of reform design, either management and/or market driven, and represents a strong commitment to decentralization. It needs to be distinguished from systems

Table 5.1
Steering Strategies

Characterization	Central agencies	Political executive
Integrated hierarchical	Transactions control	Traditional relationships Reliance on public service
Prototype steering and rowing	Strategic and selective steering	Assertion of political executive Cabinet and committees Ministerial discretion
Devolved (weak centre)	Downgraded Departments and agents prominent	Accountability management
Integrated governance	Rebalancing steering at levels of political executive, central agencies, and departments	Prime ministerial control Political and performance management and control
Strategic governance	Strategic assertion horizontally and vertically	Strategic priorities and planning Prime minister

that lack a strong centre; weak centres appear to reflect either state traditions, divided central agencies, or factors that are less determinate; see, for example, Lindquist (2004) on Canada, Lægreid and Serigstad (2004) on Norway, or Bezes (2007) on France. The dominant principle is competition whereas the more integrated conception discussed below features collaboration. The main mode of control is 'hands off' under NPM relying on contracts and 'hands on' where performance is central (Newman 2002).

The fourth model, *integrated governance*, combines the attributes of a strategic centre with active line departments. In terms of governance, it unites elements of modern governance and state-centric approaches (Richards and Smith 2006; Smith, this volume). This is a demanding option that benefits from the directive role of the political executive and relies on a system of performance management.

The final model, *strategic governance*, emphasizes strategic planning and priority setting at the centre driven by the prime minister and his department and incorporating capable ministers in key areas. Intergovernmental relations have centrality for driving the major policy agenda collaboratively but subject to performance requirements. Compared to the previous model this one ratchets up the intensity of the pursuit of strategically defined priorities. The 'steering state' dimension may still be present but the 'rowers' are knitted in more directly to the centre.

The main instruments of central steering have long been part of the machinery of government. The political executive covers: the prime minister and the PM's private office; an active cabinet and cabinet committee system; and ministers and their political advisers. For the public services there are central agencies (mainly the Department of the Prime Minister and Cabinet for policy and the Department of Finance for financial management, but also Treasury for some purposes); departments of state; and the Council of Australian Governments (COAG) for intergovernmental relationships (based on ministerial and official meetings). There are also numerous IDCs (interdepartmental committees) and task forces. The reliance on specific mechanisms or combinations has implications for governance. Various instruments are relevant to specific relationships such as conditional grants and performance management, and more generally the use of political levers for directing the public service, but very limited use of overt political appointments.

Challenges to Governance

How governance challenges are perceived depends in part on governing style and whether governments are either seeking to anticipate problems before they become full-fledged issues or are merely responding as the need arises. While simultaneous invention is possible, the articulation of problems often reflects the general influence of both a global community and the specific circulation of ideas in the Anglo-Saxon realm (Halligan 2007). In these days of assertive political executives, the definition of challenges is more often led by the government, but is subject to public debate.

External Environment

External challenges have usually been fiscal in nature, and economic factors (e.g., international competitiveness) have remained a driver, although nothing compares to the global financial crisis of 2008.

Otherwise, the most important external threat during the 2000s was the issue of security and terrorism, which dominated both the domestic and international landscape (apart from the long-term impact of 9/11, there were terrorist attacks in Bali and the commitment of forces to Iraq) and had lasting effects on public management and the community. The then-Secretary of the Department of the Prime Minister and Cabinet observed that the threat of global terrorism and the emerging challenges of counter-terrorism, protection of borders, and domestic security had transformed Australian life and identity. 'Those issues, typically "non-routine," will test bureaucratic structures. Ensuring effective coordination of intelligence, analysis and strategic policy responses will test public administration' (DPMC 2003). The security question was still resonating in late 2008 when Prime Minister Rudd (2008) presented the first national security statement to parliament as both a coherent statement of the challenges and a comprehensive approach to them.

Complex Policy Problems That Cross Boundaries

A number of whole-of-government priorities for new policy-making were adopted by Prime Minister Howard (2002); they included national security, defence and counter-terrorism, and other generally defined priorities such as sustainable environment, rural and regional affairs, and work and family life. The Rudd government has maintained and extended this emphasis, covering some similar ground (e.g., national security) and new and more specific fields (climate change and productivity).

Implementing Government Policies and Priorities

Implementation of government policy was an issue at the beginning of the reform era as a result of political concern with public service independence, which produced a sustained process of redistributing power between politicians and public servants (Halligan 2001). Despite the use of different instruments, political control and performance continued to be an issue for governments, with the concern in the 2000s being that political priorities were not being sufficiently reflected in policy directions, and were not being followed through in program implementation and delivery.

Governance Failures and Weaknesses

The governance challenges have arisen from the fallout from aspects of New Public Management, a concern with corporate governance, and public crises.

The features of NPM – disaggregation, devolution, outsourcing, and multiple services providers – supported specialization but also encouraged fragmentation and reinforced vertical structures. The range of Commonwealth public bodies was documented and the dangers of 'bureaucratic proliferation' proclaimed because departments of state employed only 22 per cent of public sector employees. The official concern was with different legislative bases, constitutions, and opaque governance. Subsequently, implementation was seen to require 'clarity of purpose, powers and relationships between ministers, public servants and boards. Good governance depends upon transparency of authority, accountability and disclosure' (Shergold 2004a). The rationalization of public bodies supported departmentalization through absorbing statutory authorities and reclaiming control of agencies with hybrid boards.

Nevertheless, two extraordinary cases during the Howard government's fourth term revealed fundamental weaknesses in the internal operations of a major department and lack of oversight of a privatized body with public policy roles.

The first case was one of internal governance failure. The Department of Immigration and Multicultural Affairs (DIMA) was found to have experienced an internal breakdown of basic operating procedures, culture, and leadership. The department had acquired a high profile because of the government's focus on keeping illegal immigrants out and locating and deporting those already in Australia. The failure of governance in the DIMA was revealed through a succession of inquiries into the handling of the detention of citizens. The two main investigations were into the illegal detention of a permanent resident, and the unlawful detention and removal from Australia of a citizen. One report recorded an astounding range of weaknesses, flaws, and disconnects within an overall managerial approach that was 'process rich' and 'outcome poor' (Halligan and Tucker 2008). The government eventually referred 247 immigration matters to the ombudsman for investigation. The head of the public service, Dr Shergold, described 'the cases as the worse thing that has happened in the public service in recent years,' blaming a number of deficiencies: failures in IT systems, record-keeping, executive leadership, and public administration (ABC Online 2006).

The combination of New Public Management and political management produced a department that was vulnerable when placed under political pressure. NPM aspects included devolution, outsourcing, risk management, outcomes, and the use of principal-agent conceptions in relationships. Political management centred on the dynamics of the relationship and interactions between politicians and public servants, and how the political executive exercised control and influence. Under these circumstances, the application of law was faulty, and the situation was compounded by the inability to apply basic governance principles (Halligan and Tucker 2008). The case had implications for other departments, and produced a reform agenda that reviewed the lessons for public administration and governance.

The second case concerned oversight of privatized public policy. The Australian Wheat Board (AWB) paid kickbacks to the Iraqi government in the form of a transport surcharge. The Department of Foreign Affairs and Trade (DFAT) claimed to have been unaware of the nature of the AWB's actions. Both DFAT and the Wheat Export Authority (WEA), a statutory body responsible for monitoring AWB, were unable to demand documents from the AWB, inhibiting their capacity to confirm or certify the AWB's claims. The AWB lied on numerous occasions to, among others, the United Nations, DFAT, and the WEA. Two issues stood out: the unwillingness of senior officials and ministers to acknowledge awareness or responsibility (including the prime minister's failure to require ministers to accept ministerial responsibility) and the limited capacity and authority of DFAT and the WEA to oversee the actions of the AWB. Neither could demand documents from AWB nor could they force it to cooperate with the U.N. investigation. Given the AWB's role in representing Australian farmers, there appeared to be serious gaps in the regulatory framework.

Government's Governing Style: Dysfunctions in Relationships and Strategic Deficit

A deterioration in governance occurred in the fourth term of the Howard government. Tensions between politicians and their public service advisers increased as party government became disengaged from the public service and pragmatic decision-making became a feature of an election year. Howard's mode of governing was now registering discontent at senior levels within the public service, with private discussion among senior officials about the policy process (Henry 2007) and the lack of strategic focus of politicians. More generally within the nation, the government was widely castigated for decision-making that was capricious, populist, short term, and ad hoc.

The nexus between the political executive and senior officials also became frayed, and there continued to be public debate about the character of the relationship. The press continued to accept some degree of 'politicization' as a given (e.g., on how public servants were constrained under the Howard government), and public debates over the handling of senior appointments. A specific issue was the impact of ministerial advisers on public servants, their lack of accountability when involved in major public policy issues (Walter 2006), and the lack of a governance framework for them (Tiernan 2007).

The most telling public disclosure was the declaration of a key central agency, Treasury, that it was bypassed by the government in the development of policy frameworks for water reform and climate (Henry 2007: 6). Secretary of the Treasury Ken Henry (2007: 13–14), observed that the election year would 'test our mettle as apolitical public servants ... Our capacity to ensure that our work is "responsible," and not just "responsive," will be put to the test. How successful we are will impact on our integrity as public servants and our long-term effectiveness.'

New Government's Identification of Challenges

The Rudd government, elected in November 2007, identified a new set of challenges around policy issues and governance problems. The five key priorities were building an Australia that is more secure (i.e., national security), stronger (economically), fairer (social democrat agenda), and capable (for twenty-first-century challenges), plus a new way of governing (Rudd 2008; Moran 2008; Australian Government 2008). There is some continuity (security and the economy), but greater differentiation with governing style, fairness (e.g., workplace relations, housing affordability, and social inclusion) and in the centrality accorded to fields (e.g., a Department of Climate Change). The wording for security was explicitly defined as 'an integrated approach based on a clear-sighted view of our long term national security interest' rather than 'a short term reactive approach,' and conveys a sense of how the government was seeking to distinguish the program from its predecessor (Rudd 2008).

The overall agenda was, of course, diverted by the global financial crisis and recession that produced an economic stimulus strategy focused on national building infrastructure (Australian Government 2009). Debate about the dysfunctions arising from a rushed drive to stimulate the economy needs to be placed alongside the indications that Australia appears to have been recovering sooner than most countries.

Evolving New Strategies

A combination of internal and external sources of change facilitated the emergence of new approaches, a combination that first applied to major reform in the 1980s (Campbell and Halligan 1993). The intensity of the Australian shift to devolution and the subsequent reassertion of the centre resulted from both system shortcomings and environmental uncertainty and threat, favouring either a weaker or stronger centre.

The general pathway for central steering has displayed features of each of the models over twenty-five years. The *integrated hierarchical*, the dominant approach of the postwar years, relied on the archetypal mechanisms of traditional coordination – the interdepartmental committee and central agency control of transactions. It was succeeded by the *prototype steering* model. The managerial culture that emerged in the 1980s 'prescribed an explicit solution … the intervention of central agencies should be minimised, which means that they had to relinquish their traditional control over line departments. They were to assume strategic directions allowing line departments to make specific resource decisions. The central agency stance should be more that of catalyst and intermittent co-ordinator' (Campbell and Halligan 1993: 43).

This was followed by an exploration of the *devolved* model (Zifcak 1994) that increasingly assumed New Public Management features. A strong commitment to market principles was associated with the neo-liberal policies of the Howard government in the 1990s. Within a philosophy that emphasized the private sector, choice for consumers and purchasers, and the use of market mechanisms, action was taken to transfer responsibilities, to privatize, and to conceptualize the public service as a business operating in a competitive environment that was to be judged by its performance. Departmental activities were reviewed using a performance management approach that incorporated competitive tendering and contracting, purchaser-provider arrangements, and business process re-engineering. Market testing of agencies sought to improve internal capacity by benchmarking and outsourcing aspects of corporate services. The result was the disestablishment of monolithic multifunctional departments, reliance on third parties for the provision of services, and an increasingly fragmented system. Under this devolved public management model, the agency was the focus, individual contracts provided the basis for public servant employment, and a disaggregated public service was the result. There was also an increase in the number of public bodies (although major enterprises were no longer in the public sector).

The impact on central agencies of management and market principles was resounding. Australia reduced the old Public Service Board to a shadow of its former self (Campbell and Halligan 1993). The Department of Finance acquired a 'strategic' role (Wanna and Bartos 2003), but its role was diminished by the pursuit of a minimalist agenda. It was so heavily purged in the second wave of market reform (the second half of the 1990s) that debate came to centre on whether it would survive organizationally (one option being to reintegrate it with Treasury from whence it originated). The Department of Prime Minister and Cabinet withdrew from active intervention except where required and was no longer providing leadership for the public service.

In Lindquist's (2001) terms, Australia moved from a strong centre to a smaller centre with a corresponding reduction in capacity, coherence, and control of coordination. At this stage it had reached a relatively extreme point on the devolved end of the spectrum that was comparable in some respects with New Zealand.

Steering Strategies: From Integrated to Strategic Governance

Movement within the public management reform cycle became apparent in the 2000s: from an intense reform agenda in the first five years of the Howard government, reflection on the results produced shifts, refinements, and revaluation of the worth of the public service under new leadership of the central agencies that suited different agendas. The *integrated governance* model emerged as a more comprehensive approach that displayed features of the earlier models with four dimensions: resurrection of the central agency as a major actor and control over departments; whole-of-government as a new expression of coordination; central monitoring of implementation and delivery; and control of non-departmental agencies.

Several themes were recurrent: delivery and implementation, performance, coherence and whole-of-government, and responsiveness to government policy. This model shifted the focus to some extent from the vertical towards the horizontal. Instead of emphasizing the individual agency, there was now a greater concern with cross-agency programs and relationships within central government. At the same time there was a reinforcement of and extension to vertical relationships. The whole-of-government agenda also had a centralizing element in that central agencies were driving policy directions or principles, either systemically or across several agencies. The result was the tempering of devolution through strategic steering and management from the centre and a rebalancing of the positions of centre and line agencies.

The significance of political control in the Australian approach to public management needs to be emphasized even though much of the story about extending the political executive's control predates this period. The consistent pattern during the past three decades has been for the political executive to challenge elements of the traditional system in the drive for a more responsive public service. Three types of changes have been important: the strengthening of ministerial influence and resources, particularly through the extensive use of ministerial advisers; the weakening of the public servant's position, including the reduction in the breadth and exclusivity of the senior public service's roles; and changes to the appointment and tenure of the senior public servant (Halligan 2001).

The Howard government tightened its grip on the centre (e.g., a political appointee headed the cabinet secretariat) and maintained close control of the appointment processes within the public service, public boards, and parliamentary positions. This reflected the leadership style of a prime minister that centred on pervasive control throughout the main political and governmental institutions. The political control aspect also underlay each dimension of change: improved financial information on a program basis for ministers; strategic coordination under cabinet; controlling major policy agendas; organizational integration through abolition of bodies and features of autonomy; and monitoring the implementation of government policy down to the delivery level.

The overall result was unprecedented potential for policy and program control and integration using the conventional machinery of cabinet, central agencies, and departments. The rebalancing 'resulted in a network of central coordinating mechanisms in place of the direct central control and institutionally based central agencies ... The system is now one in which political control of administration is coordinated by a Prime Minister whose head-of-government role exists within a strong culture of collective involvement of other ministers through the Cabinet' (Hamburger 2007: 210).

The four dimensions mentioned above can be seen as different levels within an overall strategy.

Central Steering of Departments through the Resurrected Central Agency

The overriding trend for over a decade – to devolve responsibilities to agencies – remained a feature, but it was modified in two respects involving central agencies. This occurred first through the enlarged role of the Department of the Prime Minister and Cabinet because of its revitalized role in policy coordination and other major agendas discussed below.

Second, there were more prominent roles for the other central agencies in espousing and enforcing principles, and monitoring and guiding in the areas of budgeting, performance, and values. The Department of Finance's role and capacity to oversee financial management and information was enhanced, with a greater focus on departmental programs, a renewed emphasis on cash accounting, and an expansion of staff capacity in a shrunken department to provide the necessary advice for government. The Australian Public Service Commission invested in improvements to its capacity for monitoring and evaluation, particularly through an annual report, 'State of the Service,' which surveyed employees and agencies and scrutinized public service values and practices.

Central Steering of Performance through Monitoring down to Program Delivery

A core principle of the 1980s was to require departments to manage as well as to provide policy advice. Under the market agenda of NPM, outsourcing, agents, and specialized agencies were favoured for service delivery (e.g., Centrelink). The language of the mid-2000s became to enforce effective delivery as well as policy advice, with the latter defined in terms of outcomes.

Implementation had often been the neglected end of the policy spectrum. Under the market agenda, outsourcing, agents, and specialized agencies were favoured for service delivery. The internal constraints on implementation were reviewed by the government as a result of public perceptions of the performance of delivery agencies, particularly those where ministers had direct responsibility. An Australian Cabinet Implementation Unit was established in the Department of the Prime Minister and Cabinet to seek effectiveness in program delivery by ensuring that government policies and services were delivered on a timely and responsive basis. It was depicted as a partnership with agencies in producing systematic reform to the implementation of government policies, and ensuring effective delivery.

The authority of cabinet provided a 'gateway' and a 'checkpoint.' New proposals required appropriate details regarding implementation. Cabinet submissions with a risk element had to address a delivery framework including milestones, impacts, and governance. Adopted policy proposals required formal implementation plans with progress reported to the prime minister and cabinet against milestones in 'traffic light' format. Around 200 policy implementations were monitored under the Howard government. The 'traffic light' report to the prime minister and cabinet was regarded as a powerful incentive for organizational learning for public servants. Cultural change was promoted around a project management approach that employed a methodology designed to codify and think through the connections between policy objectives, inputs, outputs, and outcomes (Shergold 2004b; Wanna 2006).

Ministerial Steering of Departments and Portfolios

An important strand of the model involved the swing back to a more comprehensive ministerial department and ministerial steering of portfolios (see Pollitt 2005). The targeting of the broader public sector derived from the election agenda and led to the review of corporate governance of statutory authorities and office holders and an agenda for ministerial departments to have tighter and more direct control over public agencies because of the extent of non-departmental organizations, and their governance.

The language of the mid-2000s had become to enforce effective delivery as well as policy advice, with the latter defined in terms of outcomes (Shergold 2004b). Departmentalization was expressed through absorbing statutory authorities and reclaiming control of agencies with hybrid boards that did not accord with a particular corporate (and therefore private sector) governance prescription. The medium-term result was a reduction in the number of agencies in the outer public sector (114 to 88 between 2003 and 2008) and an expansion in the number in the core public service (84 to 100). Similar agendas for rationalizing non-departmental organizations were apparent in other Anglo-Saxon systems (Christensen and Lægreid 2006).

The key example of agencification was also affected. Centrelink was established in the mid-1990s as a one-stop-shop, multipurpose delivery agency to provide services to several purchasing departments. This ambitious case of horizontal coordination of service delivery originally involved integrating two separate networks of regional offices for social security and employment. As an independent statutory authority responsible for delivering welfare benefits and services, it accounted for about 30 per cent of Commonwealth expenditure. Centrelink's position, however, changed in 2004 under the integrating governance agenda and Centrelink-specific matters regarding governance and relationship issues. Centrelink came under a new parent department, Human Services, created within the Finance portfolio with responsibility for six delivery agencies that operated under direct ministerial control. The rationale was still to improve the delivery of services, but within a whole-of-government approach that sought to strengthen the vertical (ministerial and departmental control) and horizontal dimensions (delivery network across agencies) (Halligan 2008).

Steering across the Public Service: Whole-of-Government and Horizontal Management

Australia was slower to adopt a systematic approach to whole-of-government issues than Canada and the United Kingdom (see Smith, this volume), which pursued these issues in the 1990s while Australia was focused on management reform. The environment created by these reforms emphasized devolution of responsibility to agency heads and each agency pursuing its own business and policy agenda. The need to temper devolution with a broader, whole-of-government perspective permeated much government activity; see Verhoest and Bouckaert (2005) for how such a trajectory was worked through elsewhere. The shift was expressed in three ways.

At the political level, the prime minister committed to a series of whole-of-government priorities for new policy-making that included national security, defence and counter-terrorism, and other generally defined priorities such as sustainable environment, rural and regional affairs, and work and family life (Howard 2002; Shergold 2004a). These priorities were pursued through a range of traditional coordinating and new whole-of-government processes including changes to cabinet processes aimed at strengthening its strategic leadership role. They involved setting aside more time in the cabinet's program to consider broader strategy and strategic issues; streamlining consideration of submissions; and giving more emphasis to following up decisions.

The priorities were also followed through a range of coordinating or whole-of-government processes, including: cabinet and ministerial processes (e.g., Ministerial Oversight Committee on Energy); the Council of Australian Governments (COAG) and Commonwealth/State arrangements (e.g., sustainable water management); interdepartmental taskforces discussed above (e.g., work and family life); integrated service delivery (e.g., stronger regions); and lead agency approaches (e.g., indigenous initiative). An example was the COAG agreement to develop a National Water Initiative to increase the productivity and efficiency of water use, sustain rural and urban communities, and to ensure the health of river and groundwater systems.

The government's organizational response to the testing external environment experienced by Australia in the 2000s was mainly to build coordinating units within current structures, particularly within the Department of the Prime Minister and Cabinet. The whole-of-government approach to national coordination covered strategic and operational levels: a National Security Committee of Cabinet, a National Counter-Terrorism Committee (for intergovernmental coordination), and a National Security Division for coordinating and applying whole-of-government principles to border protection, counter-terrorism, defence, intelligence, law enforcement, and security.

Third, the agenda was given impetus through a report on Connecting Government by the Management Advisory Committee, comprising departmental secretaries, the primary vehicle for examining and setting the reform agenda (MAC 2004), which indicated how to address issues about whole-of-government processes and structures, cultures, managing information, and budgetary frameworks. Whole-of-government was defined as denoting 'agencies working across portfolio boundaries to achieve a shared goal and an integrated government response to particular issues' (MAC 2004: 1). Despite this specific definition, the boundaries were not readily drawn for whole of government, because coordination was also viewed in terms of coordinating departments (i.e., central agencies), integration (reducing the number of departments), and cooperative federalism (MAC 2004: 6–7). Approaches could operate formally and informally, and range from policy development through program management to service delivery. There was an underlying rationalist conception suggesting that difficult policy problems and management questions could be laid out, solutions designed, and challenges managed leading to improved problem solving, service delivery, and performance.

The medium-term impact of horizontal coordination in Australia was mixed. The level of horizontal management activity expanded through a mixture of central agency push and shove using task forces, a reliance on traditional IDCs for some purposes, and some new interactive mechanisms. But until more systematic material is acquired the judgment must be qualified, as even an official verdict reported some success but 'overall implementation of the Connecting Government report has been disappointing and the report does no appear to have had a fundamental impact on the approach that the APS takes to its work' (APSC 2007a: 247; Halligan 2010); however, a major research project on whole of government at the University of Canberra is expected to provide some answers.

Reformulating Steering under Rudd through Strategic Governance

What differentiates strategic governance from integrated governance? It places greater emphasis on strategy, targeted performance, and the design of governance nationally and federally.

One indication is provided by the prime minister's style and actions. Rudd's leadership approach is closest to a 'priorities and planning style' where first ministers are 'in a strong political position and choose to pursue an ambitious, creative, and comprehensive legislative program' (Campbell 1988: 59). This style favours central agencies and their role in 'assembling coherent policies and programs.'

The government adopted innovative ways for engaging the public (a 2020 Summit of 1,000 delegates and community cabinets) and a five-point agenda, which has been reported on (Australian Government 2008). A key plank is reforming governing through engagement, building accountability and integrity, and modernizing the federation. The focus on accountability and transparency addresses the question of respect for government institutions and 'public confidence in the integrity of ministers, their staff and senior officials' (Australian Government 2008: 73). A new phase in intergovernmental relations was initiated with the intention of strengthening vertical relationships within the federation. The COAG reform agenda was at the forefront of the government's modernization and policy agenda.

A major organizational audit of the Department of the Prime Minister and Cabinet indicated that it was 'heavily focused on the day-to-day activities of government, and that [its] capacity to provide strategic policy advice could be improved' (DPMC 2008: 3). A Strategy and Delivery Division was established to advance administrative priorities that were more strategic, long term, and proactive. The overall objective was a strong department for supporting the prime minister's reform agenda for the nation with monitoring of progress assuming significance. The influence of the U.K. experience has been a constant factor, for example, the Cabinet Office delivery unit, the joined-up government agenda, and the strengthening of the strategic focus (Marsh 2009; see also Mulgan 2009, a former adviser to both Blair and Rudd).

Interpretation of the Pattern

Central steering needs to be interpreted in terms of choices made under particular circumstances. There are also several givens that constrain options. First are the basic continuities in cabinet processes: 'Australia has been unusual among Westminster systems in the strength and reach it has retained for its cabinet system ... and this has shaped the overall coordination system' (Hamburger 2007: 213–14). A second given is the dominance of the political executive, which is enforced by active ministers, leadership by the prime minister (with backup from the DPMC), and political staff. This does not, however, extend to political appointments, which are not sanctioned in general, and the exceptions have to be handled carefully in practice.

Third, Australia has a long tradition of relatively strong central agencies and of the Department of the Prime Minister and Cabinet as the primary agency. While other Anglo-Saxon systems have experienced dominance of the Treasury, the hiving off of the Australian Treasury's responsibilities for financial management and budgetary oversight in the 1970s meant that a Department of Finance has coordinated these aspects of public management. The fourth consideration is the built-in decentralization of the federal system, which means dealing with delivery systems (state governments) that have a constitutional basis, similar governmental institutions, and different electoral mandates. Finally, there is the Australian variant of an Anglo-Saxon administrative tradition and the continuing importance of responsible government, management reform, and professional relationships between politicians and public servants. These factors assist in accounting for continuities and the durability in the Australian pattern.

Nevertheless strategies change over time. Central steering over the long term involves multiple processes, alignments between components, and traditional cycles of public administration. Strategies represent a conjunction of elements. The explanation for different strategies is about the different combinations.

The factors influencing levels of centralization and decentralization assist in accounting for the emergence of different models. Both centralized and decentralized elements are normally present, and combinations of factors may push in different and contradictory ways (Mintzberg 1979). Nevertheless, environmental complexity and change appears to support decentralization, while external threat produces centralization. Political leadership style is generally important (e.g., the extent of discretion given to ministers, level of centralization in and around the prime minister, modes of control, and the place of intergovernmental questions) (Campbell and Halligan 1993).

New Public Management, in so far as it affected central agencies, was a deviation of transient significance. This is not surprising because the dictum of 'steering rather than rowing' offered few insights about central policy coordination. Most examples of 'steering organizations' were 'pitched at a much lower level than central departments of state such as cabinet offices, prime ministers' departments, or ministries of finance.' Central policy coordination was a significant issue that managerialism did not offer a theoretical or practical answer for (Pollitt 1998: 71).

The last two strategies have pursued system rebalancing as the consequence of some excesses of neo-liberal reform as well as a professional reconfiguration of central and devolved roles to produce governance models appropriate for changed environments. The new integration allowed a combination of devolved dimensions with a reactivated centre. The relational basis retained a strong hierarchical dimension underpinned by political authority but with a reliance on performance management. The components have covered a spectrum of relationships including the rebalancing of centre and line and a commitment to a whole-of-government and integrating agenda. An extensive apparatus has been installed for exacting greater coordination and whole-of-government results.

The elements that emerged in the 2000s were the search for coherence, strengthening of internal capacity, and performance improvement. One aspect was the organizing for coherence that occurred within and across portfolios and organizations with the whole-of-government agenda. The reliance was less on legislation, the management framework, and values for sustaining organizational operations – although each remains prominent – and more on bureaucratic structures and formal centres of influence (cabinet and departments of state). This has now been nationalized through the intergovernmental agenda to produce a focus on the national public sector as a whole (Moran 2008).

Second, internal capacity was strengthened through the whole-of-government agenda, enhancing the roles of central agencies in coordination, and improving implementation and capability. The previous agenda of shedding responsibilities, devolution to departments continued to be anointed as a cornerstone because it produced improved performance and productivity, but the preference was now to reincorporate, to clarify, to establish better accountability, and to improve performance. There was a reconfirmation of the three components of the traditional system: cabinet, central agency, and the department. The diminished central agencies were reconstituted with stronger roles, particularly the Department of Finance and the Department of the Prime Minister and Cabinet.

Third, there was the question of performance. This term has been used generally, as in lifting the performance of the public service and ensuring implementation of delivery. The concept of the 'performing state' was applied to a system that was 'continuously open to, and reading its environment, and learning and changing in response: a state 'inherently in transition' (Shergold 2004b). The more specific usage was in the performance management sense. The performance management has evolved over two decades, and despite limitations (Bouckaert and Halligan 2008) is being extended more explicitly to intergovernmental relationships.

Steering the public service has been integral as explained earlier. The options used have been at both individual and organizational levels: (1) reducing power of the public service; (2) expanding the resources of the political executive; (3) performance agreements for senior public servants; (4) performance oversight of departments and agencies; (5) monitoring delivery; and (6) policy interventions as required. The strength of an administrative tradition grounded in Westminster has been apparent where governments have overstepped the limits of acceptability (Labor's backpedalling on political appointees in 1983–84, the backlash to the purge of secretaries by the Coalition in 1996, and the response to the role of political advisers in the mid-1990s). System correction is again apparent with Labor's current agenda for integrity in government, including a requirement to make political advisers accountable where they have a policy role.

Ultimately, the strategic governance form of central steering is dependent on executive leadership and how the priorities and planning style is sustained over time. There are indications of the 'court government' reported for Canada to the extent that power is concentrated in the prime minister and 'carefully selected courtiers' (Savoie 2008: 16), but less clear is whether formal cabinet decision-making has been displaced by informal processes.

It is well established that high policy capacity does not necessarily translate into effective operational decision-making and implementation (Kettl 2009; Smith, this volume), and several deficits in execution have marred the Australian government's record. The prime minister was impelled to launch a new stage of public service renewal involving major reform based on a long-term blueprint for attaining world-class standing. As a consequence, a review is reporting in 2010 on reforming government administration (AGRAGA 2009).

Conclusion

Central steering of the state has a long tradition in Australia, with the strategies employed varying with circumstances and executive leadership styles. In the reform era the overall trend has been towards strengthening and extending central direction and control using a more complex array of instruments across a broader range of key policy sectors and intergovernmental relationships. This adds up to a formidable apparatus for steering and reviewing strategy and performance. The government is committed to grappling with highly challenging issues, and the effectiveness of central steering under strategic governance will depend on how the complexities are handled, the momentum is sustained, effective implementation occurs, and the outcomes are achieved in the medium term.

REFERENCES

ABC [Australia Broadcasting Corporation] Online (2006). 'Public Service' to Blame for Immigration Failures, 8 September, Accessed from Immigration Watch Canada, http://www.immigrationwatchcanada.org/.
AGRAGA (Advisory Group on the Reform of Australian Government Administration). (2009). *Reform of Australian Government Administration: Building the World's Best Public Service*. Discussion Paper. Canberra: Commonwealth of Australia.
Australian Government. (2008). *One Year Progress Report*. Canberra: Commonwealth of Australia, November.
– (2009). *Mid-Term Progress Report*. Canberra: Commonwealth of Australia, June.
APSC (Australian Public Service Commission). (2007a). *State of the Service Report 2006–07*. Canberra: Commonwealth of Australia.
– (2007b). *Tackling Wicked Problems: A Public Policy Perspective*. Canberra: Australian Public Service Commission.
Bezes, P. (2007). The 'Steering State' Model: The Emergence of a New Organizational Form in the French Public Administration. *Sociologie du Travail* 49S: 67–89.
Bouckaert, G., and J. Halligan. (2008). *Managing Performance: International Comparisons*. London: Routledge.
Bouckaert, G., B.G. Peters, and K. Verhoest. (2010). *The Coordination of Public Sector Organizations: Shifting Patterns of Public Management*. London: Palgrave.
Campbell, C. (1988). The Search for Coordination and Control: When and How are Central Agencies the Answer? In C. Campbell and B.G. Peters (eds.),

Organizing Governance and Governing Organizations. Pittsburgh: University of Pittsburgh Press.

Campbell, C., and J. Halligan. (1993). *Political Leadership in an Age of Constraint: The Australian Experience*. Pittsburgh: University of Pittsburgh Press.

Christensen, T., and P. Lægreid (eds.). (2006). *Autonomy and Regulation*. Cheltenham: Edward Elgar.

Dahlström, C., B.G. Peters, and J. Pierre. (2011). Steering from the Centre: Central Government Offices and Their Role in Governing. This volume.

Davis, G. (2008). One Big Conversation: The Australian 2020 Summit. *Australian Journal of Public Administration* 67: 370–89.

Denhardt, J.V., and R.B. Denhardt. (2003). *The New Public Service: Serving Not Steering*. Armonk, NY: M.E. Sharpe.

DPMC (Department of the Prime Minister and Cabinet). (2003). *Annual Report 2002–03*. Commonwealth of Australia, Canberra.

– (2008). *Annual Report 2007–2008*. Commonwealth Government, Canberra.

Frederickson, D.G., and H.G. Frederickson. (2006). *Measuring the Performance of the Hollow State*. Washington, DC: Georgetown University Press.

Halligan, J. (2001). Politicians, Bureaucrats and Public Sector Reform in Australia and New Zealand. In G. Peters and J. Pierre (eds.), *Politicians, Bureaucrats and Administrative Reform*. London: Routledge.

– (2006). The Reassertion of the Centre in a First Generation NPM System. In T. Christensen and P. Lægreid (eds.), *Autonomy and Regulation: Coping with Agencies in the Modern State*. Cheltenham: Edward Elgar.

– (2007). Anglo-American Systems: Easy Diffusion. In J.C.N. Raadschelders, T.A.J. Toonen, and F.M. van der Meer (eds.), *Comparative Civil Service Systems in the 21st Century*. Basingstoke: Palgrave Macmillan.

– (2008). *The Centrelink Experiment: An Innovation in Service Delivery*. Canberra: Australian National University Press.

– (2010). Post-NPM Responses to Disaggregation through Coordinating Horizontally and Integrating Governance. In P. Laegreid and K. Verhoest (eds.), *Governance of Public Sector Organizations: Autonomy, Control and Performance*. Basingstoke: Palgrave.

Halligan, J., and T. Tucker. (2008). Governance Failure in a Department of State: The Case of Immigration in Australia. Paper presented at the European Group of Public Administration Conference, Erasmus University, Rotterdam, 3–6 Sept.

Hamburger, P. (2007). Coordination and Leadership at the Centre of the Australian Public Service. In R. Koch and J. Dixon (eds.), *Public Governance and Leadership*. Wiesbaden: Deutscher Universitats-Verlag.

Henry, K. (2007). Treasury's Effectiveness in the Current Environment. Speech to [Australian] Treasury Staff, Canberra, 14 March.

Howard, J. (2002). Strategic Leadership for Australia: Policy Directions in a Complex World. Address to the Committee for Economic Development of Australia, 20 Nov.

Kernaghan, K., and D. Siegel. (1987). *Public Administration in Canada*. Toronto: Methuen.

Kettl, D.F. (2009). *The Next Government of the United States: Why Our Institutions Fail Us and How to Fix Them*. New York: W.W. Norton.

Lægreid, P., and S. Serigstad. (2004). *Organizing for Homeland Security: The Case of Norway*. Working Paper 12. Oslo: Stein Rokkan Centre for Social Studies.

Lindquist, E. (2001). Reconceiving the Centre: Leadership, Strategic Review and Coherence in Public Sector Reform. In OECD, *Government of the Future*. Paris: OECD.

– (2004). Strategy, Capacity and Horizontal Governance: Perspectives from Australia and Canada. *Optimum* 34/4: 2–12.

MAC (Management Advisory Committee). (2004). *Connecting Government: Whole of Government Responses to Australia's Priority Challenges*. Canberra: Author.

Marsh, I. (2009). The Blair Governments, Public Sector Reform and State Strategic Capacity. *Political Quarterly* 80: 33–41.

Metcalfe, L. (1994). International Policy Co-ordination and Public Management Reform. *International Review of Administrative Sciences* 60: 271–90.

Mintzberg, H. (1979). *The Structuring of Organizations: A Synthesis of the Research*. Englewood Cliffs: Prentice-Hall.

Moran, T. (2008). Splicing the Perspectives of the Commonwealth and States into a Workable Federation. Paper presented at the ANZSOG Annual Conference on Federalism, Melbourne, 11–12 Sept.

Mulgan, G. (2009). *The Art of Public Strategy: Mobilizing Power and Knowledge for the Common Good*. Oxford: Oxford University Press.

Newman, J. (2002). The New Public Management, Modernization and Institutional Change. In K. McLaughlin, S.P. Osborne, and E. Ferlie (eds.), *New Public Management: Current Trends and Future Prospects*. London: Routledge.

Painter, M. (1987). *Steering the Modern State*. Sydney: Sydney University Press.

Painter, M. and J. Pierre (eds.) (2005). *Challenges to State Policy Capacity*. Basingstoke: Palgrave.

Perri 6. (2005). Joined-Up Government in the West beyond Britain. In V. Bogdanor (ed.), *Joined-Up Government*. Oxford: Oxford University Press.

Peters, B.G. (2006). Concepts and Theories of Horizontal Policy Management. In B.G. Peters and J. Pierre (eds.), *Handbook of Public Policy*. London: Sage.

Peters, B.G., and J. Pierre. (1998). Governance without Government? Rethinking Public Administration. *Journal of Public Administration Research and Theory* 8: 223–43.

Pollitt, C. (1998). Managerialism Revisited. In B.G. Peters and D. Savoie (eds.), *Taking Stock: Assessing Public Sector Reforms*. Montreal and Kingston: Canadian Centre for Management Development and McGill-Queen's University Press.

Pollitt, C. (2005). Ministries and Agencies: Steering, Meddling, Neglect and Dependency. In M. Painter and J. Pierre (eds.), *Challenges to State Policy Capacity*. Basingstoke: Palgrave.

Richards, D., and M. Smith. (2006). The Tensions of Political Control and Administrative Autonomy: From NPM to a Reconstituted Westminster Model. In T. Christensen and P. Laegreid (eds.), *Autonomy and Regulation: Coping with Agencies in the Modern State*. Cheltenham: Edward Elgar.

Rudd, K. (2008). The First National Security Statement to the Parliament: Address by the Prime Minister of Australia. Speech, 4 December. http://pmrudd.archive.dpmc.gov.au/node/5424.

Shergold, P. (2004a). Connecting Government: Whole-of-Government Responses to Australia's Priority Challenges. Presentation, Canberra, 20 April. http://www.apsc.gov.au/mac/connectinggovernment.htm.

Shergold, P. (2004b). Plan and Deliver: Avoiding Bureaucratic Hold-Up. Presentation to the Australian Graduate School of Management/Harvard Club of Australia, Canberra, 17 November. Archived, National Library of Australia.

Tiernan, A. (2007). *Power without Responsibility? Ministerial Staffers in Australian Governments from Whitlam to Howard*. Sydney: University of NSW Press.

Verhoest, K., and G. Bouckaert. (2005). Machinery of Government and Policy Capacity. In M. Painter and J. Pierre (eds.), *Challenges to State Policy Capacity*. Basingstoke: Palgrave.

Verhoest, K., G. Bouckaert, and B.G Peters. (2007). Janus-Faced Reorganization: Specialization and Coordination in Four OECD Countries in the Period 1980–2005. *International Review of Administrative Sciences* 73: 325–48.

Walter, J. (2006). Ministers, Minders and Public Servants: Changing Parameters of Responsibility in Australia. *Australian Journal of Public Administration* 65: 22–7.

Wanna, J. (2006). From Afterthought to Afterburner: Australia's Cabinet Implementation Unit. *Journal of Comparative Policy Analysis* 8: 347–69.

Wanna, J., and S. Bartos. (2003). 'Good Practice': Does it Work in Theory? Australia's Quest for Better Outcomes. In J. Wanna, L. Jensen, and J. de Vries (eds.), *Controlling Public Expenditure: The Changing Role of Central Budget Agencies – Better Guardians?* Cheltenahm: Edward Elgar.

Zifcak, S. (1994). *New Managerialism: Administrative Reform in Whitehall and Canberra*. Buckingham: Open University Press.

6 Governing from the Centre(s): Governance Challenges in the United States

B. GUY PETERS

The government of the United States is one of the more complex in the world. Even leaving aside the complexities associated with intergovernmental relations, the federal government itself is a set of complex institutions. These institutions have always been difficult to manage, and there continue to be a number of problems in creating coordination and coherence in governing.

If one begins with the usual assumption that the presidency in the United States is perhaps the most powerful offices in the world then these difficulties in governing are somewhat surprising. In reality, however, governing from the centre in the United States is a major challenge for any President, largely because there is no single centre. The President must confront not only Congress but also the autonomy of many other federal structures as he attempts to steer public policy.

At a superficial level, the structure of the U.S. federal government appears similar to that of most other governments. The government has a number of cabinet departments, each headed by a politician. Beneath those cabinet-level structures are a range of agencies, bureaus, offices, and other subdivisions, each responsible for a particular policy area. In addition to these cabinet-level departments and their components there are a number of independent executive agencies responsible directly to the President, as well as a variety of public and quasi-public corporations, foundations, and other organizations that deliver public services (Seidman 1998). There are also a number of independent regulatory agencies that are designed not to be controlled by the President and the Congress, and are given collective leadership structures with long-term appointments to provide substantial independence. In a very fundamental sense these regulatory organizations are not intended to be coordinated by executive action but rather are intended to exercise more independent judgment over their areas of concern; in at least one case redundancy is designed into the administrative system with both the Federal Trade Commission, an independent regulatory agency, and the Antitrust Division of the Department of Justice each having some degree of jurisdiction over monopolistic practices.

Despite the structural barrier that exists, even at the constitutional level, at a superficial level it might also appear that this government would be better steered from the centre than most other governments. First, the role of the President as a leader who can wield considerable individual political power, and who can provide independent direction for policy, provides a locus for coordination and coherent policy-making. Further, the President can appoint his own loyalists to many more positions in the public sector than can most political executives (Peters 2008; Lewis 2008). That politicization of the public sector would be significant in itself, but the evidence is that an increasing number of those appointees may not so much have functional managerial responsibilities as they have responsibilities for insuring that the actions of the organization are in conformity with the program of the President (Light 1995). In addition, the President has a significant personal staff, with several thousand employees in the Executive Office of the President (Hart 2000; see below) who can assist the President in monitoring and controlling federal policy.

The Barriers to Effective Steering and Coordination

The rather superficial recounting of structures in American government above makes it appear that there would be greater steering capacity here than in other political systems. That appearance is, however, deceiving, and a number of factors combine to reduce the coordination and control capabilities of the system. Some of these factors are constitutional, some institutional, and some political, but they combine to make effective steering from the centre almost a dream within the U.S. political system. And indeed the factors do combine and interact to accentuate the difficulties that any President, or certainly any less senior official, encounters when attempting to coordinate.

As I discuss the idea of steering from the centre in this chapter I will be concerned with at least two aspects of steering. One is the capacity to impose the wishes of the political executive, or perhaps the cabinet in parliamentary systems, on the remainder of the political system. The second meaning is the capacity to govern in a coherent and coordinated manner. This interpretation of steering goes beyond the simple notion of control to consider imposing a more strategic sense of governing. This latter sense is especially important for the United States, given the extreme fragmentation of the system and the difficulties of creating a coordinated style of governing (see Bouckaert, Peters, and Verhoest 2009).

Constitutional Factors

The most important constitutional factor in the United States is the presidential system with a legislative branch that need not be coordinated with the executive, unlike that in a parliamentary system. Even when the two political branches of government are controlled by the same political party, an infrequent occurrence during the past sixty years, there is no guarantee that there will be agreement between them on policy goals; the 'divided government' argument over the capacity to govern in the face of partisan differences is inconclusive (see Mayhew 1991; Nicholson, Segura, and Woods 2002), but it does point clearly to the importance of this constitutional separation of powers. Indeed, many of the disputes over policy are related to maintaining the prerogatives of the institutions rather than genuine policy differences. A good deal of American political and policy history could be written in terms of conflicts between institutions within the federal government, and disputes over the relative powers of the central and subnational governments.

The U.S. Congress is perhaps the only truly 'transformative legislature' (Polsby 1975) in the world, and is an active participant in governing rather than a passive rubber stamp for the executive. The desires of Congress to maintain institutional independence from presidential control and to be effective are reflected, in part, in the creation of powerful committee systems in both houses. These committees enhance Congressional capacities both to legislate and to exercise oversight over the executive branch and its organizations (Aberbach 1990). In many ways Congress must be understood through the committee system as much as or more than through the two houses or the institutions as a whole. In terms of central steering the committee system largely mirrors the structure of the executive branch, and that tends to divide Congressional considerations rather than provide an integrated vision of policy.

As mentioned above, the constitutional provision of federalism further divides government. The vertical dimensions are obvious but the power granted to the subnational governments to administer federal programs often means that the same divisions that exist in Washington are replicated at state and local levels. These governments are divided just as much as the federal government and the agenda of New Public Management that enhances organizational autonomy (and minimizes central steering) has been adopted to a greater extent in the states than at the federal level (Kaboolian 1998).

Further, it is not only isomorphism with federal organizations that creates the fragmentation of policy implementation at the state and local levels. These governments all have constitutions that create many divisions between the legislative and the executive branches of government. Further, although these governments have a number of the same sorts of executive departments found in the federal government, they also have a number of independent executive organizations, many headed by *elected* officials who are not obliged to take orders from the state governors (e.g., the state of North Dakota has ten state-wide elected officials plus several elected boards). The segmentation of state and local governments charged with implementing federal legislation may therefore exacerbate the existing divisions in that legislation.

In short, the framers of the U.S. Constitution intended to design a system in which steering from the centre would not be easy, and they did an excellent job. The system they designed is highly fragmented, and was designed so that the President could not exercise control easily over the remaining parts of the system of governing. That system may have made a great deal of sense to framers concerned about the dangers of creating a constitutional monarch, but they may make much less sense in the early twenty-first century when central steering and control are crucial questions. Some of the institutional and political factors discussed below can be overcome, but the constitutional barriers to effective governance are much more difficult to address.

Institutional Factors

The institutions of the bureaucracy and the civil service reinforce the separations within the American political system. Although the cabinet departments are directly responsible to the President the internal structures of these departments are much more independent of their departments than might be expected from simply looking at the departmental organograms. The departments appear to be connected directly to the presidency through the cabinet, and subject to the personal power of the President. Perhaps the most important factor limiting the capacity of the President and cabinet secretaries from imposing their authority is the agency structure that exists within the federal bureaucracy.

Unlike agencies as discussed in the United Kingdom and other countries following the New Public Management agenda (Pollitt et al. 2004) this structure has been in place for decades. The federal bureaucracy has been built up over more than two hundred years largely through the creation of agencies, and the subsequent incorporation of those agencies into cabinet departments. Further, there are still a number of independent executive agencies not linked with cabinet departments, although they are responsible to the President and are clearly performing executive functions (Seidman 1998). As well as often predating their departments, almost all the agencies have a public law basis, and can claim rights to manage, and to make regulations about, most aspects of their policy domains. Further, leaders of the majority of these agencies are appointed by the President, so that they have some direct institutional connections to the centre of government. Their cabinet secretaries may want to control the agencies within their departments, but the leaders of the agencies often can assert their own priorities. Some agencies are more capable of exerting that influence on Congress or the public than are others. For example, despite some recent scandals, the FBI can operate rather independently of the Department of Justice, and the Internal Revenue Service has substantial autonomy from the Department of the Treasury.

The powers of the agencies are reinforced through the budgetary system. While the budget system does serve some central steering functions (see below) the federal budget also recognizes the independence of agencies, by giving them their own budgets, rather than having consolidated budgets for the whole department. Even after the adoption of the Government Performance and Results Act (Radin 2000) to reform the budget process, the emphasis remains on the performance of the individual agency rather than on the performance of departments or government as a whole. (There are some indicators of this sort developed by the Office of Management and Budget, but the dominant pattern remains to focus on the behaviour and outputs of individual organizations.) Likewise, the scrutiny of budgets in Congress remains very disaggregated, so that Congress itself does not take much interest in an integrated view of the budget. The expenditure budget is not adopted as a single act of Congress but, rather is passed as a series of twelve or thirteen appropriations acts, prepared with relatively little reference to each other. Indeed, each committee or subcommittee with the appropriate authority will fight to maintain its power over an agency budget.

Unlike other industrial democracies, the civil service system in the United States does not make very much of a contribution towards coordinating policy and improving implementation. There is a civil service, but two important aspects of the system limit the extent to which the personnel system cuts across government. First, the senior positions in government are occupied by political appointees rather than career public servants. These officials come and go with the President and the cabinet secretaries, and often spend relatively short times in government (Heclo 1983; Maranto 2005). At one time these officials were very strictly political, but they had been becoming more expert in the policy areas for which they were responsible. (During the administration of George W. Bush many presidential appointments seemed to revert to older patterns of cronyism without significant policy expertise; see below.) That expertise is a virtue in many ways, but it does mean that they are committed to a policy area, and are not likely to be especially concerned with cooperating with experts from other policy areas. There have been some changes in the appointment of these officials, with an increasing number of the appointees not having direct line authority for programs but rather being in place to attempt to impose political priorities.

The other aspect of the civil service system that tends to reduce coordination of public services is that personnel in the civil service system itself tend to spend most or all of their careers in a single department, or even a single agency. Therefore, their commitment to government is to the particular agency and its program, and not to broader policy goals. This career pattern reinforces a pattern of recruitment that focuses on specific expertise rather than general managerial capabilities. The development of the Senior Executive Service in the late 1970s and early 1980s was one attempt to create a senior civil service cadre that would be portable across the public sector and provide greater coherence and coordination in policy and administration than had been present in the past. (The legislation was passed in 1978, but was not really implemented until the early 1980s and came to be known in some circles as 'Carter's gift to Reagan' because President Reagan used the appointment powers to the fullest; 10% of the general SES positions could be appointed by the President.)

As implied above, the institutions within Congress are not well designed to pursue an integrated and comprehensive view of governing. The operational strength of Congress is its committee system, rather than the plenary sessions of the two houses. There are both functional committees that mirror the structure of the executive branch and appropriations sub-committees that also track the departments and independent executive organizations. While the committee system is very effective (especially when compared to other legislative bodies) in exercising oversight over the executive branch, it is extremely ill-suited to developing a comprehensive view. Indeed, just as Congress may defend its prerogatives against the executive branch, the individual committees also attempt to defend their own particular areas of control.

In summary, the institutional structure of both the executive and legislative branches of government in the United States is very fragmented, and adds to the fragmentation produced by the constitutional design. There are also a number of internal divisions in the bureaucracy that further fragment government, and enable individual agencies to pursue their own policy objectives and to resist pressures for conformity to presidential or Congressional priorities. Indeed, one of the most important strategies for the agencies is to play the two political branches off against each other.

Political Factors

The pronounced divisions within the bureaucratic structures of the federal government are reinforced strongly by the politics of policy. In particular, the infamous 'iron triangles' or 'sub-governments' in American politics (see Freeman 1955) create symbiotic relationships among an agency, a congressional committee or subcommittee, and interest groups. These three sets of actors all have an interest in insulating the agency and its programs from unfriendly influences, and cooperate to ensure that the interests being served by the program will continue to be treated well by government. Heclo (1978), among others, has argued that these triangles no longer are as strong as they once might have been. The growth of public interest groups and consumer groups, and the opening up of some aspects of Congressional action to great public scrutiny have reduced some of the insulation of these sub-governments from external pressures. Still, the iron triangle concept remains a good place at which to begin a discussion of the autonomy of agencies in the federal government.

It is far from uncommon for interest groups to have strong relationships with administrative agencies, but several factors in American politics tend to facilitate these relationships. One is that the pluralistic style of interest group politics in the United States that makes it easier for agencies to pick and choose which social groups they will work with, and therefore to exclude others (McFarland 2004). Likewise, the membership of committees tends to be selective and usually contains Congressmen with a direct constituency interest in the policy areas over which the committee (or subcommittee) has authority. (In practice each administrative agency is overseen by at least four subcommittees: two functional subcommittees and two appropriations subcommittees, but all four tend to be composed of politicians whose constituents are served by the agency.) Thus, the members of these 'sub-governments' all have common interests in the policy and have strong incentives to maintain its insulation from possible controls.

The American political system was designed to be consensual, but the increasing polarization of the political parties has made effective and coherent government more difficult (Peters 2007). Even when a President is fortunate to have both houses of Congress controlled by his party, such as Barack Obama did during his first two years in office, an integrated political party in opposition can often prevent effective coordinated policy being made, especially in the Senate.

Finally, even though American political parties have become more ideologically consistent and more responsible, the cabinet secretaries and other officials appointed by a President are not all necessarily his allies on policy issues. The parties are in essence coalitions of a range of factions, and some presidential appointees are made to appease geographical or partisan factions; for example, it is customary for sec-retaries of the interior to come from the West, and for secretaries of agriculture to come from major farming states in the Midwest. There-fore the President must find ways of controlling his own cabinet and appointees as well as managing in the influence of interest groups if he wants to govern effectively.

Attempting to Overcome the Fragmented State

The above discussion would not provide a great deal of hope for a President attempting to provide strong, strategic direction to Ameri-can government. Indeed, Barack Obama faced an immense challenge in governing, even when he had Democratic control of both houses of Congress. The combination of a constitutional framework designed to prevent that effective governance and the politics and institutional politics that have emerged from that design combine to make the President's life in office a difficult one. Richard Neustadt (1960) famously argued that because of these numerous barriers to direct control the President is in effect a negotiator, attempting to build agreements with a range of other powerful actors.

The President is not, however, impotent and over the past century at least the institutions in the centre of government in the United States have become elaborated and more complex in an attempt to allow the President to provide some more effective governance. There are also non-structural instruments available to the President to help control the rest of the executive establishment and with that the policies of the public sector. Further, the Congress has also developed a series of instruments and organizations that enable it to exert more control over policy. The question that then emerges from the increased capacity of both the presidency and Congress is whether two well-organized and well-staffed institutions that may not agree are able to steer from the centre, and what opportunities there may be for coordinating these alternative sources of steering.

The above discussion, and much of the literature on steering governments from the centre, assumes that all executives have the same aspirations to provide direction. The comparative evidence is certainly that they do not all have such aspirations (Peters, Rhodes, and Wright 2000). Further, different U.S. Presidents appear to have had different levels of aspirations for control. President George W. Bush invested a great deal of effort in gaining control over government (Singer 2005), while his father had been much more casual about such matters.

Organizing the Presidency

The Executive Office of the President was largely a creation of Franklin Roosevelt, as he faced the vastly expanding size and role of the federal government during the Depression and the Second World War. Previous Presidents had begun to make some additions to their staff, notably when the federal budget became an executive budget in 1921, but these changes had been relatively minor (Arnold 2000). First the Brownlow Committee and later the Hoover Commissions stressed the need to convert the President into a modern manager, responsible for a massive government. (It is customary to speak of the United States as having a 'small' government, but the federal government now employs over two million civilian employees and has another two million members of the armed forces.) Those reports argued that 'the president needs help,' and that remains as true today as when written half a century earlier.

From the relatively modest beginnings in the 1930s the Executive Office of the President (EOP) has grown into a substantial management structure (see Ragsdale and Theis 1996). In addition to the White House staff who directly advise the President and to some extent are concerned with politics as much as with steering the rest of government (assuming those functions are divisible) there are four major operational units within the EOP: the Office of Management and Budget, the National Security Council, the Council of Economic Advisers, and the Domestic Policy Council. The latter three of these organizations are designed to provide the President with independent advice about policy areas over which his cabinet departments have operational authority, while the Office of Management and Budget is responsible for system-wide control over federal spending.

All of these organizations in the EOP are staffed primarily by presidential appointees, giving the President the capacity to populate these organizations with people who are personally loyal to him. There are some career staff in these organizations, especially in the Office of Management and Budget, but the majority of these thousand or more employees serve at the pleasure of the President. These officials are in part providing the President with policy advice but also are responsible for dealing with Congress and with the agencies within the executive branch that may have their own goals distinct from those of the President.

Office of Management and Budget

The foundation of the Office of Management and Budget (OMB) was in the Bureau of the Budget, created by Budget and Accounting Act of 1921. President Franklin Roosevelt moved the bureau from the Department of the Treasury to the Executive Office of the President (EOP) in 1939 to help manage the increasing size of the federal budget. In this guise the organization was responsible for assisting the president in preparing the budget for submission to Congress, and in monitoring the implementation of that budget in the agencies. The 'M' was added during the Nixon administration, reflecting the interest of that President in making the federal government more efficient – New Public Management before it became fashionable (see Rose 1976, on Management by Objectives during the Nixon years). The management functions were to some extent ignored by subsequent Presidents, with the exception of George W. Bush who instituted something approaching performance management in the federal government; this is in addition to the Government Performance and Results Act of 1993, which was a Congressional initiative (see below).

The OMB is crucial for presidential control of policy, and Directors of the Office tend to be close political confidants of the President (Tomkin 1998). The director and the rest of the organization must have a clear view of presidential priorities as they deal with thousands of spending requests each year, and attempt to impose the President's control over a huge, complex, and often uncontrollable federal budget. The OMB does have close connections with the President, but it also has a strong professional culture stressing good budget and policy analysis as well as fiscal responsibility. There are then cases in which the value of serving the President may come into conflict with the professional values.

As noted, the Bush administration re-emphasized the management side of OMB. In particular, the introduction of the Program Assessment Rating Tool (PART) program managed by OMB has been a way to impose more presidential priorities on the remainder of the executive branch. This program, similarly to the Government Performance and Results Act (GPRA) managed by Congress (see below) seeks to link the performance of federal organizations to the budget. This follows in a line of management and budget reforms from various Presidents, none of which have had an enduring impact on either budgeting or management. It is particularly interesting given the highly politicized nature of management within the Bush administration that this program has been relatively open and managed in a relatively neutral manner (Dull 2006).

National Security Council

The National Security Council (NSC) was created by the National Security Act of 1947, and created the position of National Security Advisor to the President. The NSC shadows two large and powerful organizations – the Department of Defense and the Department of State – and attempts to place a strong presidential stamp on policy in this area. The increasing size and importance of the NSC has to some extent reflected the need to counterbalance the strong internal policy cultures of those two cabinet departments; for example, in the George W. Bush administration the Department of State was thought to be insufficiently 'neo-con' and not in line with the administration's policies in Iraq. This deviation from administration goals is a general problem for Presidents who cannot always depend upon their cabinet secretaries not to 'go native' and to accept the advice coming from the internal sources, even if this is not entirely in line with the wishes of the administration. Further, those cabinet secretaries are themselves also independent politicians who may not have been selected for loyalty and may be pursuing their own career goals.

The conduct of foreign policy has demonstrated the importance of personal confidence between a President and other officials in steering the public sector. For example, during the first part of George W. Bush's presidency the President seemed to rely on his National Security Advisor Condolezza Rice and to marginalize the State Department and Secretary of State Colin Powell. After Dr Rice was shifted to Secretary of State one has hardly heard of the NSC and its top officials. Thus, as Donald Savoie (2008) has pointed out, much of contemporary executive politics is 'court politics' with chief executives depending very much on personal loyalties to attempt to achieve their policy goals.

Council of Economic Advisors (CEA)

The Council of Economic Advisors (CEA) is the economic analog of the National Security Council. Created by the Employment Act of 1946, the CEA is designed to provide the President economic advice independent of the Department of the Treasury, as well as other less significant departments such as Commerce and Labor. The primary role of the CEA is an annual statement on the state of the economy, and to provide information for the annual round of budget negotiations. The CEA has three members, and is also staffed primarily with extremely skilled economists, albeit generally economists who also have some partisan commitment. This organization is now augmented by the National Economic Council designed (at the beginning of the Clinton Administration) to coordinate economic policy in the federal government, and perhaps especially to link domestic and foreign economic policy.

The policy role of the CEA demonstrates the complexity of economic policy-making in the United States. As well as the number of organizations within the executive branch which have a role in making economic policy (including the departments of the Treasury, Commerce and Labor, Small Business Administration, and, in addition, the Department of Energy and the Department of Agriculture, which have significant economic roles), the central bank (the Federal Reserve), a number of economic regulatory agencies, organizations such as the Federal Deposit Insurance Corporation, and quasi-governmental organizations such as Fannie Mae and Freddie Mac that have been designed to be independent from direct executive control. Thus again, even in this crucial policy area, the institutional design of the federal government tends to minimize presidential control. This may be especially true given the integration of the economic profession that would often resist overt political controls.

Domestic Policy Council

Finally, each President has developed some form of domestic policy organization to coordinate, and attempt to control, the range of domestic policies other than economic policy. These organizations have been less fully institutionalized than the three mentioned above, but are still important for managing this range of policy issues. The complexity of the range of issues involves coordination as a primary activity and again involves the challenge of overcoming entrenched policy and institutional interests. Further, lacking the legal foundation available to the other presidential organizations these organizations do not have as much clout over other organizations in government.

Other Instruments for Steering from the Centre

The above discussion of organizational weapons in the hand of the President describes a number of the more powerful instruments under his control, but there are also a number of other instruments available to a President. Further, the administration of George W. Bush had, in some instances, raised these instruments to art forms and enhanced greatly the power of the President as a central policy controller. That said, the apparent excesses of this administration may well provoke some reaction from Congress, and from the Obama administration, which appears less committed to the Imperial Presidency.

Appointments

The President has much greater power of appointment than do most other political executives. Over the first few months of his administration President Obama appointed some 4,500 people to positions in the federal government. Some are those in the Executive Office of the

President discussed above, but others occupy positions throughout the executive branch. The spoils system in the United States goes back to at least the administration of Andrew Jackson, and represents the populist tradition in American government (White 1954). More recently Richard Nixon and many subsequent Presidents, have adopted the strategy of the 'Administrative Presidency,' meaning that they attempt to steer government through controlling the personnel who make and implement policy. It must be remembered, however, that below that politicized level the vast majority of the remainder of the federal civil service is hired under a stricter merit system than is now found in many other industrialized democracies.

The appointment powers of the President are substantial, and have been increasing. Paul Light (1995; see also Gilmour and Lewis 2006) has described the increasing as the 'thickening' of government, meaning that the tier of political appointees on top of public organizations is becoming thicker. Further, many of these appointees are not responsible for managing a program or even for policy advice, but rather are primarily monitoring the actions of organizations for their compliance with the program of the President.

Presidents had been using their appointment powers to involve highly capable individuals in governing, people who even though they were committed to the program of the President were experts in the policy areas for which they would be responsible. The administration of George W, Bush turned back the clock to a more old-fashioned spoils system, appointing a number of cronies to positions for which they were manifestly unqualified. The most famous of these was Michael Brown, who was head of the Federal Emergency Management Agency (FEMA) at the time of Hurricane Katrina, but that was far from the only instance (*New Republic* 2005). In the end, the incompetence of these appointees may have reduced the capacity of the President to control policy.

Thus, appointments to the upper echelons of federal organizations have always been politicized. That politicization had effectively been decreasing somewhat given the increased emphasis on expertise (see Heclo 1975; Maranto 2005). During the Bush administration the level of politicization increased markedly (see *New Republic* 2005). The early indications are that the Obama administration is placing a great deal of importance on the competence of appointees, so that the eight years from 2001–09 may have been an aberration in a general trend towards increased competence combined with political commitment.

Although there is some element of politicization across the public sector in the United States, Presidents tend to use their appointment powers in a strategic manner. While Presidents would in principle like to control all aspects of public policy, some are more politically salient than are others. Further, Presidents may place greater emphasis on controlling organizations that are further ideologically from them (Lewis 2005), rather than making appointments more generally. Thus, although Obama created a 'government of rivals' in the Cabinet, he has been somewhat more careful about picking allies for positions further down the hierarchy.

Shaping the Remainder of Government

Presidents can influence policy by placing their own people in offices, but they can alter the structures of government itself. Although Congress is often involved in major reorganizations, the President can make a number of structural changes on his own. Making the decision to do so may be a difficult political choice, given that a new organization created without the involvement of Congress may reduce the subsequent support for that organization. Congress typically does not like to be cut out of the loop when making policy, or making organizations, so budgets and other forms of support may be harder to come by.

The President may, however, engage in some significant organizational activities using his own authority. This reorganizational capacity is most evident within the EOP, but can extend throughout government as well. As has been true in the use of the appointment powers, Presidents tend to use this power strategically and attempt to punish their enemies by abolishing organizations, or create new organizations to emphasize their own policy preferences. This strategy can run afoul of Congress and the budgetary process, but if nothing else allows the President to set the terms of the political battle.

Going Public

All politicians have the capacity to appeal to the public, but the President is in a particularly good position to do this. Theodore Roosevelt famously described the presidency as a 'bully pulpit' and when Presidents find that their capacity to negotiate is not enough, they can use that pulpit to 'go public' (Kernell 2007). That is, the President can attempt to generate public support for his policies by appealing for public support over the heads of Congress. The ability of the President to attempt to mobilize the public and to attempt to represent the public interest against the more parochial interests of individual Congressmen is to a great extent dependent upon his popularity. But for all but the most unpopular Presidents this strategy adds another weapon for the centre. (George W. Bush was, for example, largely invisible during much of the economic crisis, realizing that any attempt on his part to go public would probably be counterproductive.)

The going public strategy is one reflection of the general importance of the media for the power of the U.S. President. Going back at least to Franklin Roosevelt's 'fireside chats' on the radio, Presidents have recognized the importance of the media for getting their message to the public and shaping public opinion. Congress also uses the media but often speaks with several voices, while the White House, and to some extent the remainder of the administration, is capable of speaking with one voice.

The Czar's the Star

Beginning with the creation of the 'Energy Czar' during the Nixon administration, Presidents have used individual officials responsible for an area of policy as a management and policy device. The concept of the 'czar' is to at once give the President control over a policy area and to minimize direct personal exposure of the President. The most notable examples of the use of czars have been the drug czar begun in the Clinton administration and the national security czar initiated by President George W. Bush. As he proceeded with plans for his new administration Barack Obama for a while had an economics czar, perhaps to coordinate all the strong personalities brought into the economics organizations (see above) within the EOP (but see Wilkinson 2008). In the short run Timothy Geitner and Ben Bernancke appear to be sharing that role.

Decree Powers and Signing Statements

Finally, the President has the capacity to issue decrees that have the force of law and which he can use to circumvent the powers of Congress. This power is inherent in the constitutional responsibility of the President to administer the laws, but when the President begins to act in a more 'imperial' manner there are concerns about the extent to which this authority does in fact exceed that intended by the framers. The available evidence is that Presidents tend to use this instrument primarily in foreign affairs, a policy area in which the President has special powers (Rottinghaus and Maier 2007).

In addition to the formal powers of the President to issue executive orders, Presidents have developed the instrument of the 'signing statement' For most of the history of the United States Presidents have simply signed bills coming from Congress with which they agreed, although almost from the founding of the Republic they also have issued statements about their understanding of the laws and their intentions for implementation (see Cooper 2005). However, especially in the presidency of George W. Bush these statements have become more controversial and much more in the public eye (Bumiller 2006). The use of these statements has, to some extent, provided the President with a line-item veto that has been rejected at the constitutional level. Although less obviously, President Obama has also used signing statements to try to impose his own will over policy (O'Keefe 2009).

Summary: Managing the Centre

The above discussion should make it apparent that the President has a wealth of resources at his disposal to steer. What is perhaps most interesting is that some Presidents are so much more successful in using those resources than are others. Presidents are usually assessed in terms of their ability to make policy, but less so in terms of their ability to manage the EOP and to cope with the advice coming to them from their staff. The policy outputs of the presidency may, in turn, be a function of the ability to manage the staff within the White House (Vaughn and Villalobos 2009). Hult and Walcott (2004), for example, argued that if the President is to be successful in managing the executive establishment he must first be successful in managing the White House itself.

One aspect of the management of the Executive Office of the President is the style of the President in using advice. For example, Dwight Eisenhower rather famously wanted all advice in one-page memos with a recommended decision. Other presidents, Gerald Ford, have wanted their advisors to argue out the points in front of them and then he would make the decision (Porter 1980). Barack Obama appointed a number of heavyweight advisors, so that he will have to be able to cope with multiple streams of advice on his own and not use his chief of staff to process the information for him.

The other aspect of managing the EOP is providing direction to the staff and the organizations that are meant to provide direction to the rest of government. This is no small task, given that there are several thousand employees, many of whom are career employees who work in organizations with their own cultures and their own goals that may present the same barriers to effective management as do organizations within the line bureaucracy. Presidents generally try to overcome these barriers by appointing their own loyalists to positions that oversee the internal bureaucracies, but even then the organizational cultures in bodies such as the Office of Management and Budget may dominate.

The Other Centre: Congress and Policy Steering

By design, the majority of this chapter has been focused on the capacity of the President to control American government. In the background of that discussion, however, the Congress has been lurking. Congress represents a second centre for American government, and even when the President and the Congress are controlled by the same party there may be institutional conflicts over the control of policy. Although Congress does not have the personal mandate that a President enjoys, they can claim an equal Constitutional status in governing and also can claim somewhat closer connections to constituents and to socioeconomic interests.

The U.S. Congress is perhaps the only real transformative legislature (Polsby 1975) in the world. In addition to its constitutional rights to legislate and to exert substantial control over the executive branch, the Congress has organized itself effectively to perform those tasks. Much of the organization of Congress is not directed at steering in any comprehensive manner. The committee system is well designed to exercise oversight on the executive branch and to serve constituents, but that structure in turn makes it difficult to provide effective, coordinated steering across policy areas or regions.

Despite the generally fragmented structure of Congress, there are several important structures and procedures within Congress that enable it to provide greater central steering. The most important of these structures are related to the budget process and represent attempts to force consideration of the multiple potential uses for public money, and to reconcile annual expenditures and revenue decisions. The most important political powers of Congress are derived from its power of the purse, and hence its major steering capacities also are derived from the control of public revenue and expenditure.

The most important of the steering and control structures within Congress is the Congressional Budget Office (CBO). The CBO was established as a counterpart of the Office of Management and Budget, in order to provide a source of independent advice on expenditures and fiscal policy for Congress. The CBO is a product of the Congressional Budget and Impoundment Control Act of 1974, an act that was designed to overcome the imbalance in both expertise and control between the executive and legislative branches. This organization has become effective not only in advising Congress but also in helping the federal government as a whole to focus on the implications of expenditure policies. The CBO has been successful in part because it has operated in a relatively non-partisan manner and attempts to provide equal service to both sides of the aisle.

In addition to the Congressional Budget Office, Congress is also served by the Government Accountability Office (GAO). Created originally as the financial accounting office for the federal government, the GAO evolved into an organization that not only deals with financial issues but also with performance issues. Much of their evaluation is done on a program-by-program basis, but the GAO has also developed a greater capacity to consider the broader challenges to governance. In particular, the focus on broad policy issues that present major challenges to the system has enabled the organization, and the Congress to identify and address those challenges. Further, the GAO is responsible to Congress but is also serves government more generally and provides some common background for good governance.

Finally, in structural terms, Congress has some committees that are designed to give it a broader vision of policy. For example, the Budget Committee is staffed by the CBO and is responsible for managing the internal budget process in Congress, and especially the reconciliation process that brings together the production of the more than a dozen appropriations committees and also brings them together (twice a year) with the revenue estimates – which is an attempt to force Congress to consider the consequences of their willingness to spend and their reluctance to tax. In addition, the Joint Economic Committee comprises representatives from both the Senate and the House and its staff provides skilled advice on a range of economic issues.

In addition to the structures available to Congress the development of the Government Performance and Results Act (GPRA) provides a procedure for imposing greater control over agencies and their programs (Radin 1998, 2006). This program is a performance management program linked closely to the budget process, and is a means through which Congress can attempt to impose its priorities on the bureaucracy. Those priorities are not determined autonomously by Congress, but rather have been negotiated with the agencies. Even with those initial negotiations, however, Congress is able to use GPRA to monitor and to control federal government organizations.

Discussion: The Battle of Steering and Autonomy

The concern with steering from the centre reflects one important perspective on American government, but perhaps not the dominant perspective of the actors. That dominant perspective in the history of the public sector in the United States has been the pursuit of agency autonomy (Seidman 1998; Carpenter 2001). There are multiple roots to that pursuit of greater autonomy. One is the desire on the part of the agency leadership to be able to control their own policies and perhaps to pursue larger budgets and personnel allocations; although, perhaps, one should not take this so far as the extreme maximization logic endorsed by Niskanen (1971). The other more altruistic reason is to be able to provide better services to the clients of programs with greater flexibility and without excessive levels of control.

Given this basic dynamic in institutional politics, steering from the centre is often more difficult than Presidents would like, and easier than many people in Congress and in the agencies might like. These political battles are generally expressed in terms of the specifics of policy although much the underlying dynamic is institutional politics. Presidential responsibilities for policy, and the central role that economic and foreign policy make in evaluations of Presidents, may make control issues more relevant for the executive. The Congress, however, has its own management and control issues and wants to remain a worthy adversary for an executive that continues to seek power.

As implied above, Congress plays something of a double role in the process of steering from the centre. On the one hand the committees and the individual Congressmen have strong incentives to support the autonomy of the programs in the executive branch that provide services to their constituents. Much of the political logic of Congress has been to support constituents, and that may mean avoiding priority setting by either the President or coordinating structures in Congress. On the other hand, however, the party leadership in Congress and some of the central organizations do have an interest in creating a more coherent style of governing across programs and agencies.

Politically steering from the centre has become easier in the United States because of several major external shocks to the system. The first was the attack of 9/11 and the perceived need to strengthen government in general, and security in particular (Naff and Newman 2004). Some the intelligence failures leading to the success of the 9/11 attacks was thought to be a product of poor coordination, and there have been attempts to improve the cooperation of the various intelligence organizations. Likewise, some of the failures in coping with Hurricane Katrina were products of bureaucratic infighting, with resulting pressures from the centre for greater control. Recall that on the fourth anniversary of Hurricane Katrina, President Barack Obama promised in his weekly radio address to use his office and his power to end bureaucratic turf-fighting.

The economic crisis beginning in 2008 has also helped to solidify the steering position of the centre, and to reduce the autonomy of some actors. In particular the Federal Reserve Bank has become more of a part of the executive branch rather than an autonomous economic regulator. Further, the Council of Economic Advisors and the National Economic Council have taken an even stronger position in guiding economic policy from the White House, overcoming some of the organizational resistance in the executive branch and from Congress.

Conclusion

The numerous actors involved in governance in the United States must attempt to steer the economy and society, as well as the remainder of government, within a very complex system that is not designed to facilitate that steering. Even if there were a single actor or institution that were attempting to exert control through this complex system it would be difficult, but there are several institutional actors, and their interactions exacerbate the complexity of the governance problems. Therefore, the steering from the centre involves negotiation as much as it involves command, although Presidents often come to office not realizing just how limited the powers of the office may be.

Steering from the centre also involves using the vast array of information and ideas that bubble up from the system, both from the bureaucracy as a whole and more particularly from the several organizations within the Executive Office of the President. Somewhat paradoxically, managing information in the centre might best be done in a less centralized manner than most Presidents attempt. That said, Presidents, like any other leaders, will have their own styles of managing and their own endowments of skills. What is clear, however, is that to be successful as a President one of the most important skills is the ability to negotiate and to work effectively with others in this labyrinth of a government.

REFERENCES

Aberbach, J.D. (1990). *Keeping a Watchful Eye: The Politics of Congressional Oversight*. Washington, DC: Brookings Institution.

Arnold, P.E. (2000). *Making the Managerial Presidency: Comprehensive Reorganization Planning*. Lawrence: University Press of Kansas.

Bouckaert, G., B.G. Peters, and K. Verhoest. (2009). *Specialization and Coordination in Advanced Democracies*. London: Palgrave.

Bumiller, E. (2006). For President, Final Say Comes after the Bill Is Signed. *New York Times* (16 Jan.).

Burke, J.P. (1992). *The Institutional President*. Baltimore: Johns Hopkins University Press.

Carey, J.M., and M.S. Shugart. (1998). *Executive Decree Authority*. Cambridge: Cambridge University Press.

Carpenter, D.P. (2001). *Forging Bureaucratic Autonomy*. Princeton: Princeton University Press.

Cooper, P.J. (2005). George W. Bush, Edgar Allan Poe and the Use and Abuse of Presidential Signing Statement. *Presidential Studies Quarterly* 35: 515–35.

Dull, M. (2006). Why PART? The Institutional Politics of Presidential Budget Reforms. *Journal of Public Administration Research and Theory* 16: 187–215.

Freeman, J.L. (1955). *The Political Process*. New York: Doubleday.

Gilmour, J.B., and D.E. Lewis. (2006). Political Appointees and the Competence of Federal Program Management. *American Politics Research* 34: 22–50.

Hart, J. (1996). *The Presidential System*, 2nd ed. Chatham, NJ: Chatham House.

Heclo, H. (1977). *A Government of Strangers? Executive Politics in Washington*. Washington, DC: Brookings Institution.

Heclo, H. (1983). One Executive Branch or Many? In A. King (ed.), *Both Ends of the Avenue*. Washington, DC: American Enterprise Institute.

Howell, W.G., and D.E. Lewis. (2003). Agencies by Presidential Design. *Journal of Politics* 64: 1095–1114.

Hult, K.M., and C.E. Walcott. (2004). *Empowering the White House: Governance under Nixon, Ford and Carter*. Lawrence: University Press of Kansas.

Kaboolian, L. (1998). The New Public Management: Challenging the Boundaries of the Management vs Administration Debate. *Public Administration Review* 58: 189–97.

Kernell, S. (2007). *Going Public: New Strategies for Presidential Leadership*. Washington, DC: CQ Press.

Kerwin, C. (2004). *Rulemaking*, 3rd ed. Washington, DC: CQ Press.

Kettl, D.F. (2004). *System under Stress: Homeland Security and American Politics*. Washington, DC: CQ Press.

Leeuw, F.L., R.C. Rist, and R.C. Sonnichsen. (1994). *Can Government Learn? Comparative Perspectives on Evaluation and Organizational Learning*. New Brunswick, NJ: Transaction Publishers.

Lewis, D.E. (2005). Staffing Alone: Unilateral Action and the Politicization of the Executive Office of the President. *Presidential Studies Quarterly* 35: 496–514.

– (2008). *The Politics of Presidential Appointments: Political Control and Bureaucratic Performance*. Princeton: Princeton University Press.

Light, P.C. (1995). *Thickening Government*. Washington, DC: Brookings Institution.

Maranto, R. (2005). *Beyond a Government of Strangers: How Career Executives and Political Appointees Can Turn Conflict into Cooperation*. Lanham, MD: Lexington Books.

Mayhew, D.R. (1991). *Divided We Govern: Party Control, Lawmaking and Investigations, 1946–90*. New Haven: Yale University Press.

McFarland, A. (2004). *Neopluralism: The Evolution of Political Process Theory* Lawrence: University Press of Kansas.

Neustadt, R. (1960). *Presidential Power: The Politics of Leadership*. New York: Doubleday.

New Republic. (2005). Welcome to the Hackocracy. *New Republic* (17 Oct.).

Nicholson, S.P., G.M. Segura, and N.D. Woods. (2002). Presidential Approval and the Mixed Blessings of Divided Government. *Journal of Politics* 64: 701–20.

Niskanen, W. (1971). *Bureaucracy and Representative Government*. Chicago: Aldine/Atherton.

O'Keefe, E. (2009). The Latest Obama Signing Statement. *Washington Post* (31 March).

Peters, B.G. (2001). *The Future of Governing*, 2nd ed. Lawrence: University Press of Kansas.

– (2007). Conclusion: From Consensus to Majoritarian Government. In G. Peele et al. (eds.), *Developments in American Politics V*. Basingstoke: Macmillan.

– (2008). Political Advisors in the United States. In R. Shaw and C. Eichbaum (eds.), *The Role of Policy Advisors*. Oxford: Oxford University Press.

Peters, B.G., R.A.W. Wright, and V. Wright. (2000). *Administering the Summit.*
 Basingstoke: Macmillan.
Polsby, N.W. (1975). Legislatures. In F.I. Greenstein and N.W. Polsby (eds.),
 Handbook of Political Science, vol. 5. Reading, MA: Addison-Wesley.
Porter, R.B. (1980). *Presidential Decision-Making: The Economic Policy Board.*
 Cambridge: Cambridge University Press.
Radin, B.S. (1998). The Government Performance and Results Act (GPRA):
 Hydra-Headed Monster or Flexible Management Tool? *Public Administration
 Review* 58: 307–16.
Radin, B. (2006). *Challenging the Performance Movement: Accountability, Complex-
 ity and Democratic Values.* Washington, DC: Georgetown University Press.
Rose, R. (1976). *Managing Presidential Objectives.* New York: Free Press.
Saldarini, K. (1999). 'Results Act Could Prevent Overlap,' GAO Says.
 GovExec, Daily Briefing, 30 March. Available at http://www.govexec.com/
 dailyfed/0399/.
Savoie, D.J. (1994). *Reagan, Thatcher, Mulroney; The Search for a New Bureaucracy.*
 Pittsburgh: University of Pittsburgh Press.
– (2008). *Court Government and the Decline of Accountability in Canada and the
 United Kingdom.* Toronto: University of Toronto Press.
Seidman, H.B. (1998). *Politics, Power and Position: The Dynamics of Federal
 Organizations*, 5th ed. New York: Oxford University Press.
Singer, P. (2005). Bush and the Bureaucracy: Crusade for Control. *National
 Journal* (25 March).
Tomkin, S.L. (1998). *Inside OMB: Politics and Process in the President's Budget
 Office.* Armonk, NY: M.E. Sharpe.
United States General Accounting Office. (2000a). *Managing in the New Millen-
 nium.* GAO/T-OGC-00-9. Washington, DC: USGAO.
– (2000b). *Managing for Results: Barriers to Interagency Coordination.* GAO/
 GGD-00-106. Washington, DC: USGAO.
Vaughn, J.S., and J.D. Villalobos. (2009). The Managing of the Presidency:
 Applying Theory-Driven Empirical Models to the Study of White House
 Bureaucratic Performance. *Political Research Quarterly.* 62: 158–63.
White, L.D. (1954). *The Jacksonians: A Study in Administrative History.* New
 York: Macmillan.
Wilkinson, W. (2008). America Doesn't Need More Czars. *Marketplace* (19
 Nov.).
Wolf, P.J. (1997). Why Must We Reinvent the Federal Government? Putting
 Historical Developmental Claims to the Test. *Journal of Public Administration
 Research and Theory* 7: 353–88.

7 Steering from the Centre: The Canadian Way

DONALD J. SAVOIE

Canada has hardly been immune to fashions and fads in public policy, and public Canada has hardly been immune to fashions and fads in public policy and public administration. The Canadian government borrowed more than a page from Britain in introducing special operating agencies, new approaches to financial management, and measures to empower front line managers and their employees. Canada, as is well known, is the world's second largest country by land mass and has a federal system of government. Its national public service is spread over 9,330,970 square kilometers, and something like 65 per cent of federal public servants are located outside the nation's capital in regional and field offices.

Canada also has a parliamentary system based on the Westminster model, and British influence informed virtually every major development in the development of Canada's machinery of government and the public service. The Westminster and Whitehall models provided the inspiration not just for the Canadian government, but also for the ten provincial governments. W.A. Carrothers wrote in the very first issue of the *Canadian Journal of Economics and Political Science* that 'it is to be hoped that before long we shall, in all of the provinces, have developed a permanent public service of high character and efficiency, which will carry on its work regardless of the party in power. There is no doubt that the efficiency of government service in Great Britain is to be attributed largely to an efficient permanent public service. Were this evil remedied in Canada, a great many of the charges of corruption on the part of governments would disappear and, incidentally, there would be a greater respect for government, on the part of the Canadian people' (Carrothers 1935: 29).

Still, Canadian public servants had to deal with something that British public servants did not: geography. They had to come up with ways to provide services over a vast territory and so had no choice but to experiment with decentralization. This is difficult enough in mature governments with well-oiled administrative and financial processes already in place. On the very day that Canada was born, in 1867, public servants had to decentralize operations while creating a departmental structure. The fact that they were unable to look to Britain for guidance here did not help matters. As a result, major problems soon surfaced in regional and local offices. Canada's dean of the public administration discipline, Ted Hodgetts, writes that 'it would be a tenable thesis that the history of the developing federal public service reveals a gradual curtailment of powers delegated to local agents ... and has tended to place a few key officials under an unbearably heavy burden' (1955: 278). The political and administrative difficulties associated with decentralization in Canada's early years gave rise to an institutional memory that, I believe, lingers still.

Thus, Canadian public servants had to adapt British-inspired institutions to Canada's political reality. Britain is, or at least was, a unitary state and its regional dimension is not nearly as difficult to manage as are Canada's regional and linguistic tensions. Consider this: Canada has two official languages, ten provinces and three northern territories, and its geography covers five time zones.

Geography and other factors, however, have not prevented the government of Canada from looking to Britain in recent years for inspiration in reforming government operations. For example, a few years after Margaret Thatcher established executive agencies to deliver services, Canada introduced special operating agencies (SOAs) to do the same thing. The similarities do not end there. We have seen prime ministers, dating back to Pierre Trudeau in Canada and James Callaghan in Britain, make every effort to centralize more and more power in their own offices and at the centre of government.

In this chapter, we look at the Canadian experience in managing a growing public sector at a time when the new fashion in public administration is to empower front-line managers and workers. Like other governments, the Canadian government has, over the past thirty years or so, introduced measure after measure to empower program managers. Yet, at the same time, we have also seen politicians intensify their efforts to locate more power in their own hands and offices – a contradiction of sorts. Public policies and government decisions, however, are never struck in a vacuum. There are a number of reasons that have led Canadian prime ministers to centralize power in their own offices and we need to explore these. We also need to review strategies to empower program managers and how the centre of government holds managers to account.

Trudeau Leads the Way

Canadian politicians, like their counterparts in other Anglo-American democracies, have sought to strengthen their hands in shaping policy. Trudeau was the first to deliberately set out in a systematic fashion to wrestle policy influence away from departments and to give Cabinet the ability to make policy based on competing advice. Indeed, Trudeau decided to overhaul the Cabinet process precisely to break the stranglehold ministers and long-serving deputy ministers had on departments. He felt that major policy decisions and all administrative issues had become the preserve of line departments and that the centre was left ill-equipped to challenge them. The solution – strengthen the centre considerably. Richard French explains, 'The Prime Minister's often expressed conviction is that Cabinet is less easily captured by the bureaucracy than are ministers operating independently' (French 1979: 365). Peter Aucoin writes that Trudeau launched a major assault on the centre of government to correct 'the abuses and excesses of individual ministerial autonomy which had to be replaced by a rigorous system of checks and balances within the Cabinet as a collective executive.' He adds, 'The influence of the bureaucracy had to be countered to ensure that the organizational interests of departments and agencies did not take precedence over required policy innovation and policy coherence' (Aucoin 1986: 8).

Trudeau wanted policy-making to be placed firmly in the hands of Cabinet and removed from those of a few powerful ministers and mandarins running government departments. This, in turn, explains why he decided to strengthen the centre of government by enlarging his own office, expanding the Privy Council Office (PCO), and establishing new Cabinet committees, effectively giving them the authority to make decisions. The reforms did wrestle policy influence away from departments and senior public servants, but in the end power flowed to the prime minister and central agencies rather than to Cabinet (Savoie 1999: chapters 4 and 10).

Trudeau's decision to curb the power of the mandarins gave rise to a new breed of deputy minister in Ottawa that is still evident today. Have-policy-will-travel became the new credential that created deputy ministers capable of serving in virtually any department. It is now not uncommon for deputy ministers to serve in several departments before they retire. Deputy ministers are no longer specialists in one sector or in the policies and programs of a single department. They take pride in being able to manage any department and any situation. They are what one former senior public servant labelled 'careerists, and their careers are paramount' (Savoie 1999: 254). Moreover, the single most important determining factor on career prospects for current and aspiring deputy ministers is how well they are perceived at the centre of government.

The PCO also attaches a great deal of importance on 'being corporate' when it looks at the work of a deputy minister. One former deputy minister reports that at one of his performance reviews a senior PCO official observed, 'You are doing great, and everybody is saying so from your minister to other deputy ministers. You are strong on both the policy and management front. But you are not being corporate enough' (Savoie 1999: 255). It is important to note that in this case the individual became a senior deputy minister without having worked in a central agency, a rare occurrence.

The PCO also stresses in print the importance of being 'corporate.' In its document *Responsibility in the Constitution*, it states that 'Deputy ministers are, of course, responsible to their respective ministers, but their appointment by the Prime Minister reinforces their commitment to ensure the successful functioning of ministerial government.' It then adds that 'the system would be unstable without the collective responsibility necessary to Cabinet solidarity, and the deputy must also play a role in and be affected by means that are used to ensure the maintenance of collective responsibility among ministers' (Privy Council Office 1993: 58 and 62).

If the Head Goes, So Does the Government

Former Prime Minister Chrétien told his ministers at their very first Cabinet meeting that 'above all they should always strive to protect the prime minister' and added that 'if the prime minister should fall, then the government would likely follow' (Savoie 1999: 97). In short, ministers were dispensable but not the prime minister. Chrétien learned about governing at the feet of former Prime Minister Pierre Trudeau, who he called 'the boss' when he served in the Trudeau cabinet (Savoie

1999). Trudeau, as already noted, put in place measures to strengthen the centre of government in its dealings with line departments and agencies. No prime minister after Trudeau has sought to turn back the clock. If anything, prime ministers since Trudeau have sought to strengthen further the centre of government.

Canadian prime ministers now have in their own hands many instruments to protect themselves from the media, the opposition, and even their Cabinet colleagues. Yet Canadian prime ministers feel increasingly vulnerable and less in control than was the case forty years ago.

In Canada, preoccupation with national unity, particularly since the Trudeau years, has pushed prime ministers and their political advisers to intervene or keep a watchful eye in areas that in years past would have been left to ministers and their departments. It is no exaggeration to write that national unity tends to recast substantive policy issues into the question of their impact on Quebec and the likelihood of securing federal-provincial agreements. This invariably brings issues to the attention of the prime minister and his or her advisers. There are plenty of examples. Andrew Cooper, for example, in his comparative study of Canadian and Australian foreign affairs, writes, 'a tell-tale sign of how Canada's economic and diplomatic strategy was subordinated to political tactics in agricultural trade was the routing of all important decisions in this area ... through the central agencies of the Prime Minister's Office (PMO) and the Privy Council Office (PCO). The decisive impact of the constitutional issue in this matter inevitably stymied the government's ability to perform effectively in the concluding phase of the Uruguay Round' (Cooper 1997: 217). The participants directly involved in recasting or rerouting the issues are for the most part political strategists or generalists operating at the centre and are not usually specialists in health care, social or economic development policy, and so on (Cameron and Simeon 2000: 58–118). They are also often directly tied to the prime minister and his office in one fashion or another.

All important files have the potential of bringing the centre of government into play. In this sense, the centre not only steers but also rows whenever it thinks that it should. What makes a file important is not at all clear and very often it depends on the circumstances. Media attention can, on very short notice, turn an issue, however trivial, into an important file. When this happens, there is no distinction made between policy and administration. A file that receives media attention becomes political, and at that point the prime minister and his advisers will want to oversee its development. Without putting too fine a point on it, what the front page of the national media reports can make a file important, no matter its scope or nature. Today, the media, much like society itself, are far less deferential to political leaders and political institutions. Nothing is off limits anymore, and political leaders and government officials must continually be cautious of letting their guard down when meeting the press. Ministers and their senior departmental officials know that officials in the PMO will be monitoring very carefully what they say to the media and how they say it.

The Media

The media have undergone a sea change in recent years with the advent of twenty-four-hour television news, radio talk shows, TV punditry, the Internet, and political blogs. Forty years ago, political columnists were rare. Today, according to a leading Canadian columnist, they are 'almost a dime a dozen.' Forty years ago, journalists 'worked hard on collecting facts, cross-checking them, reading documents and talking to people. This kind of work is now considered hopelessly old-fashioned' (Simpson 2006: A13).

Douglas Fisher, a member of Parliament in the 1950s and 1960s and later a columnist and a television commentator for more than forty years, reflected on his time in Ottawa as he took his leave from journalism in 2006. He noted that, over the years, the 'House of Commons has withered almost to insignificance ... that the influence of cabinet ministers has declined most of all,' and that 'the prime minister and his office now dominate government' (Fisher 2006). The media, he insists, have also changed. He reports that 'television in almost every sense has altered the behaviour in the House. Part of Question Period every day is kind of an arranged farce, a drama ... The TV people do somewhat a different chore than the print people. The print people are less important and less well known now, but in some ways they remain the basic people in terms of providing the story. You very rarely get, consecutively, from the television coverage of parliament, much information of worth or weight about, say, an important bill that's coming through. Television tends to report on politics as though it's a game and every day has winners and losers' (*Hill Times* 2006). Consequently, governments have had to learn the business of news management, to develop an instinct for political survival so as to be perceived as winners or able to take decisions quickly before the television cameras. This, in turn, has extended the scope and influence of those operating at the centre of government.

Prime ministers are at the heart of the news management mode, a circumstance that has strengthened their hand in dealing with their parties and ministers. Indeed, judging by the media focus, the incumbent prime minister and party leaders now appear to be the only substantial candidates in an election race. How one does in an election campaign and in the televised leaders' debate can affect the election itself (Johnson et al. 1997). Increasingly, the objective of all parties at election time is to sell their leaders rather than their ideas, policies, or party. A study by leading students of election campaigns observes that 'Canadian elections, in common with elections in other Westminster-style systems, as well as with presidential elections in the United States, inevitably turn on the question of who – which individual – shall form the government' (Johnston et al. 1992: 84). If the leader secures a majority, it is generally assumed that the party is in his or her debt, not the other way around.

This, in turn, explains the rise of what Christopher Hood and Martin Lodge describe as 'a new politico-bureaucratic class of spin doctors shouldering aside public servants with more traditional analytic skills' (Hood and Lodge 2006: viii). Their purpose essentially is to promote or protect the head of government. They are a key component of a government's news-management model. They are the hired hands whose job is to manage the media. In the process, they have become important voices in their own right inside government, trying to control a powerful voice on the outside always lurking to spot a weakness in the prime minister.

Letting Managers Manage

There is an old cliché that has been part of the Ottawa vocabulary for the past forty years or more – let managers manage. Brian Mulroney, in the mid-1980s, borrowed a page from his Conservative soul mate, Margaret Thatcher, and introduced a number of private sector inspired measures to turn bureaucrats into managers. Like Thatcher, Mulroney sought to distinguish the role of policy formulation from the role of management. This would serve two purposes: it would upgrade the importance of management in government and enable politicians to carve out a large role in shaping policy.

Barely a year in office, Mulroney unveiled a plan to overhaul government management practices. He labelled the initiative Increased Ministerial Authority and Accountability (IMAA). The objective was to give departmental managers more latitude and direct responsibility to manage financial and human resources. This would be accomplished by reducing centrally-prescribed rules and controls and give managers greater freedom of action and flexibility in the use of funds voted to them by Parliament.

The Mulroney government borrowed still another page from Thatcher when it introduced special operating agencies to deliver services. The government readily admitted that its decision 'was spurred by the Executive Agency, or Next Steps initiative in the United Kingdom' (Clarke 1992: 13). The scope of the Canadian initiative was considerably less ambitious than Britain's Next Steps, but it did provide more autonomy and a sharper mandate to managers.

There have been other measures introduced by successive prime ministers to let managers manage. Pay for performance schemes have been introduced and financial controls have been streamlined and made more flexible. As in other Anglo-American democracies, empowerment has become the buzzword in the government of Canada. Empowerment signalled the search for doers rather than thinkers and emphasized the importance of managers taking the lead, getting things done, and dealing effectively with customers and their needs. Bureaucracy, red tape, and centrally prescribed rules were to be replaced by a new delegation of authority to managers in line departments, much as in the private sector.

There is some evidence that the government was able to reduce red tape and financial control. The result is that departments and managers have a great deal more freedom than they have ever had to move financial resources around and to manage human resources. One has only to look at the number of Treasury Board decisions over a period of twenty-five years to see that there have been some changes. In 1983, the Treasury Board issued 6,000 decisions. By 1987 the number had dropped to 3,500. By 1997 the number had dropped still further, to about 1,100 (Savoie 1999: 233). By 2007 the number dropped to less than 1,000.[1]

Some of management reforms in Canada look like reforms in other jurisdictions. To be sure, the political-management environment that Martin Smith describes in his 'The Paradoxes of Britain's Strong Centre: Delegating Decisions and Re-claiming Control' in this volume does resonate in the Canadian context. Although Finland's political context

Table 7.1
Number of Staff in Central Agencies, 1970 and 2005, Government of Canada

	1970	2005
PMO-PCO	287	1,032
Treasury Board	479	1,259
Finance	417	966

Sources: Canada, Budget des dépenses 2005–2008, partie III – Rapport sur les plans et les priorités (Ottawa: Public Works and Government Services, 2005); Canada, Budget des dépenses (Ottawa: Ministry of Finance, 13T 31–2, 1970).

differs substantially from the Canadian context, one can draw a parallel between Canadian and Finnish efforts to coordinate better sectoral policies and strengthen the hand of managers as outlined in Sirpa Kekkonen 'and Tapio Raunio's 'Towards Stronger Political Steering: Program Management Reform in the Finnish Government.'

Falling On Hand Grenades

At the same time, front-line managers were given more freedom to manage financial and human resources, central agencies saw their role, mandate and size expand. Table 7.1 below reports on the growth of central agencies in Canada between 1970 and 2005.

The centre of government has not only grown in the government of Canada, but people who work in central agencies enjoy more senior classifications and higher pay than officials occupying similar positions in line departments. There are many officials, for example, in the Privy Council Office in Ottawa who enjoy a deputy minister-level classification. Nor do these central agency officials have programs to manage and deliver. Thus, they can spend all of their time on policy issues, working on briefing material and micro-managing specific files whenever a crisis flares up, and demanding more and more information from the front line (Savoie 1999).

Central agencies have a much stronger policy capacity than they had forty years ago. They have strategic planning capacities and, if need be, a direct hand in the day-to-day work of departments. At times, their officials can be heavily involved in transactions or specific departmental files; at other times, not at all. It depends. If it involves the prime minister's interest or if the government's political standing may be in jeopardy, then central agency officials will be present – even, if necessary, physically in the department directing things (Savoie 1999: chapter 9). Departments know full well that the centre has them on constant watch to protect the prime minister and the government's political interests, that it also has the human and financial resources to monitor departments – or at least what the media have to say about them – and that, if necessary, it will intervene.

Still, officials in central agencies need to rely on data provided by line departments, and this explains in part the constant stream of requests for information. It should surprise no one that if you add positions in central agencies, as the government of Canada has done in more recent years, you will also give rise to more requests for information to line departments and agencies. But that is not all. Ministers need to be briefed on proposed new initiatives and on anticipated questions, both in Parliament and from the media. Just responding to access to information requests and any difficulties they may create for the minister and department can consume a great deal of ministerial time and that of department officials. Andy Scott, the minister of Indian Affairs and Northern Development in Paul Martin's government (2004–6), reports that the department's communications branch employed 118 officials and that 111 of them spent most of their time on work related to access to information requests.[2] A number of new requirements, notably whistle-blowing legislation, will only add to briefing requirements.

Consultations with front-line employees suggest that Canadian officials spend more time on providing briefing material for the system than in dealing with citizens. In Canada, there are more central agencies than, say, Britain, and access to information legislation has been in place for more than twenty years. In addition, federal-provincial relations generate a great many policy papers and a great deal of briefing material. Canada has, by last count, nine oversight bodies reporting to Parliament and these also generate paperwork. A government survey of 221,434 positions was carried out in the late 1980s to identify all jobs that had at least some responsibility for dealing with the general public, even if that 'some' amounted to only 10 per cent. The survey found only 92,481 such positions or 41.8 per cent of the total number of positions (Savoie 1990: 213).

Officials in central agencies report that they have to develop an ability to keep ministers out of trouble and a capacity to 'fall on hand grenades to be successful in their work' (Savoie 2008: 157). They insist that they have to monitor and at times manage what they call 'visible and invisible' errors in line departments and agencies. In this sense, senior public servants are more politicized today than before. This is not to suggest, however, that they are more partisan. Indeed, there is little to make the case that senior public servants in Canada, at least at the federal government level, are more politically 'partisan' than in years past (Savoie 2003).

Visible errors occur when gaffes are committed by a minister or a department and are widely reported in the media. Invisible errors, of which there are always many lurking, are never uncovered by the media or the opposition. The media are all too willing to hunt for exploding hand grenades, and Canada's access to information legislation has made the hunting a great deal easier. The role of the media and the right to information legislation has transformed the relationship between the centre and line department and agencies and between politicians and public servants. Public servants with an ability to assist putting out political fires are now highly sought after in central agencies and in senior positions in line departments.

An instinct for political survival, when overseeing large sprawling bureaucracies that have lost their capacity to work both in relatively secrecy and in a clear hierarchical structure, also explains why Canadian prime ministers have sought to control things from the centre. The view at the very top is that problems are less likely to surface if the centre keeps a tight rein on things when dealing with the prime minister's priorities or high profile issues. The system can manage the rest, or those issues that matter less to the centre, and ensure that departments and agencies keep running on their tracks.

This, again, calls for a different relationship at the top. It explains why prime ministers look for senior public servants with different skills than were preferred forty years ago. Having an intimate knowledge of a sector or a government department has become less important. Although senior public servants in Canada still prefer working on policy issues rather than on administration, there is limited capacity in government to evaluate the quality of policy work (Page and Jenkins 2005: 167). It is quite different today than it was forty years ago. Networking in support of horizontal government has become an important policy skill. In addition, elected politicians, starting with the prime minister, are demanding that public servants be much more responsive to their policy agenda, able to assist in managing political crises and in dealing with the media. I asked a senior Canadian official who retired from the federal public service in November 2006 to reflect on the most important change during his time in government. His response: 'There was a time when the most senior public servants would not only pursue what the Prime Minister wanted, but also told him what he should want, not just what he wanted to hear, but what he should hear, not just respond to a short term political agenda, but also present a much longer term perspective for him to reflect on. All of this has changed.'[3] This has come at a price. As Christopher Hood argues, demand-led authority and demand-led policy work have led to impoverished policy expertise (Hood et al. 2002: 30).

The policy role of public servants now is less about having an intimate knowledge of a relevant sector and being able to offer policy options and more about finding empirical justification for what the elected politicians have decided to do (Travers 2006). In brief, the ability to know when to proceed, when to delay, when to be bold, and when to be prudent; to sense a looming political crisis; to navigate through a multitude of horizontal processes and networks; and then to justify what elected politicians have decided – these have come to matter a great deal (Axworthy 1988: 252). These skills, however, are much more akin to the political world than those found in Weber's bureaucratic model. The centre of government now values these skills and if a public servant does not possess them, then it is highly unlikely that he or she will rise to the top.

From Management to Measurement

Management can never trump politics, if the two should ever come into conflict. One high-profile scandal can undo the effect of any number of speeches about modernizing government and empowering government managers and their staff. Yet no matter the approach, politicians continue to hammer home the same message – the pursuit of good management.

In speech after speech, Trudeau, Mulroney, Chrétien, Martin, and Harper all talked about 'sound public sector management, accountability and transparency.' Prime Minister Paul Martin and his Treasury Board president, Reg Alcock, in response to the sponsorship scandal, declared that the government of Canada was unable to articulate how well its administrative and financial control mechanisms were working and that important changes were needed. Harper spoke about good management practices when he introduced legislation to strengthen accountability. Mulroney had also talked about good management when he introduced IMAA. In brief, although they all voiced the same message, they offered different prescriptions, at times conflicting ones.

Martin and Alcock, it will be recalled, decided to make internal audit committees 'independent' from line management, to introduce new 'key control' requirements across government, and to put in place a number of new reporting requirements. They also decided to strengthen the role of the Treasury Board Secretariat and to introduce a 'rigorous process to prevent re-employment of or contracting with individuals who were terminated from the public service' (Canada 2005b: 17, 1–21, 30–9). They added an 'oversight committee of independent leaders' to provide advice to the president of the Treasury Board on the necessary 'measures to implement management improvements' (Canada 2005b: 38). All in all, the Martin government, by its own count, introduced '158 measures' to clean up management in government within ten months of coming to power and pledged to introduce 'another 80' (Canada 2005b: 38 and *National Post* 2005: A8). Martin and Alcock thus served notice to senior public servants that they could not be fully trusted on management and that the government would be looking outside their ranks for advice. Empowerment was now taking a back seat to scoring political points. Thus, it does not matter what they do – introduce or remove centrally prescribed rules – the intent remains the same: to improve and strengthen management and accountability.

The Martin-Alcock reforms added still more demands for information from line-department managers. The demand for information to fuel performance measurement and evaluation initiatives by senior departmental and central agency officials in Canada has increased substantially in recent years, although few are able or even willing to make the case that these efforts have been very fruitful or led to better management practices.

The Canadian government introduced in 2003 an elaborate management accountability framework (MAF) designed to identify strengths and weaknesses in management practices in line departments and agencies. The MAF process essentially is built around key elements that define good management and establishes performance targets. The Treasury Board reports that it invariably turns to MAF generated information to assess the management performance of departments and agencies. It also reports that MAF has improved reporting to Parliament on departmental plans and performance. Treasury Board officials maintain that MAF is necessary and that the government has been willing to invest the necessary resources to make it work. They add that given that government operations are spread over a very large territory and that managers have been given considerable flexibility in managing human and financial resources in recent years, a sophisticated management reporting process is necessary to ensure that the centre of government can promote policy and program coherence and accountability (Treasury Board, undated). The MAF process, however, requires government managers to produce a great deal of material and data for central agency officials.

In my recent research for a book on accountability, I heard one complaint after another from departments, from citizens, and from communities about the never-ending demand for reporting documents (Savoie 2008). I was informed, for example, that Aboriginal communities in Canada need to submit '60,000 reports a year' to the federal government (Good 2003). A federal task force reports that an Aboriginal community in the north, with a population of sixty-three, had fifty-one contribution agreements, each requiring a year-end report (Canada 2002: 12). Associations and groups with frequent dealings with the Canadian government also report a sharp increase in demands for 'paper,' 'reports,' 'justification,' and 'evaluations' on the part of public servants after the 'HRDC and sponsorship scandals' (Good 2003).

If one removes centrally prescribed rules and attaches more importance to horizontal government and less to hierarchy, then one has to identify other means to ensure accountability. Establishing management targets by central agencies and producing evaluation reports appear to be the solutions of choice. The view is that targets and performance evaluations of one kind or other both motivate staff and promote accountability.

However, public servants, by tradition, do not wish to draw attention to their work, particularly if the verdict may be critical. Management targets, internal audit reports, and evaluation reports are now accessible to those outside government. Performance in government is now the product of many hands, from the political level down to the most junior front-line worker. There is no incentive for public servants to draw attention to problems, to explain what has gone wrong, or to suggest why performance targets may not be realistic. Michael Warnick, deputy minister of Indian Affairs and Northern Development, summed up very well how line departments have learned to deal with central agency requirements. He reports that departments do produce 'fake stuff' and explained that 'fake stuff is the stuff you pretend to do and that you feed to the central agencies to get them off your back' (Warnick 2009).

Oversight Bodies

Front-line managers and central agencies have also had to learn to deal with a growing number of oversight bodies. In Canada especially, there is no shortage of oversight bodies looking over the shoulders of front-line managers at their work. They sit in judgment on managers and are always ready to point to flaws in their decisions and work. As government managers go about their work in Canada, they must bear in mind what the auditor general, the commissioner of official languages, the access to information commissioner, the Public Service Commission, internal auditors, judicial reviews, the privacy commissioner, whistle-blowing legislation, the Treasury Board Secretariat, and the media have to say about their performance, employing any number of criteria to determine success. Central agencies officials, meanwhile, have to monitor the work of oversight bodies just to keep a watch on exploding hand grenades.

Strengthening the Political Centre: You Dance with the One Who Brung You

Former Canadian Prime Minister Brian Mulroney was very fond of the old saying 'you dance with the one who brung you.' Those who gave of their time and resources to help secure the party leadership for the prime minister and who played an important role in the general election campaign would be rewarded either by being offered a position in government or by having access to its most senior levels. As is well known, loyalty is a much valued asset in partisan politics. Modern election campaigns are today less dependent on foot soldiers than in years past and are now heavily dependent on money, expertise in developing political and policy strategies, and a strong capacity to deal with the media.

A prime minister's immediate political court is partisan and consists of a mixture of outsiders and insiders. The outsiders include media relations specialists, selected lobbyists or government relations specialists, and close political confidants who have contributed money or expertise to the prime minister's political success. They have the skills necessary to staff a political war room, to spin messages to the media, and to craft political and policy positions on short notice.

Those who opt to serve in the PMO or in ministerial offices are politically partisan. There are now more of them in Canada than in years past, and they too enjoy higher pay and status. They also enjoy greater influence, especially in their dealings with senior public servants. It is much more difficult for partisan advisers to have influence in a formal setting with clearly defined rules and processes than when the prime minister brings key decisions to his office or his court (Savoie, 2008). Public servants must learn to respond to the court and its members rather than to cabinet and its formal processes. This and the growing importance of news management have considerably strengthened the hand of politically partisan advisers.

Governments, in response to a more aggressive media, appear to be fighting a permanent election campaign; hence the need to manage the news on a daily basis (Foster 2005: 177). News management is also often regarded by many public servants as a partisan activity, and some have simply decided to turn the steering wheel over to the politicians and say, 'OK, now you drive.' But spinning tomorrow's headlines is not without implications for how power and influence are distributed in government or for relations between elected politicians, their partisan advisers, and public servants or between the centre, line departments, and regional offices.

Warren Kinsella, the chief of staff for the minister at Public Works and Government Services (DPWGS), the department that housed the sponsorship program, wrote to the deputy minister stating that 'in my view, Mr J.C. Guité, current Director General of Advertising and Public Opinion research, should be assigned to carry out a review of advertising and sponsorship activities on a full-time basis. It is requested that he be assigned to a position that will allow him to carry out these tasks and that he be provided with the appropriate resources consistent with such an initiative' (Canada 2005a: 10,509). The minister, David Dingwall, said that he 'certainly instructed Mr. Kinsella to write the note' (Canada 2005a: 10,600). Long-serving public servants report that this kind of political interventions in government operations would not have been as easily tolerated in Ottawa some twenty or thirty years ago (Savoie 2008).

Looking Back

The Canadian prime minister and central agencies have gained the upper hand in establishing government priorities, in managing high profile issues and in dealing with political crisis. They are able to bring to the centre of government all the necessary material and data to make decisions and to control information going to the media and Parliament, at least in the short term. As for the rest, they appear content to let departments and agencies run on their track.

Accordingly, there are now two fairly distinct policy and decision-making processes in the government of Canada. One is under the direct control of the prime minister, his immediate political advisers, and central agencies. They govern from the centre in that they can easily have their way on things that matter to them. Formal processes, machinery of government, and bureaucratic hierarchy are easily pushed aside.

The other process is designed to keep things under control, to avoid or, failing that, to manage political or bureaucratic gaffes. The process is slow, cumbersome, and the product of many hands. It is laden with elaborate reporting requirements. Its purpose is in part to assess the management performance of line departments and agencies, but also to enable those at the centre to steer departments away from political or bureaucratic gaffes and to establish an early warning signal to manage politically difficult situations caused by the access to information legislation. However, the track record of this process in assessing management performance or evaluating the impact of government's policies and programs has not lived up to expectations.

The Canadian government has never embraced New Public Management measures to the extent that governments in other Westminster-style parliamentary systems have. For example, Canada only created a handful of executive or special operating agencies and never gave them the same management authority Britain gave to its executive agencies (Savoie 1994). Political and bureaucratic scandals have also led central agencies to impose either new centrally prescribed administrative controls or reporting requirements (Savoie 2008).

All of the above makes the case that the centre in the government of Canada has grown in size and influence in recent years. Prime ministers, starting with Pierre Trudeau, have preferred it this way. It has enabled to them to gain the upper hand in managing relations with the media, in pursuing initiatives that truly matter to them (Trudeau and patriating the constitution, Mulroney and free-trade agreement with the United States, and Chrétien and deficit reduction) and in keeping an eye on things from the centre in the era of permanent election campaigns.

NOTES

1 Consultation with a senior Treasury Board official, Ottawa, 14 March 2008.
2 Consultation with the Hon. Andy Scott, Sussex, New Brunswick, 9 Sept. 2006.

3 Consultation with a former senior Canadian Government official, Moncton, New Brunswick, 21 Nov. 2006.

REFERENCES

Aucoin, P. (1986). Organizational Change in the Machinery of Canadian Government: From Rational Management to Brokerage Politics. *Canadian Journal of Political Science* 9/1: 8.

Axworthy, T. (1988). Of Secretaries to Princes. *Canadian Public Administration*. 31: 252.

Cameron, D., and R. Simeon. (2000). Intergovernmental Relations and Democratic Citizenship. In B.G. Peters and D.J. Savoie (eds.), *Revitalizing the Public Service: A Governance Vision for the XXIst Century.* Montreal and Kingston: McGill-Queen's University Press.

Privy Council Office. (1993). *Responsibility in the Constitution.* Ottawa: Minister of Supply and Services.

Canada, Task Force on the Coordination of Federal Activities in the Regions. (2002). *Delivering Federal Policies in the Regions: Partnership in Action,* Final Report. Ottawa: Author.

Canada, Commission of Inquiry into the Sponsorship Program and Advertising Activities. (2005a). Report Two: Restoring Accountability, vol. 60. Ottawa: Author.

Canada, Treasury Board Secretariat. (2005b). *Management in the Government of Canada: A Commitment to Continuous Improvement.* Ottawa: Author.

Carrothers, W.A. (1935). Problems of the Canadian Federation. *Canadian Journal of Economics and Political Science* 1: 29.

Clarke, I.D. (1992). Special Operating Agencies: The Challenges of Innovation. *Optimum.* 22: 13.

Cooper, A.F. (1997). *In Between Countries: Australia, Canada and the Search for Order in Agricultural Trade.* Montreal and Kingston: McGill-Queen's University Press.

Fisher, D. (2006). A Celebration of 50 Great Years. *Sun News.* Available at http://www.ottsun.canoe.ca, 30 July.

French, R.D. (1979). The Privy Council Office: Support for Cabinet Decision-Making. In R. Schultz et al. (eds.), *The Canadian Political Process,* 2nd ed. Toronto: Holt, Reinhart and Winston.

Foster, C. (2005). *British Government in Crisis.* Oxford: Hart.

Good, D. (2003). *The Politics of Public Management: The HRDC Audit of Grants and Contributions.* Toronto: University of Toronto Press.

Hill Times. (2006). 'I Was in Love and Still Am' with Centre Block, Says Douglas Fisher. Available at http://www.thehilltimes.ca, 7 Aug.

Hodgetts, J.E. (1955). *Pioneer Public Service: An Administrative History of the United Canadas, 1841–1867.* Toronto: University of Toronto Press.

Hood, C., and M. Lodge. (2006). *The Politics of Public Service Bargains: Reward, Competency, Loyalty and Blame.* Oxford: Oxford University Press.

Hood, C., M. Lodge, and C. Clifford. (2002). *Public Service Policy-Making Competencies in the German BMWi and British DTI: A Comparative Analysis Based on Six Case Studies.* London: Smith Institute.

Johnson, R., A. Blais, H. Brady, and J. Crête. (1997). *Letting the People Decide: Dynamics of a Canadian Election.* Montreal and Kingston: McGill-Queen's University Press.

National Post. (2005). Bureaucrats Warned of Total Constipation. *National Post* (17 Nov.): A8.

Page, E.C., and B. Jenkins. (2005). *Policy Bureaucracy: Government with a Cast of Thousands.* Oxford: Oxford University Press.

Savoie, D.J. (1990). *The Politics of Public Spending in Canada.* Toronto: University of Toronto Press.

– (1994). *Thatcher, Reagan, Mulroney: In Search of a New Bureaucracy.* Pittsburgh: University of Pittsburgh Press.

– (1999). *Governing from the Centre: The Concentration of Power in Canadian Politics.* Toronto: University of Toronto Press.

– (2003). *Breaking the Bargain: Public Servants, Ministers, and Parliament.* Toronto: University of Toronto Press.

– (2008). *Court Government and the Collapse of Accountability in Canada and the United Kingdom.* Toronto: University of Toronto Press.

Simpson, J. (2006). The Brain of Our Existence: A Lot of Imitators but No Equals. *Globe and Mail* (16 May): A13.

Travers, J. (2006). Mandarins Learning to Like Harper. *Toronto Star.* Available at http://www.thestar.com, 22 Aug.

Treasury Board Management Accountability Framework. Available at http://www.tbs-sct.gc.ca/maf, undated.

Warnick, M. (2009). In Ralph Heintzman, *Measurement in Public Management: The Case for the Defence.* Available at http://www.optimumonline, 39/1 (March).

8 The Paradoxes of Britain's Strong Centre: Delegating Decisions and Reclaiming Control

MARTIN SMITH

Britain has long been at the forefront of public sector reform. It initiated a long process of privatization, developed a large number of agencies for the delivery of policy, and a complementary set of regulatory bodies, refined the development of new management techniques, and encouraged a belief in the need to delegate decision-making to managers on the ground. Since 1979 there has been something of a permanent revolution in terms of the reform of public services. This has led, in many people's eyes, to the fragmentation of central government and what Rhodes (1997) calls the hollowing out of the state leading to the creation of a differentiated polity. For others, what we have seen in recent years is an increased centralization of the prime minister's power and a shift to a process of presidentialization of British politics (see Pryce 1997; Hennessy 1998; Foley 2004). Rhodes and Bevir (2006) argue that this paradox is a consequence of conflicting interpretations of the ambiguities of government, with the Westminster model being used to blind us to the complex realities of government. While there is no doubt that the Westminster model is intended to sustain the myth of a unified state with undiminished sovereignty (see Migdal 2001), the paradoxes emerge not from problems of interpretation but as a consequence of the strength of personalism and the problematic relationship between policy-making and policy delivery. While British governments have supported delegation and fragmentation, they have not managed to shake off the imperatives of the Westminster model, which place responsibility and, power, with ministers. The aim of this chapter is to briefly outline the ways in which the British state has fragmented and to demonstrate how the British core executive has attempted to re-impose the Westminster model on the fragmented, New Public Management state. The chapter outlines the institutional developments that have occurred in Britain, before examining the ways in which the centre has built up capacity that has done little to resolve the problems of the central British state. The chapter argues that while considerable efforts have gone into increasing the policy-making capacity of the prime minister, the Blair government was not able to resolve the contradiction of centralizing power within the core executive with greater managerial autonomy. This is essentially a consequence of the British political system, which places considerable authority in the centre of government but leaves processes of implementation at the local level. The chapter briefly outlines how these dilemmas have returned to haunt the new Coalition government.

The Westminster Model and the Paradox of Prime Ministerial Power

The British political system is paradoxical in terms of power. On one side, the idea of Parliamentary sovereignty, combined with party discipline and a winner takes all electoral system, concentrates power within the centre of Whitehall. It is a cliché that Britain is the most centralized country in the world and that power is concentrated within the core executive. It is undoubtedly the case that the centre of government is involved in details of policy which in most other political systems would be left to local or regional government, such as the implementation of particular policies in areas like anti-social behaviour. In addition, there are very few constraints on a government's legislative program; there are no constitutional limits on what British governments can do. The Westminster model legitimizes highly centralized power by locating sovereignty within Parliament. Sovereignty is essentially appropriated to the executive on the basis that it is accountable to Parliament and through Parliament to voters.

However, while power is focused to a high degree on the centre, the prime minister traditionally has limited resources. British central government attempts to do a lot but its capability is limited and consequently government failure may occur because the centre is overwhelmed. The Prime Minister's Office (PMO) has always been smaller than most comparators. Traditionally, British prime ministers have lacked institutional resources, and their power has been based on personalism. They have had power to the extent that they are able to persuade their colleagues to undertake their policy goals. This was always an ineffective mechanism because prime ministerial activism only lasted as long as the prime minister focused on a particular issue and without an institutional framework, prime ministers lacked the capacity for systematic intervention in a range of policy areas. Consequently, the main focus of policy-making and implementation in British government has been departments (see Marsh, Richards, and Smith 2001). However, it also the case that while departments have traditionally had a near monopoly of policy-making powers, the delivery of policy has occurred largely at local level (see Rhodes 1988). So, the situation is one where policy-making power has been concentrated within the core executive yet the centre has often lacked the mechanisms to control the implementation of policy. This paradox has been exaggerated over the last twenty years, with reforms further fragmenting the system and the centre attempting to reassert control. What defined New Labour's period in office (1997–2010) was a combination of a number of contradictory reform efforts. On one hand, there has been a strong belief that centrally led reform is one of the key ways of improving the delivery of public service, and therefore the need to strengthen the capabilities at the centre has driven a number of reforms. On the other hand, there has been the belief that improving local management of delivery, increasing the choice of consumers of public services, and devolving political power are the means of improving the effectiveness of government. These contradictory reforms are reinforcing the paradoxes that have traditionally underpinned British government. New Labour has been in a continual tension between the decentralizing impact of market-led reforms and the political imperative within the British political system for power to be centralized and for politicians to be in control.

The Fragmentation of the Westminster Model

Governments in Britain have been involved in a permanent revolution in terms of public sector reform that has seen the development of privatization, agencification, contracting out, the pluralization of service delivery, and, more recently, devolution in Scotland and Wales. Flinders (2008) suggests that these new developments have led to a situation of 'walking without order.' What has occurred in Britain is the ad hoc proliferation of bodies: 'Government now takes place within a broader context of governance in which governmental actors operate within an increasingly fragmented, complex and delegated administrative environment involving private, voluntary, and parastatal organizations' (Flinders 2008: 1).Within this framework, the logic and mechanisms of accountability behind these bodies is unclear. For Flinders the extent and degree of devolution is so great that it has effectively undermined the principles of the Westminster model (Flinders 2008: 131–2) because the core executive is no longer in control. The ad hoc nature of this development means that the mechanisms of control are obfuscated. This is a view shared by an ex-Cabinet Minister, David Blunkett, who recently informed a Parliamentary Select Committee:

in the 1980s with the next steps, with the obsession with agencies and then with decentralisation from trying to do too much from the centre to doing things through agencies or through local institutions without any clear accountability either administratively or politically at that level. So what we end up with is secretaries of state standing at the dispatch box declin- ing to answer questions on things that are no longer directly their respon- sibility without anyone knowing who carries the responsibility publicly and who can legitimately be held to account. To give you an example, if you ask the Department of Health about what a primary care trust is up to in terms of its interpretation of regulations laid down by the DoH because the regulations have been devolved downwards to the PCT, it will be the PCT's fault, but the PCT will tell you that they are only following what they thought were the regulations that the DoH had laid down and the secretary of state at the dispatch box (although the present one I am sure would carry responsibility for whatever he felt was needed) would quite legitimately say, 'It's nothing to do with me, Guv.' In the end if 'it's noth- ing to do with me, Guv' and it is nothing to do with government and it is nothing to do with us as elected representatives to hold to account those who theoretically have their hands on more than just the distribution of resources, we are getting ourselves in a muddle. (Public Administration Committee 2008)

This quote highlights the problem within the British government: a desire to delegate yet retain accountability at the centre. The account- ability imperative – reinforced by electoral and media pressures – often forces ministers into taking back control of problems even after they have been formally contracted out to external agencies.

The fragmentation of New Public Management (NPM) both under- mined the simple lines of accountability that existed within the West- minster model, but also frustrated ministers who continually felt the need to try to control policy outcomes. These frustrations were particu- larly felt by the New Labour government. Fragmentation had emasculated the ability of the core executive to pursue holistic policy programs that cut across different functional areas of government (see Richards and Smith 2000). In particular, Labour subscribed to the notion that the key issue was the inability of elected governments to control and coordinate policy across Whitehall. Their view was that the policy arena had become a more crowded environment with numerous actors competing for political space, curtailing government's ability to maintain some semblance of control. This can be referred to as the pathology of governance (ibid.). One effect of this changed environment was that policy was being developed in a more isolated, segmented manner, often leading to unintended and unforeseen consequences; most notably when different departments pursued conflicting policy goals (see Smith 1998). Consequently, Labour on one side bought into the rhetoric of the NPM and giving power to frontline staff, but on the other the need to reassert central control and reimpose the Westminster model (see Richards and Smith 2006).

From Joined-Up Government to Prime Minister's Delivery Unit

Two and a half years into his first term, Tony Blair complained of having 'scars on my back' from his attempts to get Whitehall departments to improve on policy delivery; public servants, he implied, were concentrating on operating in 'policy chimneys,' protecting their turf and their own interests rather than advancing government programs (see Kavanagh and Richards 2000). This is an issue that has been raised again by the Conservatives who, despite Labour's reforms, still see policy silos as a problem (*Guardian*, 2 July 2009). New Labour implicitly accepted the NPM critique and were concerned to develop alternative mechanisms of policy delivery.

The signs that the Labour Government was to take up the challenge of reforming the policy process were clearly discernible prior to their coming to power in 1997. In opposition, key Labour figures believed that at a general level, government had lost the ability to operate in a single, unified, coordinated manner across the whole policy spectrum (see Blair 1996; Mandelson and Liddell 1996; Gould 1998). This in turn, they concluded, was leading to policy failure. Underpinning this view was a narrative Labour embraced that suggested that the British state had become increasingly fragmented.

Not surprisingly, as with its predecessors, the response of the Labour government since 1997 has been to implement a series of reforms that aim to increase the power that the centre wields. As Richards and Smith (2000: 146) observe: 'Labour politicians have been conditioned, as much as Conservatives, by the Westminster model.' They therefore drew from within the confines of this model in order to find a solution to the problem of fragmentation, a loss of central controlling capacity, and implementation failure. Implicit within Labour's strategy was a reinforcment of the Westminster model where new patterns of governance would not necessary lead to a loss of political control Thus, in the year before Labour won the election, Blair declared that: 'People have to know that we will run from the centre and govern from the centre' (see Richards 2004: 37).

From 1997, the response of the Labour Government was to try and wire the system back up, and so reimpose a reformed version of the Westminster model. This was an attempt to bring together the many, often disparate, elements that constitute the policy arena. Thus, Labour's antidote to failings in policy-making was 'joined-up-government' and 'improvement in service delivery' based on a model of strong central control from Number 10 and the Cabinet Office (see Cm 4310 1999; Cabinet Office 2000, 2002). At the same time, it set in place what appears to be a countervailing force at the street-level, by continuing to pursue a policy of semi-detaching delivery agencies from government [boutique bureaucracy] and increasing the local autonomy of the multiple service deliverers – a modern governance approach (see Office of Public Service Reform 2002; Peters 2000). This raises the key issue of whether or not increasing central control while at the same time attempting to enhance local autonomy creates diametrically opposed goals which are difficult to reconcile.

Labour's reform program produced a further paradox – Labour was concerned with improving policy delivery by enhancing its central controlling mechanisms (a top-down, state-centric strategy approach). At the same time, it had, rhetorically at least, continued to argue for the need to increase the level of autonomy for officials charged with delivering services (a bottom-up, modern governance strategy based on NPM). As we saw above, the British political system is not designed in such a way as to afford the centre hands-on control over street-level bureaucrats. Therefore, while formal targets and audit programs imposed by central government can be quantitatively measured, control over the actual process of delivery still often remains with street-level bureaucrats based on their own subjective interpretation of a particular policy. As Lipsky (1980: xii) observes, street-level bureaucrats: 'believe themselves to be doing the best they can under adverse circumstances and they develop techniques to salvage service and decision-making values within the limits imposed upon them by the structure of work.' This can lead to an array of unforeseen or unintended consequences for a government aiming to reimpose control over the policy-making arena. In other words, there is a fundamental contradiction between the WM and the NPM models.

Reimposing the Centre

The rhetoric of the Blair government rejected the statist approaches of past Labour governments for achieving its policy goals. Instead, the emphasis was to be on control: 'the era of "big government means better government" is over' – 'control' was to become its new mantra (Blair 2003: 132) (although there is little doubt that New Labour considerably increased the size of the state in terms of expenditure and personnel). As Blair (2003: 132) observed: 'Leverage, not size, is what counts. What government does, and how well, not how much, is the key to its role in modern society,' sentiments not far removed from the 'reinventing government' discourse associated ten years earlier with the American centre-right commentators Osborne and Gaebler (1992). Nevertheless, Blair was concerned to provide the means to ensure that he could run government from the centre.

The first attempt to reimpose central control was through coordination. The British core executive has always been hampered by the weakness of central coordination. Strong departments have faced a plurality of coordination mechanisms through the Cabinet Office, the prime minister, and the Treasury (Smith 1999). The fragmentation of coordination combined with powerful departments has meant that policy has often been contradictory and there has been little sense of overall strategy. Consequently, Blair attempted to create joined-up government with the aim of ensuring that departmental goals were linked to overall strategy. However, the attempt at joined-up government failed to overcome departmental barons and led the prime minister to focus on strengthening the centre and improving delivery.

Initially, pursuing joined up government was a mechanism for increasing the control of the centre because it was a way of ensuring that strategies developed in Number 10 were not undermined by the conflicting goals of departments. As Blair told the Liaison Select Committee in July 2002: 'I make no apology for having a strong centre, particularly in circumstances where, one, the focus is on delivering better services.' Since 1997, an important development has been the way in which the resources of the prime minister have increased. When Blair came into office, he expanded the size of the Policy Unit (now the Policy Directorate), almost doubling the personnel compared to the time John Major was prime minister (see Kavanagh and Seldon 2000). Crucially, the role of the Policy Directorate was not so much making policy but ensuring that departments were aware of the Blair agenda and are delivering policy in line with Number 10's wishes. As one political adviser said: 'the Prime Minister and his closest advisers in Downing Street felt that they had to evolve an architecture which would give them more reach into the Whitehall set-up.' They wanted to ensure that the prime minister's decisions were followed up by departments. Blair reinforced this policy steer through regular bilateral meetings with ministers to ensure that they and the prime minister were agreed on policy objectives. This was an important development because it meant that there was an institutional relationship between departments and Number 10. In addition the prime minister – through his advisers – often became involved in detailed aspects of policy-making. As one former policy directorate adviser revealed:

> In respect of – for example school behaviour – we would talk to the director general of the schools section of the Department for Education and Science very regularly. But even then, as DG in that role, he is obviously juggling a huge number of different tasks day-by-day. It would reach the stage where even he wanted to – not disengage – but he almost preferred it that we had conversations with civil servants lower down the chain. So we would often talk to, in terms of hierarchy, certainly with Grade 5s we would have a lot of contact, and they would be the people who you would basically be working with through the detail.

Blair's mechanism for overcoming departmentalism was to give the Prime Minister's Office access to departments and to ensure that the departments worked for the prime minister rather than their departmental ministers. This was a significant change in the resource structure of the core executive and changed the balance of power between the premier and departments. Prime ministerial policy activism does not rely solely on the whim or attention span of the prime minister. The strategy was similar to that developed in the Australian case examined in this volume with Number 10 developing capabilities to direct department. This capacity depended on the special advisers within Number 10 overseeing and commenting on the policy proposals that were coming from departments. Again, this was an important change in the patterns of dependency between departments and the prime minister, with departments becoming more dependent on the prime minister for policy initiatives.

While the role of the Policy Directorate was largely oversight, strategic policy capability was provided by the Strategy Unit created in 2002. The stated aim of the Strategy Unit was to: 'improve Government's capacity to address strategic, cross-cutting issues and promote innovation in the development of policy and the delivery of the Government's objectives' (see http://www.strategy.gov.uk/output/page82. asp). When the unit was established, it brought together the Performance and Innovation Unit (PIU), the Prime Minister's Forward Strategy Unit (FSU), and parts of the Centre for Management and Policy Studies (CMPS). The Strategy Unit had three main roles: 'to provide strategy and policy advice, to carry out occasional strategic audits and to help build departments' strategic capability (see http://www.strategy.gov. uk/output/page82.asp). Again, this can be seen as an attempt to consolidate control over the policy process at Number 10, with the unit reporting to the prime minister through the chancellor of the Duchy of Lancaster and the Cabinet secretary. Nevertheless, the period under Gordon Brown illustrated the fragility of this machinery. In the face of a series of political and economic crises, Brown was not able to set the agenda of the government and was forced on a number of occasions to make significant concessions in terms of policy.

One important aspect of Labour's attempt to strengthen the centre was an increased use of special advisers. Labour developed some distrust of traditional officials. This was not related to the ideological disposition of officials; instead Labour questioned Whitehall's ability to develop and deliver policy. The element of distrust was revealed in significant changes in policy-making. Labour looked much more to outside sources for policy advice. This took the form of greater use of task forces, tsars, and special advisers (and increasingly under Gordon Brown the appointment of ministers from outside of Parliament). In addition, in terms of the former, the government created an array of ad hoc bodies – task forces – with the intention of crossing departmental boundaries and providing a range of sources of advice. Tsars are an eclectic mix of outside appointments, bearing an array of informal titles as 'Drugs Tsar,' 'Health Tsar,' 'Transport Tsar,' 'Anti-Cancer Tsar,' 'Children's Tsar,' etc. They are appointed by the prime minister, but then work within individual Whitehall departments. Probably the most important aspect of the changing policy process was the increased role of special advisers, who more than doubled in number since the Conservative government of John Major. These political appointees offer an alternative source of advice to ministers. When Ed Balls and David Miliband (later both Cabinet ministers) were special advisers in the Treasury they changed the traditional relationships between ministers and officials. They were acting: 'as gatekeepers, letting civil servants know what the Chancellor is interested in and acting as a filter for policy ideas coming from below. An official knows that he or she is getting somewhere when they get a half-hour slot with Ed Balls.' Political advisers became brokers between ministers and officials (Gains and Stoker 2009). More importantly, the prime minister increasingly surrounded himself with political advisers providing independent policy capability inside Number 10. Moreover, early in New Labour's development there was a considerable concern with controlling the media and ensuring that all parts of the government were 'on message.' This has had the effect of further strengthening the control over the centre over departments.

The most important development in terms of strengthening the centre was the creation of the Prime Minister's Delivery Unit (PMDU). This was a crucial second term innovation intended to overcome what was seen as the core failure of the first term, the inability to deliver on promises. The PMDU, set up by Michael Barber, was intended to focus on ensuring the delivery of the Prime Ministers core objective (see Table 8.1) by focusing directly on what government departments were doing in terms of actually achieving government goals on the ground. Consequently, the unit focused on developing 'real time data' with which to observe the operation of policy delivery (Barber 2007: 88). Following the collection of date there were regular stocktakes including the prime minister, the unit, and the senior members of the team where the performance of a department in terms of delivery was closely examined. The PMDU ensured that prime ministerial engagement occurred not just in the process of policy-making but also policy delivery. It was an attempt to force the traditional civil service bureaucracies into effectively implementing policy goals. The prime minister was involved in stocking meetings every two weeks with departments (Barber 2007: 121). What is interesting about the PMDU is that it added a new logic to the process of policy-making in Britain. First, it assumed that policy comes from the prime minister – directly from the core – rather than departments. Second, it extended the traditional empiricism of Brit-

Table 8.1
Priorities of Prime Minister's Delivery Unit

Department	Priority
Health	Disease mortality
	Cancer mortality
	Waiting lists
	Waiting times
	Accident and emergency
Education	Literacy and numeracy at age 11
	Maths and English at 14
	5+ A*-C GCSEs*
	Truancy
Home Office	Overall crime
	Likelihood of being a victim
	Offenders brought to justice
Transportation	Road congestion
	Rail punctuality

*GCSE is the general certificate in secondary education taken by school pupils at 16.
Grades A*-C are the top grades and are necessary for going on to further education.
They were set as what the average pupil should obtain by the end of secondary
education by the Labour Government.

ish government beyond policy-making to policy delivery. The belief
of those within the PMDU was that if they had the facts about policy
delivery they could analyse and resolve any problems; in that sense
delivery was not political. Third, the PMDU with the policy unit created a source of policy that came outside of departments. In key areas
of health and education, Number 10 developed policy with advisers
and external think tanks which was implemented by the delivery unit.
The traditional departmental structures of British government – which
as we saw – had been dominant in policy-making were by-passed.

The empiricism of the PMDU and the attempt of the centre to regain
control over policy-making and delivery were reflected in the use of
targets. Targets and audit became crucial tools in ensuring that departments were responding to the policy goals of the centre.

The growth in the use of targets and audit mechanisms reflected an
attempt by central government to ensure it maintained control over
those agencies or actors delivering services to the public (see Hyndman and Eden 2002). The most obvious institutional form in which
target-setting pursued by the Labour Government were Public Service
Agreements (PSAs), set up after the 1998 Comprehensive Spending
Review. PSAs established in one document the aims, objectives, and

Figure 8.1: The Prime Minister's Delivery Unit

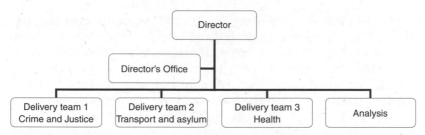

performance targets for each of the main Government departments. They included value for money targets and a statement of who was responsible for the delivery of these targets. PSAs were agreed on by the individual department following discussions with the Treasury and the Prime Minister's Delivery Unit. According to Matthews (2009: 6): 'Spending became linked to the achievement of policy outcomes, such as improvements in literacy standards amongst primary school pupils or reduction in teen conceptions, rather than individual departmental processes and outputs. Fixing the public expenditure envelope for a three year period was intended to enable department to manage their resources more effectively and strategically ... The PSA framework was also intended to bring about greater governmental co-ordination.'

Where organizations failed to meet the prescribed targets laid down by government, they could incur an array of prescribed penalties ranging from a simple cut in government funding to the outright closure of an organization, such as has occurred, for example, with a number of 'failed' secondary schools. The practice of target-setting became the key tool of control now exerted by government, as a report by the comptroller and auditor general, focusing specifically on Next Steps Agencies testifies: 'performance measurement and reporting are intrinsic to the whole process of public management, including planning, monitoring, evaluation and public accountability' (HM Government 2000: 2).

New Labour developed specific mechanisms aimed at improving policy delivery, which has effectively created a highly interventionist approach by central government on managers and 'street level bureaucrats.' However, while the Labour leadership was particularly concerned to increase the coherence and capacity at the centre what we have actually seen is a continuation of the reform and the development of a growing number of overlapping bodies at the centre. To some extent there is confusion as to what the bodies are, and those lower down the chain can find themselves subject to competing demands.

Centralizing Power

During the Blair years there was a two-fold process of centralization. First, the Blair government centralized power within the core executive. Power essentially shifted from departments and the Cabinet to the Prime Minister's Office. As Peter Hennessy has pointed out (House of Lords Constitution Committee 2010): 'In fact what we have had since May 1997 (and Tony Blair's people would say this privately, as do Gordon Brown's) is a Prime Minister's Department in all but name pretty well a fusing of the Cabinet Office and Number Ten but they treat both Parliament and public and scholars as if we had not noticed.'

As we have seen there has been gradual development of policy-making capacity within Number 10 which has to some degree been based on political appointments rather than the traditional civil service individuals and structures based in the Cabinet Office. What the Butler Report on the events leading up to the war in Iraq pointed out was the way in which the traditional structures of the Cabinet did not play a role even in a major strategic decision such as that as going to war. As Butler (2004) reported in terms of the war in Iraq there was an intention:

> to limit wider collective discussion and consideration by the Cabinet to the frequent but unscripted occasions when the Prime Minister, Foreign Secretary and Defence Secretary briefed the Cabinet orally. Excellent quality papers were written by officials, but these were not discussed in Cabinet or in Cabinet Committee. Without papers circulated in advance, it remains possible but is obviously much more difficult for members of the Cabinet outside the small circle directly involved to bring their political judgement and experience to bear on the major decisions for which the Cabinet as a whole must carry responsibility. The absence of papers on the Cabinet agenda so that Ministers could obtain briefings in advance from the Cabinet Office, their own departments or from the intelligence agencies plainly reduced their ability to prepare properly for such discussions, while the changes to key posts at the head of the Cabinet Secretariat lessened the support of the machinery of government for the collective responsibility of the Cabinet in the vital matter of war and peace.

The Iraq war was not unique, but reflected the way that under Blair major decisions by-passed the Cabinet. For instance, on the first day of the Labour government in 1997 the constitutionally significant decision to make the Bank of England independent was made without reference to the Cabinet.

However, what is even more significant is that not only was power centralized within the Core Executive but the Labour Government saw increasing intervention in the detail of policy implementation. One example is related to the issue of street crime. The Street Crime Initiative (SCI) used the Delivery Unit within the Cabinet Office and PSAs as mechanisms for attempting to encourage action on street crime. Moreover, the SCI was applied to particular areas, and specific funding was made available for tackling street crime (Smith et al. 2011). The development of the SCI from policy idea to implementation demonstrates the importance of political saliency and authority to the delivery of policy goals and the way that the prime minister, unusually, united talk, decision, and action. A PSA target for reducing robbery was in existence before the SCI but it was missed by a large margin. In 2001 robbery had increased by 24 per cent. For some time the official in charge of street crime had been trying with minimal resources to deal with the rise in mobile phone theft. The five biggest metropolitan police forces were given the full budget, £20m, to try to deal with street crime, but this was having little impact. The *Evening Standard* then made the street crime figures a *cause celebre* in the autumn of 2001 with headlines berating the New Labour government for increased street crime in London. According to one official interviewed:

> The pressure for action I think was partly mediated through the press because robbery numbers were going up. Robbery is a very sensitive issue partly because it is highly concentrated in a handful of urban areas and those urban areas coincide with ones where you have higher proportions of non-white populations. Certainly with the mobile phone work which we published in January the ethnic dimension to that was uppermost ... one of the things which really pushed ministers into tackling street crime (robbery) was that the Christmas period was relatively light on news and when that happens and there's a big crime story the ramifications and amplifications can have quite serious implications ... Bearing in mind what had started to happen in that Christmas period, late 2001, early 2002, is that the Met police, month after month after month were coming out with crime figures and the big story was 'yet another increase in robbery.' The Evening Standard as a vehicle for getting that story a lot of attention and then some nasty very high profile street robberies at Christmas time so big public/media debate was an important preamble to the whole story.

The consensus among officials was that these headlines captured the attention of the prime minister and his advisers and led to the decision to commit considerable resources into a drive to bring them down quickly. It is a further example of personalism in British government (see Richards and Smith 2006) and the strong institutional incentives within British government for ministers and prime ministers to be involved in the minutiae of government. Blair, for instance, told the Secretary of State for Education to get to grip with truancy as part of dealing with street crime (Barber 2007: 149). Prime ministerial and ministerial authority can rapidly transform perceptions of an issue within the political system. That the issue was picked up by the prime minister and the home secretary transformed how the policy was delivered.

As a consequence of prime ministerial pressure, the delivery unit and the Home Office quickly established new targets for street robbery. Key performance indicators, targets, and objectives were introduced as mechanisms for achieving goals. The SCI was designed to use these tools to maximum efficiency to tackle a well-defined problem in a short time. The aim was to show a demonstrable reduction in street crime within six months. However, the development and scope of these targets was almost accidental in nature. As one senior official said in an interview: 'In one meeting [i.e., of Prime Minister's Committee] the ACPO representatives were challenged on what they could achieve, and they said something along the lines of they'd have street crime down by September, and the Prime Minister announced it that day in Parliament and that was the target.'

As Barber admitted, the targets in terms of street crime were plucked out of the air (Public Administration Committee 2007) The development of the figures also illustrates the ad hoc nature of the process. One senior official admitted in an interview that in developing targets: 'At that stage it wasn't quite that scientific.' The eventual target was a 14 per cent reduction – from 68,782 in 1999–2000 to 59,153 by March 2005. However, while the process of governing has been based on institutionalizing prime ministerial power, the reality is that the process was one of personalism, and emphasis on this problem lasted only as long as prime ministerial attention. The point is that prime ministers do not have the ability of government departments to ensure a sustained and essentially bureaucratic approach to particular issues.

Street crime illustrates how the changing structures of central government have led to prime ministers becoming involved in the minutiae of policy. How has this change come about? There are a number of factors which explain this process of centralization and why, despite the NPM pressures for greater managerial autonomy, the prime minister has in fact increased his or her control over the making and delivery of policy. First, British politics has always been highly adversarial. This is partly a consequence of the party system but also a consequence of the system of accountability, which locates power almost solely with politicians at the apex of the system (Judge 1993). As a consequence there is an expectation for politicians to act. So while a number of commentators have argued that the British political system has been subject to a process of depoliticization (see Burnham 2001; Buller and Flinders 2005; Hay 2007), policy in Britain is highly political because ministers are expected to act and to do something. Policy in Britain is often led by demand, not by supply, with ministers responding to what are seen as public and media pressure. One journalist said that Tony Blair based policy on tomorrow's headlines (House of Lords 2010). Street crime became a central issue of the Prime Minister's agenda because it was a big issue in the media and so following a line of policy initiatives (on knives, NHS waiting lists, dangerous dogs) that owe little to strategic policy goals and a lot to the demands of the electorate as filtered through the media. As one journalist, Simon Jenkins, (House of Lords 2010) has commented:

> To a certain extent when Blair came in – when Major came in really the change was absolute – suddenly my profession set the agenda, and it did set the agenda by the way in which it managed the news to require Downing Street to respond and from that moment onwards the central capability was devoted to that requirement of Downing Street to respond to the news. Inevitably a department which is institutional, continuous, responsible and accountable downwards was out of the loop and from that moment on the Cabinet Office exploded in size. I am just saying get rid of it.

The combination of adversarial politics, the system of accountability and increased media responsiveness has politicized policy and in, Moran's (2003) term led to hyper-innovation, with ministers and in particular the prime minister feeling the need to intervene in all aspects of policy-making.

New Labour was very much a response to the failure of the previous Labour government and a strong desire to see that the government must remain in charge of events (something that started to unravel with the economic crisis of 2008) and the sense that in order to win an election they needed to control the media (Campbell 2008; Gould 1998). This was also based on more substantive critique of Old Labour's social democracy. There was a belief that previous Labour governments failed because they did not deliver and therefore the new Labour government had to ensure major improvements in key public services. Considerable amounts of extra public spending were committed to health and education, and the prime minister was concerned to ensure that the spending had an impact on service delivery; hence the focus on targets. This development is partly a reaction to the notion that the solutions to the problems of British society were technocratic rather than ideological.

New Labour's policies were also based on an acceptance of the fundamentals of the market economy. Labour abandoned the traditional social democratic notions of economic intervention and planning. Partly, as a consequence Labour shifted its focus increasingly away from collective approaches to the economy and welfare and onto individual solutions to social problems (Smith 2009). This led the Labour government to develop a whole range of policies which are concerned with modifying individual behaviours (see Smith 2009) rather than developing policies that tackle broader social problems. Hence, problems of social conflict are not seen as a consequence of social inequalities but as anti-social behaviour. This, then, involved central government in a complex set of policies which focused on changing the behaviour of individuals through social behaviour orders and contracts.

Institutional reform has, then, become inbuilt into the British process of government, and the Labour government clearly had a number of reasons for pursuing innovation in the structure of government. It is also the case that one of the powers that the British prime minister does have is to change the structure of government without restraint. As Colin Talbot told the Public Administration Committee (2007: 10): 'Tony Blair can get out of bed tomorrow morning and think: I should amalgamate a couple of departments and it is done. There is no review process; there is no consideration of whether it has worked or not; there is no evaluation afterwards.'

So while policy may be difficult to control, institutional innovation is a way that prime ministers can effect change and without any effective scrutiny. Hence, hyper-innovation in terms of organizational change and public sector reform has occurred because, in a sense, it can and at relatively low cost. Consequently, we can see that a range of factors led the Labour government to attempt to increase its control over both policy-making and policy delivery.

Moreover, that control was increasingly concentrated within the Office of the Prime Minister, although the concentration had some adverse policy consequences. For instance, the focus of capacity with the prime minister meant that Labour's reforms were not been able to eliminate personalism. As we can see with the PMDU and the Street Crime Initiative, priorities were based on prime ministerial desires, and consequently policy was effective only as long as the premier's attention was focused on those issues. In a number of areas targets produced perverse outcomes. In other areas there was significant policy drift. So, for example, in the cases of anti-social behaviour the policy was not controlled effectively by the centre – despite a relatively complex apparatus – and it was implemented differently in various regions of the country. As in the case of the Street Crime Initiative, a policy existed but it was very patchily implemented. There were often conflicts between partners over the policy. In Sheffield, the police felt they were not supported by the judiciary, and indeed one senior law official believed that ASBOs were a mallet to crack a nut. In Manchester, one police officer believed that the local authority were too keen on the use of ASBOs. These examples, demonstrate the difficulty of partnerships as implementation mechanisms. As one interviewee said: 'We're trying to corral cats here, trying to get people together to work on a common issue; crime and disorder, from different points of view – philosophical as well as statutory, work really hard at it and in come the inspectors and it's only the council that's inspected … What price partnership? Surely the lot should be in the dock together … You should be jointly accountable.'

Central control has had only partial success. There has been considerable opposition to targets and central control, with many critics pointing to their distorting effects and unintended consequences (see Marquand 2008).

Reasserting the Local and Departments: The Conservative Approach to the Centre

The Conservatives in opposition were highly critical of what they argued was Labour's highly centralizing and overbearing approach to government. This built on a growing awarness within the Labour government that there was a need to develop greater local input into the policy process.

The latest developments on the reform process emphasize a return to local control: 'The next stage of public service reform will involve unlocking the creativity and ambition of public sector workers and establishing new relationships between the Government and professionals' (Cabinet Office 2008). Throughout the period of the Blair government there has been an awareness of the tension between central control and local autonomy (Richards and Smith 2006). However, as we have seen it has been central control that has been dominant. Yet with the apparent failure of, and resistance to, some central measures there has at least been a rhetorical attempt to re-emphasize localism. A Cabinet Office (2008) paper on the effective provision of public service emphasizes localism and professionalism:

> We know that services need clear standards but that, following our first phase of reform, persisting with too many top-down targets can be counterproductive; we know services must value professionals if we are to foster innovation and excellence; we know that while central government must be a key player in driving better public services there are limits to what it can achieve and if it seeks to do too much it will stifle local initiative; and we know that vital though user choice is, it needs to be complemented with other approaches if we are really to empower citizens.

There are two important points here. One is that the emphasis on localism is not new but has been developing for a number of years. Second, the new focus on professionalism is in a sense a reversal of public sector reforms of the past twenty years. The nature of the reform process since the Thatcher government has been to shift power away from professionals and to use targets and managerial processes to reduce their autonomy. Now government seems to want to increase their control. It is also uncertain how these new developments will fit with the structure of central control that is now in place. There is little sign that the central capabilities are to be wound down. The Labour government essentially failed to resolve the tension between ideas of local autonomy and its attempts to increase central capacity. This challenge has re-emerged to haunt the new Coalition government.

The Conservative-Liberal Democratic Coalition government elected in 2010 emphasized the need to reduce the centralizing power of Whitehall in two ways. First, in terms of local government the government has stated the need to reduce the power of Whitehall over local government and proposed that budgets will increasingly be devolved to local authorities with citizens having a greater say over how resources are distributed locally. The Localism Bill introduced in late 2010 makes a commitment to pushing decisions down to the lowest possible level. This approach has been underpinned by the commitment to the Big Society, the idea that social organizations can have a greater role in the provision of collective goods and therefore reducing dependence on the central state.

Second, at central government level, the Coalition government has abolished the performance indicators and league table introduced by the Labour government replacing them with much greater transparency of government data in order to allow the people to hold government to account. Many of the targets introduced by Labour have been abolished, with the government arguing that it is up to local people to determine what sort of services they require. In effect the Coalition government sees markets as better than top-down mechanism as ways of improving the effectiveness of public services.

Perhaps one of the most suprising aspects of the new administration was that the Prime Minister David Cameron started to dismantle some of the new capacity created by the New Labour Government in Number 10 as part of Cameron's commitment to reducing the power of the centre (*The Guardian* 25 May 2009). Cameron abolished the Delivery Unit and reduced considerably the number of special advisers. In the prime minister's view ministers were there to make policy and therefore the prime minister only needed limited policy capacity. However, after almost a year in office, and with a number of policy problems appearing, Cameron restructured the operation within Downing Street. For instance, Number 10 was surprised by the extent of the health reforms proposed by Health Secretary Andrew Lansbury. There had been no oversight by Number 10 in the development of health reform and the prime minister was not prepared for either the scale of the reforms or the reaction to them. As a consequence, Cameron recreated a ten-strong policy unit in order to shadow departments in Whitehall and reintroduced an Implemenation Unit which appears similar to the PMDU. Without capacity within Number 10 it was very difficult for the Prime Minister to control events and policy within the government (*The Guardian* 18 Febuary 2011, *The Independent* 17 Feburary 2011). Consequently the new government has higlighed the persistant tension within British government between the desire to return power to the locality at the same time ensuring the implementation of governmental goals which results in political leaders looking to enhance their central capacities. The fact is that political opposition rebounds on the prime minister and so creates an incentive for policy activism.

Conclusion

British government has been caught between the tension of New Public Management and the traditions of the Westminster model. Public sector reform has fragmented the processes of governance, frustrating a government concerned to implement its policy goals. Consequently, New Labour put considerable effort into institutionalizing the power of the prime minister and increasing the policy and delivery capability of the centre. Through targets, the use of personal advisers, bilaterals and the Prime Minister's Delivery Unit, the Prime Minister's Office became integrated into departments to an extent that is much greater than in the past. Departments have traditionally controlled much of the policy-making and implementation resources, but these have shifted to the prime minister to a significant degree. Despite these new mechanisms the ability of the prime minister and those around him to control outcomes has been problematic. For example, the Street Crime Initiative case highlighted how even with a basically simple set of ideas about policy, implementation depended on a high level of political will, command and authority, directed resources, and attention that could not be sustained for a long period. This produces an unsettling conclusion that in many cases implementation depends on politics rather than administration. The examples discussed here illustrate the continuing importance of personalism in the British political system. If a prime minister or minister wants something done it happens. If they reduce their attention then the implementation of the policy can grind to a halt. Policies often fit closely to the 'garbage can' model or organizational choice, where items come onto the agenda with a particular mix within the 'garbage can' of problems, solutions, and politics. An issue becomes salient when 'a problem is recognized, a solution is available and the political climate make the time right for change' (Kingdon 1984: 93). In the cases of street crime and anti-social behaviour it was a combination of problem, solution, and climate that produced a focus on policy delivery.

In terms of issues of command and control and levels of autonomy there are some interesting contradictions. In many ways, and despite the governments' commitment to local autonomy, the SCI demonstrates that successful policy delivery from the centre's point of view depends on the suppression of autonomy. In the case of ASBOs, the government was dependent on a whole range of street-level bureaucrats to identify anti-social behaviour and then to take action and ensure some measure of compliance. However, many bureaucrats on the ground interpreted the policy differently from the government.

One of problems of the Prime Minister's Delivery Unit was that while it did effectively break out of the paradox of executive power but delivery weakness it only did so by building on elements of the traditional Whitehall model. It reinforced and extended the power of the central executive over policy to delivery and often the minutiae of delivery (train times, hospital waiting lists), and it did so on the basis of prime ministerial authority – the PMDU works while the prime minister supports it; its authority is completely dependent on the prime minister, and hence it was actually a new form of personalism (institutionalised personalism). The priorities of the PMDU are not a set of strategic government goals but the particular priorities of the prime minister, and this in effect was the continuation of the notion that prime ministers become involved in policy by dipping in and out of particular issues. This also leads to the suspicion that what the PMDU is about is not extending central capability in order to produce good government but to create a mechanism that quickly responds to the aspects of public service that are annoying voters and therefore are electorally problematic. Moreover, the ability to control departments continues to depend on the authority of the prime minister. Hence, a prime minister with less autonomy will be in a weaker position to control departments leading to further failures of coordination. The problem is that power of the prime minister has been increased, but not within the context of the wider structure of British government.

REFERENCES

Barber, M. (2007). *Instruction to Deliver: Fighting to Transform Britain*'s Public Services. London: Methuen.

Blair, T. (1996). *New Britain: My Vision of a Young Country*. London: Fourth Estate.

– (2003). The Third Way: New Politics for the New Century. In A. Chadwick and R. Heffernan (eds.), *The New Labour Reader*. London: Polity.

Buller, J., and M. Flinders. (2005). The Domestic Origins of Depoliticisation in the Area of British Economic Policy. *British Journal of Political Science and International Relations*, 7: 526–43.

Butler, Lord R. (2004). *Review of Intelligence on Weapons of Mass Destruction.* London: Stationery Office

Burnham, P. (2001). New Labour and the Politics of Depoliticisation. *British Journal of Politics and International Relations* 3: 127–49.

Cabinet Office. (2000). *Wiring It Up: Whitehall's* Management of Cross-Cutting Policies and Services. London: Stationery Office.

– (2002). *Organising to Deliver.* Available at http://www.cabinet-office.gov.uk/innovation/2000/delivery/organisingtodeliver/content.htm.

– (2008). *Excellence and Fairness: Achieving World Class Public Services.* London: Stationery Office.

Campbell, A. (2008). *The Blair Years.* London: Arrow Books.

Cm 4310. (1999). *Modernising Government.* London: Stationery Office.

Cm 5571. (2002). *2002 Spending Review: Public Service Agreements.* London: Stationery Office.

Flinders, M. (2008). *Delegated Governance and the British State.* Oxford: Oxford University Press.

Foley, M. (2004). Presidential Attribution as an Agency of Prime Ministerial Critique in a Parliamentary Democracy. *British Journal of Politics and International Relations* 6(3): 292–311.

Gains, F., and G. Stoker. (2009). Special Advisers and the Transmission of Ideas from the Policy Primeval Soup. Paper prepared for the Governmentality after Neo Liberalism, Conference, 26 June, Winston House, London.

Gould, P. (1998). *The Unfinished Revolution.* London: Little Brown.

Hay, C. (2007). *Why We Hate Politics.* Oxford: Polity.

Hay, C., and D. Richards. (2000). The Tangled Webs of Westminster and Whitehall: The Discourse, Strategy and Practice of Networking within the British Core Executive. *Public Administration* 78(1): 1–28.

Hennessy, P. (1998). The Blair Style of Government: An Historical Perspective and an Interim Audit. *Government and Opposition.*

Hindmoor, A. (2004). Public Policy: But Domestic Policy Didn't Stop. *Parliamentary Affairs* 57: 315–28.

HM Treasury. (2005a). *Public Service Performance Index.* Available from http://www.hm-treasury.gov.uk/performance/index.cfm.

– (2005b). *Performance: Department of Health.* Available from http://www.hm-treasury.gov.uk/performance/Health.cfm.

Hood, C., C. Scott, O. James, G. Jones, and T. Travers. (1999). *Regulation Inside Government: Waste Watchers, Quality Police and Sleazebusters.* Oxford: Oxford University Press.

House of Lords Constitution Committee. (2010). *The Cabinet Office and the Centre of Government.* London: Stationery Office.

Hyndman, N., and R. Eden. (2002). Executive Agencies, Performance Targets and External Reporting. *Public Money and Management* 22(3): 17–24.

Judge, D. (1993). *The Parliamentary State*. London: Sage.

Kavanagh, D., and D. Richards. (2000). Departmentalism and Joined-Up Government: Back to the Future? *Parliamentary Affairs* 54(1): 1–18.

Kavanagh, D., and A. Seldon. (2000). *The Powers behind the Prime Minister*. London: HarperCollins.

Kingdon, John W. (1984). *Agendas, Alternatives, and Public Policies*. Boston: Little, Brown.

Kooiman, J. (ed.). (1993). *Modern Governance: Government-Society Interactions*. London: Sage.

Lipsky, M. (1980). *Street-Level Bureaucracy: Dilemmas of the Individual in Public Services*. New York: Russell Sage Foundation.

Machin, S., and O. Marie. (2004). Crime and Police Resources: The Street Crime Initiative. Unpublished paper, London School of Economics.

Mandelson, P., and R. Liddell. (1996). *The Blair Revolution: Can New Labour Deliver?* London: Faber and Faber.

Marquand, D. (2008). *Britain since 1918: The Strange Case of British Democracy*. London: Weidenfeld and Nicholson.

Marsh, D., D. Richards, and M.J. Smith. (2001). *Changing Patterns of Governance: Reinventing Whitehall*. Basingstoke: Palgrave.

Matthews, F. (2009). Developing Delivery: The Evolution of the PSA Framework and its Response to Emeregent Societal and Geopolitical Challenges. Paper presented at the PSA Conference, Manchester, 7–9 April.

Migdal, J. (2001). *State in Society: Studying How States and Societies Transform and Constitute One Another*. Cambridge: Cambridge University Press.

Moran, M. (2003). *The British Regulatory State: High Modernism and Hyper-Innovation*. Oxford: Oxford University Press.

Mulgan, G. (2005). Joined-Up Government: Past, Present and Future. In V. Bogdanor (ed.), *Joined-Up Government*. Oxford: Oxford University Press.

Osborne, D. and Gaebler, T. (1991). *Reinventing Government*. Reading, Mass.: Addison Wesley.

Office of Public Service Reform. (2002). *Reforming Public Services: Principles into Practice March*. London: Stationery Office.

Painter, C. (1999). Public Service Reform from Thatcher to Blair: A Third Way. *Parliamentary Affairs* 52: 94–112.

Perri 6, and E. Peck. (2004). New Labour's Modernization in the Public Sector: A Neo-Durkheimian Approach and the Case of Mental Health Services. *Public Administration* 82/1: 83–108.

Peters, B.G. (2000). Governance and Comparative Politics. In J. Pierre, *Debating Governance*. Oxford: Oxford University Press.

Pryce, S. (1997). *The Presendentialism the Premiership*. London: Macmillan.

Public Administration Committee. (2007). *Machinery of Government Changes*. London: Stationery Office.

– (2008a). *Good Governance, Minutes of Evidence*.

– (2008b). Good Governance – Corrected Evidence. Available at http://www.publications.parliament.uk/pa/cm200708/cmselect/cmpubadm/c983-iii/c98301.htm.

Rhodes, R., and M. Bevir. (2006). *Governance Stories*. London: Routledge.

Rhodes, R.A.W. (1988). *Beyond Westminster and Whitehall*. London: Allen and Unwin.

– (1997). *Understanding Governance: Policy Networks, Governance, Reflexivity and Accountability*. Buckingham: Open University Press.

Richards, D. (2004). The Civil Service in Britain: A Case-Study in Path Dependency. In J. Halligan (ed.), *Civil Service Systems in Anglo-American Countries*, 30–71. London: Edward Elgar.

Richards, D., and M.J. Smith. (2000). New Labour, the Constitution and Reforming the State. In S. Ludlam and M.J. Smith (eds.), *New Labour in Government*, 145–66. Basingstoke: Macmillan.

– (2002). *Governance and Public Policy in the United Kingdom*. Oxford: Oxford University Press.

– (2004). Interpreting the World of Political Elites. *Public Administration* 82/4: 777–800.

– (2006). The Tensions of Political Control and Administrative Autonomy: From NPM to a Reconstituted Westminister Model. In T. Christensen and P. Laegreid (eds.), *Autonomy and Regulation*. London: Edward Elgar.

Smith, M.J. (1999). *The Core Executive in Britian*. London: Macmillan.

– (2009). *Power and the State*. London: Palgrave.

Smith, M.J., D. Richards, A. Geddes, and H. Mathers. (2011). 'Analysing Policy Delivery in the United Kingdom,' *Public Administration*, forthcoming.

PART FOUR

Scandinavia

9 Steering the Swedish State: Politicization as a Coordination Strategy

CARL DAHLSTRÖM and JON PIERRE

During the past few decades, the steering capacity of the Swedish state has come under increasing internal and external pressure. Some of the challenges facing the administrative system can be related to deeply rooted features of the Swedish model, including agencies and autonomous regions and local authorities, which in many national contexts have been a defining feature of reform, but has characterized the Swedish system of government for centuries (Jacobsson and Sundström 2009; Pierre 1995). Other challenges have more recent sources; in the context of management reform there has been a massive interest in performance measurement and management as well as management by objectives and results in Sweden (Pierre 2001; Sundström 2006) and the pressure at the centre from the media has also grown dramatically during the same period (Erlandsson 2008; Ullström 2008). Finally, and for the findings in this chapter perhaps most important, the pressure for political coordination at the centre has grown, as Sweden has since the 1970s gone from an internationally unique but stable system of Social Democratic one-party governments, to a more normal system for countries with proportional representation, with recurrent periods of coalition governments.

At the same time, recent reform of the administrative centre has been largely aimed at procedures and processes and only to a limited extent at institutional arrangements (but see Erlandsson 2007; Persson 2004; SOU 2008: 118). During the 1990s and 2000s, administrative reform in Sweden has emphasized performance measurement and management. Similarly, management by objectives and results more broadly, an organizational philosophy which appears to be past its peak in many countries, is still the predominant mechanism of administrative steering and control, and has been so since the early 1990s (Pierre 2001; Sundström 2006).

In this chapter we briefly describe the challenges outlined above and we point to an often neglected development of the core executive in Sweden: the dramatic growth of the number of political appointees in the government offices. Sweden has since the early 1970s gone from about a dozen political appointees in the government offices to almost two hundred at the peak in 2006 (Larsson 1986: 72–5; see also Table 9.1). We argue that this growth has been one way of creating more coordinating capacity in order to strengthen the capacity of the centre. Tentatively, we suggest that this echoes a process similar to that in countries like Norway, Australia, and New Zealand, commonly referred to as 'post-NPM' reforms, guided by a desire to create, or recreate, organizational capacity close to the political executive (Christensen and Lægreid 2008).

Before going any further in the discussion about politicization of the Swedish government offices it is, however, important to note that the Swedish government offices in comparative terms are not very politicized, and that the increase described in this chapter departs from, comparatively speaking, low figures (Dahlström 2011a). Another characteristic, important to bear in mind, is that the increase in the number of political appointees in the government offices in Sweden has taken the form of a thickening layer of political appointees rather than substitution of them for civil servants. Thus, the political appointees are added to the existing organization, which is a pattern that we recognize from other, much more politicized countries, like the United States (Light 1995; see also Peters, this volume).

In sum, this chapter suggests that the politicization of the centre to some extent is caused by pressures to enhance its coordinating capacity, which in turn is related to challenges like growing media attention, coordinating coalition governments, and administrative reform. Coordination remains the unrivalled problem facing the government offices. In 2009 and 2010, intra-organizational reviews and commissions have presented extensive programs for reform aiming at improving interdepartmental coordination. At the time of writing (September 2009), these measures are about to be implemented.

The two key concepts sustaining our analysis are politicization and coordination. There are at least three ways of defining politicization, which Hans-Ulrich Derlien refers to as functional, role, and personal politicization (Derlien 1996: 149; see also Rouban 2007). We confine

Table 9.1
Employees in the Swedish Government Offices, 1981–2008

Year	Ministers	State secretaries	Political appointees, excluding State secretaries	Total number of political appointees, excluding Foreign Affairs	Total number of political appointees, including Foreign Affairs	Employees, Ministries*	Employees, Government Offices**
1981	21	21	65	83	86		
1982	18	18	55	69	73	2022	
1983	23	24	65	83	89		
1984	23	24	45	63	69	1942	
1985	23	21	59	80			
1986	19	23	67	90		1856	
1987	19	21	70	91		1799	
1988	19	21	76	97		1782	
1989	22	21	76	97			
1990	22	21	73	94		1786	
1991	22	21	65	86		1803	
1992	20	26	91	106	117	1720	
1993	21	25	117	130	142	1849	
1994	20	25	125	136	150	1846	
1995	22	24	102	110	126		
1996	22	24	117	128	141	2157	
1997	22	26	107	117	133	2233	
1998	22	25	107	116	132		
1999	19	29	107	119	136	2307	
2000	17	24	112	119	136	2435	
2001	20	25	121		146	2550	
2002	20	25	120		145	2558	
2003	22	27	145	160	172	2659	3550
2004	23	27	140	155	167	2734	3642
2005	22	30	151	168	181	2766	3615
2006	22	28	162		190	2829	3608
2007	22	33	128		161	2842	3590
2008	22	34	139		173	3109	3854

Data for 1981–2008 are from the Parliamentary Committee on the Constitution, yearly publications from 1980/81–2008/09. See also Statskontoret (1997), Regeringskansliet, yearly publications 1998–2008. For the years 1985 to 1991 the Ministry for Foreign Affairs is not included in the reports from the Parliamentary Committee on the Constitution.
* Total number of employees in the Swedish Government Offices, excluding committees and the Ministry of Foreign Affairs.
** Total number of employees in the Swedish Government Offices, including the Ministry of Foreign Affairs but excluding committees.

our analysis to the third type, where politicization of the government offices refers to the increasing number of political appointees. This also fits the definition of politicization suggested by Guy Peters and one of the present authors (Peters and Pierre 2004: 2). Practically, this means that we analyse the terms of employment, as appointments are commonly viewed as the 'primary locus of politicization' (Eichbaum and Shaw 2008: 341; Dahlström 2011b). Thus, in our analysis, more political appointees in the government offices lead to more politicization.

Coordination is a broad and slippery concept in which we include phenomena like political coordination among the political parties in coalition governments and policy coordination between the government and external actors. To give more precision to the concept we will make a distinction between vertical and horizontal coordination. Vertical coordination denotes coordination efforts from the government offices towards the parliament, party organizations, interest groups and agencies. Horizontal coordination is, in turn, used for describing coordination efforts within the government offices, among different ministries, and among different parties within the same coalition government (for a similar approach see Jensen; Stolfi, this volume).

Challenges to the Core Executive in Sweden

On the surface, not much appears to have happened in the government offices over the past century or so. True, the system of government departments is frequently altered; new departments are created, others are merged, and so on (Erlandsson 2007; Persson 2004). And, in the 1990s the core of European Union (EU) matters was transferred from the Ministry of Foreign Affairs to the Prime Minister's Office. Except for these changes, the institutional setup of the political and administrative centre has remained intact.

This stability becomes all the more intriguing when considering the rather profound changes that have taken place in the external environment of the government offices. The external environment that the Swedish government is supposed to steer and regulate looks vastly different today compared to fifty or even twenty-five years ago (Kooiman 1993, 2003). Sweden is deeply embedded in international, if not global, contingencies that shape its economic development and political autonomy. Almost all of the major corporate players who account for a very significant share of the GDP are integrated in international corporate conglomerates and take their cues to a much larger extent from those hierarchies than from domestic political institutions. The government's capacity to govern the economy is clearly constrained by the globalized corporate sector.

Another source of complexity relates to Sweden's membership in the European Union. Estimates suggest that in the early 2000s, about two-thirds of domestic regulation had its origin within the EU, not from domestic institutions. Sweden's insertion into the EU in 1995 had profound ramifications across the board; it has influenced both politics and administration at all levels of government and also the relationship between institutions at these different levels. Translating (in an organizational and regulatory sense) the EU's policy-making and regulations has added an important dimension of complexity to the Swedish political system (Jacobsson and Sundström 2006). Indeed, it could be argued that because of its neutrality and therefore its limited experience of being a member of a regulatory international union – something which, for instance, the North Atlantic Treaty Organization (NATO) member states are more accustomed to – this has been a bigger challenge for Sweden than for most of other member states of the EU.

Furthermore, as mentioned earlier in this chapter, coordination across departmental borders has been a long-standing problem in the Swedish government offices. The management of a severe financial crisis in the early 1990s, coupled with management reform emphasizing performance measurement and management by objectives, reduced the role of line departments and strengthened the role of the Ministry of Finance and agencies designated to oversee performance management. The coordination problems become even more intriguing when considering the growing number of 'mainstreaming' policies that the departments have set up for themselves during the past twenty years. These policies define overarching policy goals such as economic growth, gender equality, ethnicity, ethnic integration, and sustainable development that are to be considered by all departments when drafting governmental bills, appointing royal commissions, or allocating budgetary resources. Today, there are all in all sixteen such mainstreamed policies. Needless to say, proper handling of these objectives would require extensive coordination. However, except for gender equality there is very little issue ownership for these policies, and therefore the impact of the mainstreamed objectives could be assumed to be rather limited. Again, however, they do add considerably to the challenges to which the government offices must respond.

As other chapters in this volume demonstrate, New Public Management has been an important source of coordinating problems and erosion of central control in many countries. In Sweden, with its long tradition of autonomous agencies, this problem was much less noticeable (Jacobsson and Sundström 2009). To be sure, Sweden never adopted NPM reform on a full scale (see Pierre 2008; Pollitt and Bouckaert 2004). Thus, Swedish agencies operate under considerable autonomy from the political echelons of government. Policy-making appears to be more a matter of dialogue among departments and agencies than one of command and control.

The aspect of NPM that speaks to the present context is its effect on the centre's capacity to steer. In that respect, the NPM measures that were introduced did not in and of themselves significantly reduce the steering or coordinating capacity of the government offices. The design of the Swedish administrative system is such that detailed central steering of agencies and subnational government was never intended. However, it appears clear that NPM added to the overall complexity of the system, or systems, that the government offices are to coordinate.

The capacity to steer from the centre has also been affected by growing pressure from the media. If asked about important changes during the past decades, policy-makers and politicians often mention the media (see, e.g., Carlsson 2003). This is also noted by scholars who study the core executive, internationally as well as in Sweden. Politicians and other policy-makers need to consider how to 'spin' new policy issues already on the drawing board. They also know that they cannot hope to control the media discussion and that the success or failure of a policy proposal very much depends on how it is received by the media (Jacobsson and Pierre 2008; Ruin 2007: 204). A similar development has been observed in several other countries (see the chapters by Savoie and Smith, this volume). In the Swedish government offices this growing media pressure has led to a considerable strengthening of professional communication personal and a growing attention to the media's handling of issues among politicians and managerial ranks in the ministries (Erlandsson 2008; Ullström 2008).

Finally, the composition of the government has changed during the period studied. Sweden was for a long time been dominated by Social Democratic one-party governments. In 1976 the first government since 1936 not led by a Social Democrat was elected. After 1976 Sweden had a centre-right coalition government from 1976 to 1978, a liberal minority government in 1978–79, and two centre-right coalition governments between 1979 and 1982. In 1982 the Social Democrats returned to power and formed a one-party minority government. After the 1991 election a new centre-right coalition government came into power, and in 1994 the Social Democrats returned. Between 1995 and 1998 the Social Democrats received long-term cooperation from the Centre Party, but it was never included in government. A similar, but more formalized arrangement was introduced again, this time between the Social Democrats, the Green Party and the Left Party, between 2002 and 2006. After the election in 2006 a centre-right coalition came into power again. Coalition governments or more or less formalized long-term cooperation between the Social Democrats and other parties are today a political reality, and have created more strain on political coordination, both within the government and between the government and the parliament.

Thus, to sum up the discussion so far, the capacity of the Swedish centre to steer, which had never been very strong compared to other unitary states like the United Kingdom or France, was further constrained by developments within the five areas we pointed out. Sweden is today more involved in international organizations, policy issues are more often cross-departmental, administrative reforms inspired by NPM have further added to the already complex administrative system, the pressure on the centre from the media has grown, and internal coordination problems are more common because there is often more than one political party in government. In the next section we will analyse if these five challenges to the core executive have contributed, together or a part, to the politicization of the government offices in Sweden.

Politicization as a Strategy for Coordination

During the past decades, the number of political appointees in the Swedish government offices has grown, although from a comparatively low level (Dahlström 2011a; Pierre 2004: 46). However, it is important to note that political appointees have generally not replaced civil servants. Instead, a 'thickening' layer of political appointees has been added to the existing civil service organization (Light 1995: 7).

We will describe three different aspects of the politicization of the government offices. First, we give a general picture of the trend, describing the development of the total number of political appointees in the government offices over time. Secondly, we will describe the four different categories of political appointees and their development over time. Finally, we will show where within the government most political appointees are employed. Throughout the analysis we will relate these three aspects of the politicization to the pressures on coordination described in the previous section, and point out when it has resulted in more or less need for vertical and/or horizontal coordination.

Political appointments have been used in the government offices at least since the 1930s, but for a long time only on a small scale (Erlander 1972: 231; Larsson 1986: 72, 1990: 210). In the 1970s this pattern changed, and the number of political appointees rose dramatically. As already mentioned, in 1976, a non-socialist government was elected for the first time since 1936. The new centre-right coalition government (the first Fälldin government of 1976–78) employed almost twice as many political appointees as the Social Democrats had done before the election (the Palme government of 1973–76) (Larsson 1986: 101). This shift is probably explained by two factors. The first was a growing need for horizontal coordination. Naturally, the coalition government had a greater need for coordination within the government itself, because several parties were involved. To solve this coordination problem within the government they created political coordination units within each ministry, each with several political appointees, which in turn created an increase in political appointees. The second factor was a growing need for vertical coordination, also created by the fact of a new coalition government. The centre-right coalition was more dependent on coordination between the government and the party groups in the parliament. This coordination problem was largely handled by members of parliament temporarily employed as political appointees within the government offices, again contributing to the increasing politicization (Bergström 1987: 398; Larsson 1986: 72, 101).

There are no comparable data available for the years before 1981, so the analysis above is based on secondary sources, but the overall picture of the number of political appointees in the government offices between 1981 and 2008 is presented in Figure 9.1. We also provide the exact figures for each year in Table 9.1, on the next page, together with information on the total number of employees in the government offices.

Figure 9.1 shows how the number of political appointees first dropped after the Social Democrats' return to power in 1982, and then increased in 1983, only to decline again in 1984. After that the number of political appointees continued to rise, but stayed at more or less at the same levels as before the election in 1982 during the rest of the 1980s.

The biggest change in the number of political appointees represent-

Figure 9.1: Political appointees in the Swedish Government Offices, 1981–2008, including and excluding the Ministry for Foreign Affairs

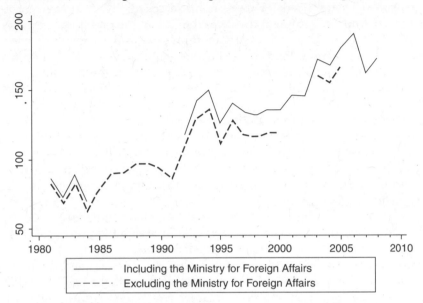

Including the Ministry for Foreign Affairs

Excluding the Ministry for Foreign Affairs

Source: Data for 1981–2008 are from the Parliamentary Committee on the Constitution, yearly publications 1980/81–2008/09. For the years 1985–1991 the Ministry for Foreign Affairs is not included in the reports from the Parliamentary Committee on the Constitution.

Note: The solid line reports the number of political appointees including the Ministry for Foreign Affairs, while the dashed line reports the numbers excluding the Ministry for Foreign Affairs. See also Regeringskansliet, annual publications 1998–2007 and Statskontoret (1997).

ed in our data appears with the new centre-right government, elected in 1991 (the Bildt government of 1991–94). This was the first coalition government since the centre-right government of the early 1980s. By March 1992, when the Bildt government had been in office for only seven months, it had increased the number of political appointees from 86 to 106, and when it left office in 1994 the number of political appointees had increased to 136. All figures excluding the Ministry for Foreign Affairs, reported with the dash line in Figure 9.1. The leap from

86 political appointees to 106 in 1992 represents a 23 per cent increase, and to 136 in 1994 a 58 per cent increase. Again, this is most probably explained by the need for more political coordination in the centre-right coalition government then was the case in the previous one-party Social Democratic government. The Bildt government created a coordination unit within the Prime Minister's Office, to handle horizontal coordination problems between the four parties in the coalition. This unit was led by a political appointee, State Secretary Peter Egardt from the Conservatives, and all the other parties in the government were represented in this unit by political appointees. Like the previous coalition governments during the late 1970s and early 1980s, the Bildt government also temporarily employed members of parliament as political appointees in the government offices to make the vertical coordination with the parliament run smoother (Parliamentary Committee on the Constitution 1993/94: KU30, 99).

In 1994 the Social Democrats were re-elected, and the number of political appointees declined but stayed far above the pre-1991 levels. However, in 2001 such appointments started increasing again. This can probably be explained by two factors. In 2001, Sweden had the presidency of the European Union. It has been shown that the relationship between political appointees and career civil servants in the government offices is particularly sensitive when it comes to EU issues. The political appointees are more actively involved in, and monitor more closely, EU-related issues, than those in other areas (Ullström 2009: 41). Therefore it is plausible that the Swedish EU presidency called for more of both horizontal and vertical coordination, and thereby more political appointees. This view is shared by the permanent secretary in the government offices, Jan Landahl. He says that the increase during the EU presidency is 'simply a workload related issue' (interview with Jan Landahl, 11 May 2009). After the presidency the number of political appointees could have gone down again but it did not, because of the coalition-like cooperation between the Social Democrats, the Green Party, and the Left Party starting after the 2002 election. There were no formal coalition between the three parties, but the Greens and the Left Party got a significant number of political appointees within the government offices (Olsen 2007: 116–17). It is true that the Social Democrats had previously – between 1995 and 1998 – had a similar arrangement with the Centre Party, but on a much smaller scale. In total, three political appointees from the Centre Party were employed before the 1998 election (Persson 2008: 90). This should be compared with a total of

18 to 19 employees from the Greens and the Left in the government offices after the 2002 elections. As with the coalition governments of the 1970s and 1990s, the increase is probably driven by a need for coordination both between the parties and with their representatives in the parliament.

In 2006, a new centre-right coalition government was elected. Compared with the Social Democratic/Green/Left cooperation, the number of political appointees declined directly after the election, but increased again, and two years after the election the number of political appointees is almost at the same level as it was in 2006.

Taken together, our interpretation is that there is a trend towards a more politicized executive in Sweden. The absolute numbers, presented in Figure 9.1, strongly support this interpretation. Since 1981, the number of political appointees in the government offices has more then doubled, and as of September 2008, 173 persons were politically employed there. The growing number of political appointees is most probably both a strategy to infuse ideology into the political centre and a means of increasing the capacity to coordinate policy between different parties in the government. As we have pointed out, the growth has especially occurred during times of coalition governments, with a larger need for horizontal coordination between the parties and vertical coordination with the parliament.

If, however, we also take the growth of the total number of employees in the government offices into account, we get a more mixed picture. This is presented in Table 9.1, both including and excluding the Ministry of Foreign Affairs. If we take the number of political appointees relative to the total employees excluding committees and Ministry of Foreign Affairs (the longer of the two employee time series), the development goes from 3.6 per cent in 1982 to 6.7 per cent in 2006. Using this measure, there is still an increase over time but the percentage of political appointees peaks in 1994 and not in the mid-2000s. The percentage of political appointees declines after 1994, although stays well over the pre-1992 levels.

We now turn to analysis of the different kinds of political appointees. Generally, there are four different categories of political appointees in the Swedish government offices: (1) state secretaries (*statssekreterare*), (2) press secretaries (*pressekreterare*), (3) assistants (*assistenter*), and (4) political advisers (*politiskt sakkunniga*; in this category we also include the few higher ranked political advisers called *planeringschefer*).

The state secretary position that was created in 1917 is roughly equal to a deputy minister, that is, it is second in command in a ministry. State secretaries were introduced as an attempt to reduce the workload at the top of the ministry by dividing the top position in two; the director general for administrative affairs, who was supposed to handle the administrative issues, and the State Secretary, who should handle political issues. The state secretary position was therefore already from the beginning a hybrid between a civil servant and a politician, and its status was not made clear (Larsson 1990: 200–2). However, scholars seem to agree that the actual politicization of this position was relatively low in the early twentieth century, but that this gradually became more politicized. With the Social Democratic leader Olof Palme's first cabinet in 1969, the group of state secretaries for the first time almost all belonged to the ruling Social Democratic Party. This system of politically appointed state secretaries was confirmed after the election of Torbjörn Fälldin's centre-right government in 1976, when more or less all state secretaries were exchanged, which has since then become standard procedure (Larsson 1986: 72; Larsson 1990: 208; see also Bergström 1987: 244).

The number of state secretaries has increased over the years. Between the 1920s and the 1960s about ten state secretaries were employed in the government offices. In the 1970s it increased to fifteen and in the beginning of the 1980s to around twenty (Larsson 1990: 206). As is reported in Table 9.1 the number has increased after that, to twenty-five in the 1990s and to between thirty and thirty-four in the mid-2000s. Permanent Secretary Jan Landahl explains this increase with what he calls the 'growing complexity of the political environment'; he points especially to the more cross-departmental nature of policy issues and the EU membership (interview with Jan Landahl, 11 May 2009). State secretaries fill several different tasks. Primarily, they are responsible for the day-to-day work in the ministry, but they are also involved in dialogues on several levels: between the minister and the civil service, the ministry and the parliament, and if there is a coalition government between the different parties. The state secretary has also over the years been given a more public role. She often represents the minister in Brussels and sometimes comments on policy issues in the media (Ullström 2009).

The first press secretary was employed in the Prime Minister's Office in 1963, and by the beginning of the 1970s almost all ministries employed at least one press secretary (Hadenius 1990: 337). This is the first group of employees directly connected to the minister (Larsson

1990: 210). Their exact number is not reported here (they are included in the politically appointed column in Table 9.1), but there are normally one or two in each ministry. During a short period in the beginning and mid-1990s there have, however, been three press secretaries in the Prime Minister's Office (Parliamentary Committee on the Constitution 1993/94: KU20; 1994/95: KU30; 1995/96: KU30). In total, the number of press secretaries has stayed between twenty and thirty since the beginning of the 1980s (see, e.g, Parliamentary Committee on the Constitution 1981/82: KU35; 2001/02: KU10; Premfors and Sundström 2007: 72). There are several scholarly reports of how the growing pressure from the media has created the need for more active media contacts from the government offices and especially from the Prime Minister's Office (Premfors and Sundström 2007; Erlandsson 2008; Ullström 2008). Consequently, this has amplified the need for coordination of media management in different policy issues, both within and between ministries (Ullström 2008: 363–4).The group of politically appointed assistants is the smallest category, and according to the literature first appeared in 1982, when the Social Democratic government was elected (Bergström 1987: 398). There have been between five and fifteen since then; they normally assist the ministers with less conspicuous matters such as answering letters from the public.

From the 1980s and onwards, the bulk of political appointees have been political advisers. There are examples of politically appointed advisers as early as the late 1930s, but the number of political appointees increased especially during the coalition governments of the 1970s and early 1980s. The system with political advisers was formalized in 1979 with the introduction of a 'political contract' that tied the employee's terms of employment to the minister (Statskontoret 1997: 180). Since the early 1980s, the number of political advisers has increased by almost 150 per cent, with the peak in 2006. The development of the number of political advisers follows the same pattern as for the total number of political appointees, discussed above, with leaps to higher levels during coalition governments. As already discussed this indicates that the need for more vertical coordination between the parties in coalition governments and a growing need for horizontal coordination with the parliament contributes to the increasing number of political advisers.

Generally, individual political advisers follow one or a small number of policy issues. One important task is to establish contacts with interest groups and the party organization, in order to gain information of how they would react on different potential policy suggestions. As Mr Landahl points out, the political advisers have a possibility to make such contacts informally, which is not possible for the minister. Therefore they can gain valuable information without being seen as taking position for or against the preferred policy position of the interest group. This type of informal vertical coordination is probably one of the more important tasks of the political advisers.

Nevertheless, we get an important indication that horizontal coordination is also an important driver of politicization by observing where within the government offices the political appointees are employed. In Figure 9.2, the numbers of political advisers are reported for the Prime Minister's Office, the Ministry of Finance, and the Ministry of Defence. The three ministries represent three different levels of politicization.

Most of the political appointees in the government offices are employed in the Prime Minister's Office. The Prime Minister's Office employs about thirty political advisers, or about 40 per cent of the total employed in the government offices. The Prime Minister's Office is followed by the Ministry of Finance, with ten to fifteen political advisers. After that, most of the other ministries follow with generally between two and four political advisers. In Figure 9.2, the 'other' ministries are represented by the Ministry of Defence.

It is no surprise that it is the Prime Minister's Office and the Ministry of Finance that employ the most political advisers. The Prime Minister's Office is the 'hub' of the government offices, and the pressure for policy coordination is strongest there. The Ministry of Finance is the coordinator in the budgetary process, itself a key instrument of coordination. It is well known, in both Sweden and other countries, that this gives the Ministry of Finance an important policy-coordinating role (Larsson 1986: 168; Premfors and Sundström 2007: 174; for the Danish experience, see Jensen 2003). The concentration of policy advisers in the Prime Minister's Office and the Ministry of Finance indicates that even though policy coordination within the government offices is probably not their main concern, the political advisers are also involved in this process.

We should, however, note that historically speaking the Prime Minister's Office has not been the centre of politicization in the Swedish government offices. When the Social Democrat Tage Erlander was appointed prime minister in 1946 his office only employed one part-time civil servant and one porter. In 1953, Erlander started to employ a small staff, starting with Bo Johansson (later a known Swedish political scientist under the last name Särlvik) and later including Olof Palme

Figure 9.2: Political advisers in the Ministry of Finance, the Ministry of Defence, and the Prime Minister's Office, 1981–1999

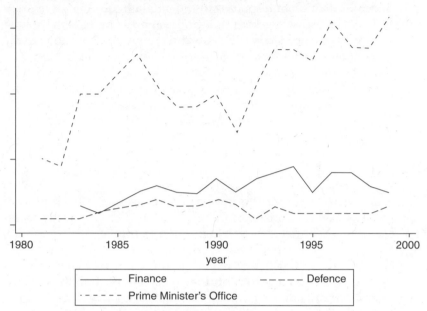

Source: Data from the Parliamentary Committee on the Constitution, yearly publications 1980/81–1999/2000.

Note: Data are only reported for the years between 1981 and 1999, because we only have comparative data for the different ministries for this period.

(who would be Erlander's successor in 1969) (Östberg 2008: 126). The development towards a more politicized and also more active summit continued during the 1960s. This was quite criticized and was even debated in the Riksdag in 1961 (Larsson 1986; Ruin 1986: 141–7; Swedish Parliament AK 1961: 9, 36). However, the trend continued; fifteen years later, when the centre-right government came into office in 1976, the system with a policy coordination capacity in the Prime Minister's Office was established (Larsson 1986: 184–5).

Summing up, the number of political appointees in the Swedish government offices has increased during the last decades, and we suggest that this is linked to the pressure for more coordination from the centre. This is true with regard to policy coordination and political coordination between different parties within coalition governments (both of them creating the need for more state secretaries and political advisers), and coordination of responses to the media (requiring more press secretaries). Generally speaking, the political appointees seem for the most part to be involved in vertical coordination with actors outside the government offices, but there are also some indications suggesting that political appointees are involved in horizontal coordination within the government offices, especially during periods of coalition government. Politicization has most of all increased during coalition governments and most noticeably in the Prime Minister's Office, where the pressure for coordination is strongest.

Conclusion

This chapter has attempted to uncover the causes of politicization of the centre as well as its manifestations. Together, changes in the political (coalition governments), administrative (administrative reforms), international (EU), policy (mainstreaming), and medial (growing media pressure) environments created a growing need to beef up and reassert the political centre to coordinate processes within the government offices (horizontal coordination), and even more importantly with other external actors such as the parliament, the media, and interest organizations (vertical coordination).

Governments of different ideological orientations have resorted to the same solution to this problem: to increase the number of political advisers and other political appointees. We believe that this politicization represents more than merely the infusion of ideology into the government offices. Coordination can often be a politically sensitive matter that should not be left to career civil servants. Also, there has to be close and continuous contact between Cabinet ministers and the coordinators. The logical arrangement therefore has been to bring in political advisers to solve, or at least mitigate, the coordination problems. Thus, it is a type of politicization which is not only partisan in nature; it is also a matter of ensuring control and integrity in the process of coordinating policy.

Nevertheless, the chapter suggests that the most important reason for the growing politicization is that political changes – more specifically, going from one-party governments to coalition governments – generate a need for coordination, both horizontal between the parties in the government and vertical with the parliament, party organizations, and interest groups. Politicization became the preferred solution to this coordination problem also, for both social democratic and centre-right governments.

REFERENCES

Bergström, H. (1987). *Rivstart?* Stockholm: Tidens Förlag.

Carlsson, I. (2003). *Så tänkte jag*. Stockholm: Hjalmarson and Högberg.

Christensen, T., and P. Lægreid. (2008). Increased Complexity in Public Organizations: The Challenges and Implications of Combining NPM and Post-NPM Features. Paper presented at the SOG/IPSA Conference, Gothenburg, 13–15 Nov.

Dahlström, C. (2011a). Who Takes the Hit? Ministerial Advisers and the Distribution of Welfare State Cuts. *Journal of European Public Policy* 18: 294–310.

– (2011b). Politicization of Civil Service. In B. Badie, D. Berg-Schlosser, and L. Morlino (eds.), *Encyclopedia of Political Science*. London: Sage.

Derlien, H.-U. (1996). The Politicization of Bureaucracies in Historical and Comparative Perspective. In B.G. Peters and B.A. Rockman (eds.), *Agenda for Excellence*, vol. 2. Cheltham: Cheltham House.

Eichbaum, C., and R. Shaw. (2008). Revisiting Politicization: Political Advisers and Public Servants in Westminster Systems. *Governance* 21: 337–63.

Erlander, T. (1972). *Tage Erlander 1901–1939*. Stockholm: Tidens Förlag.

Erlandsson, M. (2007). *Striderna i Rosenbad: Om 30 års försök att förändra Regeringskansliet*. Stockholm: Department of Political Science, University of Stockholm.

Erlandsson, M. (2008). Regeringskansliet och medierna. *Statsvetenskaplig tidskrift* 110: 335–49.

Hadenius, S. (1990). Regeringen och massmedierna. Departementshistoriekommittén. *Att styra riket*. Stockholm: Allmänna Förlaget.

Jacobsson, B., and J. Pierre. (2008). Politikens medialisering: Introduktion. *Statsvetenskaplig tidskrift* 110: 335–49.

Jacobsson, B., and G. Sundström. (2006). *Från hemvävd till invävd*. Malmö: Liber.

– (2009). Between Autonomy and Control: Transformation of the Swedish Administrative Model. In P.G. Roness and H. Stætren (eds.), *Change and Continuity in Public Sector Organizations*. Bergen: Fagbokforlaget.

Jensen, L. (2003). *Den store koordinator*. Copenhagen: Jurist-og Økonomforbundets Forlag.

Kooiman, J. (2003). *Governing as Governance*. London: Sage.

Kooiman, J. (ed.). (1993). *Modern Governance: New Government-Society Interactions*. London: Sage.
Larsson, T. (1986). *Regeringen och dess kansli*. Lund: Studentlitteratur.
Larsson, U. (1990). Människorna i kanslihuset. Departementshistoriekommittén. *Att styra riket*. Stockholm: Allmänna Förlaget.
Light, P. (1995). *Thickening Government: Federal Hierarchy and the Diffusion of Accountability*. Washington, DC: Brookings Institution.
Olsen, L. (2007). *Rödgrön reda: Regeringssamverkan 1998–2006*. Stockholm: Hjalmarsson and Högberg.
Östberg, K. (2008). *I takt med tiden: Olof Palme 1927–1969*. Stockholm: Leopart förlag.
Parliamentary Committee on the Constitution (1981/82). KU35.
– (1993/94). KU20.
– (1993/94). KU30.
– (1994/95). KU30.
– (1995/96). KU30.
– (2001/02). KU10.
– (2007/08). KU20.
Persson, G. (2008). *Min väg, mina val*. Stockholm: Albert Bonniers Förlag.
Persson, T. (2004). *Regeringskansliets omvandling: Från förhandlingsorganisation till stabsorganisation*. Stockholm: KKR.
Peters, B.G., and J. Pierre. (2004). Introduction. In B.G. Peters and J. Pierre (eds.), *Politicization of the Civil service in Comparative Perspective*. London: Routledge.
Pierre, J. (1995). Governing the Welfare State: Public Administration, the State, and Society in Sweden. In J. Pierre (ed.), *Bureaucracy in the Modern State: An Introduction to Comparative Public Administration*. Aldershot: Edward Elgar.
– (2001). Parallel Paths? Administrative Reform, Public Policy and Politico-Bureaucratic Relationships in Sweden. In B.G. Peters and J. Pierre (eds.), *Politicians, Bureaucrats and Administrative Reform*. London: Routledge.
– (2004). Politicization of the Swedish Civil Service: A Necessary Evil – or Just Evil? In B.G. Peters and J. Pierre (eds.), *Politicization of the Civil service in Comparative Perspective*. London: Routledge.
– (2008). Stealth Economy? A Comparative Assessment of the Influence of Economic Theory on Public Administration. Paper presented at a conference on Economics and Democracy, Australian National University, 5–6 Dec.
Pollitt, C., and G. Bouckaert. (2004). *Public Management Reform. A Comparative Analysis*. Oxford: Oxford University Press.
Premfors, R., and G. Sundström. (2007). *Regeringskansliet*. Malmo: Liber.

Regeringskansliet (various years 1998–2007). *Rekeringskansliets årsbok*. Stockholm: Regeringskansliet.

Rouban, L. (2007). Politico-Administrative Relations. In J.C.N. Raadschelders, T.A.J. Toonen, and F.M. Van der Meer (eds.), *The Civil Service in the 21st Century: Comparative Perspectives*. Basingstoke: Palgrave Macmillan.

Ruin, O. (1986). *I välfärdens tjänst: Tage Erlander 1946–1969*. Stockholm: Tidens förlag.

– (2007). *Statsministern*. Hedemora: Gidlunds förlag.

SOU 2008: 118. (2008). *Styra och ställa: Förslag till en effektivare statsförvaltning*. Stockholm: Fritzes.

Statskontoret. (1997). *Staten i omvandling 1997*. Stockholm: Statskontoret.

Sundström, G. (2006). Management by Results: Its Origin and Development in the Case of the Swedish State. *International Public Management Journal* 9: 399–427.

Swedish Parliament. AK 1961: 9.

Ullström, A. (2008). Medierna ökar pressen. *Statsvetenskaplig tidskrift* 110: 351–67.

– (2009). Styrning i maktens centrum. In J. Pierre and G. Sundström (eds.), *Samhällsstyrning i förändring*. Malmö: Liber.

10 Steering from the Centre in Denmark

LOTTE JENSEN

Decentring and the Drivers of Recentralization in Denmark in the 2000s

The central hypothesis of this volume (see chapter 1) is that reforms of the past decade, inspired by the New Public Management, promoted a differentiation and decentring of Western political systems, to which central government actors must now respond. They respond, either by strategies designed to *hold on* to their power through political appointments or to *let go* through extended delegation of power, autonomy, and accountability to non-central actors, be they agencies, substate governments, private providers, non-state actors, and partnerships. The Danish case differs in two significant ways: The polity was differentiated long before the NPM era and the 'holding on' strategies do not encompass political appointments.

The Danish policy has a long history of differentiation, both politically and administratively. Some reforms towards managerial decentralization have just added further complexity to this pre-existing decentralization. Attributing the response of the centre to post-NPM hangovers is therefore unhelpful. Indeed, Denmark may not have reformed the public sector according to dogmatic NPM ideology, and a general judgment is that the adaptation to the fashions of the Organisation for Economic Co-operation and Development (OECD) is at best pragmatic and clearly path dependent (Greve 2006).

Over at least the past decade, however, a variety of centralization tendencies are increasingly discernible as responses to strengthened demands on, as well as the preferences of, central political actors to appear as pragmatic managers: They want to appear to be forceful decision-makers, who take problems and demands of the electorate seriously, and demonstrate the ability to create and change policy to which they can claim credit and appear accountable. These preferences and demands have several diverse sources.

The first is the escalating personalism – or even presidentialization – of politics (Poguntke and Webb 2005) fuelled by the media and a general focus on celebrities and public individuals on television and in journalism. In this vein, the wave of biographical studies of Danish politicians, with titles like *The Prince,* a direct reference to Machiavelli (about the former Social Democratic finance minister, Lykketoft, 1993–2000), and *The President* (on former Liberal Prime Minister Fogh Rasmussen, 2001–09), conveys a personalized picture of decision-makers as heroic individuals in a vacuum ruling the world (Holstein 2003; Mylenberg and Steensbeck 2009).

The second source is the breakdown of the traditional party system since the 1970s, the decline of party membership, and the increasing prominence of swing voters. A response has been marketization of politics, where parties derive their key policy issues from analyses of voter preferences (Knudsen 2009). This trend is also magnified by more and faster media communication through ever-competing channels, constant polling of voter responses to hot policy issues, and shifting support of government and opposition. Government cannot appear indecisive or internally divided for too long, although the de facto policies may be – even intentionally – inconsistent to court different constituencies (Grønnegard Christensen and Jensen 2009). Central control of the framing, priming, and timing of the government narrative and its projects in the media has become an important concern – and object of steering (Brink Lund 2006; Langer 2006; Grønnegard Christensen et al. 2009).

The third source of centralization is the prominence of the welfare issue in contemporary politics. Polls show that the proportion of voters nominating welfare as the most important issue rose from 20 per cent to 60 per cent between the 1990 and the 2007 elections (Goul Andersen 2008: 12). Hence, the competition among government and opposition to deliver policies and to act when appropriate in the welfare arena has grown significantly. Denmark has one of the largest public sectors in the OECD, so welfare policy affects not only users and clients but also public service personnel (Grønnegard Christensen et al. 2009: 14), and public-sector unions are also strong players on the arena. As the welfare sector is, to a large extent, decentralized to local government and regions since the 1970s, national government actors implement their welfare policy action in areas formally out of their reach. This policy centralization entails an extreme potential for conflict between central steering and local autonomy.

A fourth factor, related to the third, is that Denmark has had almost a decade of Liberal-Conservative rule. Welfare policy theory states that Liberal-Conservative governments historically own the issue of 'tough on budgets' and have had to work hard to claim ownership of the welfare issue (Ross 2000; Green-Pedersen 2002). Since 2001 the Liberal Party has been particularly keen to take leadership in welfare policy. Like those in other Western welfare states the generous Danish welfare system faced a medium-term fiscal and demographic challenge even *before* the financial crisis. Therefore, attention to aggregate fiscal discipline is unavoidable, yet problematic in the short term. This has fuelled a need for fiscal coordination, either overtly as political decisions or more subtly as administrative maneuvers outside public scrutiny, not the least to cover increasing welfare expenditure without raising taxes, because the government defined a 'tax freeze' as its political flagship in 2001. At the same time, the business cycle peaked and an increased public surplus (significantly generated by oil income, high tax revenue, and low unemployment) enabled the government to deliver on policy promises, particularly in the welfare sector.

Fifth, since 2001 Denmark has had a permanent operational majority in Parliament composed of the Liberal-Conservative government and the Danish People's Party with its nationalist welfare focus. The coalition has provided unprecedented opportunities for driving through systemic changes to control local decision-makers, service delivery, and institutions, through political 'guarantees' and monitoring systems – a tendency lamented by liberal and socialist critics alike. The stable majority created a parliamentary platform for bargains between liberal, national-conservative, and welfare-oriented issues, regarding which central control policies have proliferated simultaneously to accommodate different hinterland preferences.

In sum, over the past decade, central government has had all of pressure, incentives, ambitions, and the opportunity to pursue centralization policies in public governance to some degree. The policy in the 2000s has both profited and learned from the 1990s centralization of government decision structures, to which the chapter draws the attention after having sketched the countervailing centrifugal and centripetal mechanisms of the Danish polity.

Logic of This Chapter

When assessing trends towards centralization, this chapter addresses the following three dimensions of steering from the centre (for a similar approach see Stolfi, this volume): horizontal coordination within government, vertical coordination between the political and administrative levels of government, and the scope of the relationship between state and substate levels.

First the chapter maps the decentring mechanisms in the Danish policy, distinguishing between the historical heritage and what can reasonably be considered recent reforms of the type addressed in chapter 1. This paints the picture of a challenge to central steering rooted in systemic traits, to which some NPM elements have been added.

Following this, the preceding decade of attempts to strengthen central steering within these three dimensions will be discussed, while taking into account the inherited centripetal forces on which this endeavour is premised. The analysis elaborates further on the framework – by distinguishing between centralization strategies targeting different phases of the policy process – *agenda setting, discourse and narrative, decision-making, implementation,* and *evaluation* in order to show the multifaceted nature of the Danish version of the 'holding on' strategy. The analysis presents a historically embedded overview of the specific Danish case after 2000. The changing approach to horizontal coordination also has a significant impact on the vertical and scope dimensions, which are subsequently analysed before the megatrends of centralization are integrated in the conclusion. I also raise the question whether central government actors strive for substantive coordination of policy outcomes minimizing overlaps, lacunae, and redundancy (Peters 1998) or employ a more pragmatic and selective logic accommodated to the strategic context and political opportunities of the day.

Centrifugal Mechanisms: Historical Paths and Recent Reforms

In the *horizontal coordination* of government, I distinguish between *political* coordination addressing party political interests in the coalition and *functional* coordination ensuring alignment of technical standards, budgetary discipline, and foreign policy consistency (Wolf 1997: 8). *Politically,* Denmark is a multiparty parliamentary system with proportional representation and a historical record of minority coalition governments. Hence, political coordination within government itself, as well as in Parliament is a long-standing art form. The expression 'the art of counting to 90' (given 179 seats in Parliament) is the basic logic of political argumentation as well as 'reality check' of political advice.

Functionally, the system displays a high degree of ministerial autonomy. The Danish Constitution (ss. 14, 15, 16) states that once nominated by the prime minister, ministers are politically and legally responsible for their ministry, its organization, and administration. Underlining this, each ministry has a separate entry in the budget document. The system is therefore marked by political complexity and a strong territorial structure and culture, posing challenges to functional coordination of crosscutting policies and fiscal coordination.

In *vertical coordination* I distinguish between *positional* coordination addressing political control over bureaucratic positions through recruitment and incentives and *organizational* coordination addressing the steering of organizational processes and outcomes. Denmark has a long-standing tradition of a merit-based bureaucracy as well as keen parliamentary scrutiny of undue party politicization (Grønnegard Christensen 2006a). It has therefore been controversial whenever ministers have appointed staff with known compatible political sympathies.

On the *organizational aspect*, since 1985 agencies have enjoyed considerable budgetary autonomy within envelopes in line with early OECD recommendations (Schick 1998: chapter 1). Since the 1960s each ministry has successively been reconstructed to a unitary departmental system. Each of the now eighteen ministries has one minister and one permanent secretary, to whom a varying number of agencies – fifty-nine in total – report. Other bodies have enjoyed a more independent status with independent competencies, their own executive boards, or legally defined autonomy. For example, universities have historically operated at arm's-length from government. In general agencies have been regarded as functional entities based on professional autonomy, from which the more politically attuned echelons around the minister could acquire technical support.

The steering relationships between ministries and agencies have been reformed repeatedly. Since the 1980s a performance management regime ('the contract chain') based on contracts, measurement, and annual reports, fleshed out with controller functions and benchmarks, has been developed with the initial aim to enhance efficient and effective performance in accordance with agreed targets, with more managerial freedom as a quid pro quo. As a consequence, performance payment related to aggregate agency targets was introduced for agency heads and cascaded down to internal reward structures (Ejersbo and Greve 2005: 89 ff; Binderkrantz and Grønnegard Christensen 2009).

On the *scope* dimension, I distinguish between the *political* aspect of conflict between central and local government concerning ownership of the political agenda and the local decision capacity, and the *institutional* aspect concerning the autonomy of institutional leadership and profession in, for example, hospitals, kindergartens, and schools.

As for the *political* aspect, local government and regions are both independent political systems, integrated into the national political hierarchy (Grønnegard Christensen et al. 2007: 249ff). Comparatively, Denmark has a significant heritage of local autonomy and democracy (Knudsen 1995: chapter 25). Their status is mentioned in the Constitution (s. 82) which states that the 'right of local government to govern local matters under the supervision of the state is regulated by law' – that is, parliament. Local government has historically stressed the 'right' element, while national government focuses on '*supervision*' and particularly 'regulated by law.' Postwar policy has decentralized the majority of welfare tasks to counties and municipalities, covering about half of the total expenditure budget and 75 per cent of public consumption, mainly spent on welfare. Local government account for around 50 per cent by local taxes, while regions have had, after 2007, no right to levy taxes and are primarily financed by state grants (Blom-Hansen and Serritslew 2008: 154ff.). The economic conditions (tax and expenditure levels) of substate levels of government are negotiated annually between the interest organizations Local Government Denmark (LGD) and Danish Regions (DR) and the minister of finance. The negotiations are tense processes that attract significant annual media attention when agreements turn into concrete budgets. Blame shifting between state and local levels when *realpolitik* demands prioritization is part of the routine battles.

Institutionally, two subsequent 'reform waves' decentralized decision competences further. First, budgetary and substantive professional autonomy was delegated to individual institutions such as kindergartens and homes for the elderly. Second, user boards were introduced in the mid-1990s, integrating users of childcare, schools, and services for the elderly in decision-making (Floris and Bidsted 1996). Contracting out, competitive tendering, and purchaser/provider splits on the welfare area were gently introduced during Social Democratic rule in the 1990s but never to any significant degree other than in exemplary liberal municipalities (Ejersbo and Greve 2005: chapter 5).

Table 10.1
Centrifugal and Centripetal Mechanisms

Centrifugal mechanisms

Perspective	Horizontal		Vertical		Scope	
Aspect	Political	Functional	Positional	Organizational	Political	Institutional
Heritage	Multiparty system Coaltion- minority government	Ministerial autonomy Individual budget entries	Merit bureaucracy with strong loyalty culture	Decentralized budgets Institutional autonomy in universities	Local government autonomy Right to levy taxes at county and local government level Welfare areas decentralized Institutionalized negotiations on sub-state economy	Professional autonomy
Reforms prior to 2000				Agency contracts Performance management Performance pay Annual reports SOEs and privatization		Budget and substantive competence devolved to individual institutions. User boards

Table 10.1
Centrifugal and Centripetal Mechanisms (*concluded*)

Centripetal mechanisms

Heritage	Strong PM position Council of State Quasi-formalized committee system	Annual budget round	Functional politicization Ministers appoint senior civil servants	Parliament/government decides scope of local government autonomy and economy	Parliament/government issues legislation on concrete conditions for governance and policy in welfare institutions
Reforms prior to 2000			Performance contracts	Agency Contract negotiations	

Taken together, due to institutional heritage and reforms between 1980s and 2000, Denmark can be described as a differentiated system with considerable centrifugal forces challenging the picture of 'strong government' and the conditions for central steering. At the central government level, coalition parties cater for their constituencies and ministries defend their autonomy; on the vertical dimension, a merit culture prevents party political appointments and ministries enjoy budgetary autonomy and preside over agency contracts. In terms of scope, substate actors were always strong political players in large policy areas, and diversity has been fuelled by institutional autonomy in welfare provision, user empowerment, and union involvement. Table 10.1 summarizes the centrifugal mechanisms as well as the countervailing centripetal ones sketched in the following section.

Centripetal Mechanisms: Existing Tools for Central Steering

Although characterized as a decentred policy, a number of mechanisms enable central players to actively build up central capacity. For *political horizontal* coordination, the prime minister holds a rather strong formal position, as he can hire and fire all ministers, distribute portfolios, call elections, and hire top officials (Knudsen 2000). The 'council of state' – a very formal meeting, chaired by the queen, where no strategic debate and decision making takes place – is the sole formally codified coordination forum (Constitution s. 17). The weekly meetings of ministers, used for debates and internal discipline, are more important depending on the authority and clout of the prime minister and the relationship between coalition partners (Hegelund and Mose 2006: 20). Historically, an institutionalized practice of government committees has evolved (Knudsen 2000). In terms of interior policy, two committees are most important. The Coordination Committee (CC) dates back to the 1970s, is chaired by the prime minister, and includes key ministers in the coalition. The Economic Committee (EC) originates from postwar economic regulation and was chaired by the minister of economic affairs from 1947 until 1993, when a move to the minister of finance changed the rules of the game. The backbone of the EC is the economic ministers, but different governments have included other ministers for strategic reasons or to secure coalition balance. For *functional coordination*, the annual budget is compulsory according to the Constitution (ss. 43, 45, 46). The budget is a normal law, passing three readings in parliament between September and the New Year. This implies that the budget process can be employed as a coordination device for striking deals and log rolling in complex political situations.

Thus, horizontal coordination has two formal strongholds: the prime minister's constitutional position and the compulsory nature of the budget agreement. To this a quasi-formalized system of committees and meetings is added, the function of which depends on the power of and between core ministers, notably the prime minister and the finance minister. What the Danish prime minister does *not* have is a large Prime Minister's Office. Until the 1960s it was rather insignificant in size and competence. Since the 1990s the size has stabilized around thirty academic staff, which is in a comparative perspective pretty slim. However, a notable professionalization has occurred as top staff are recruited on contract from other ministries, notably the Ministry of Finance and the Foreign Office (Knudsen 2000). Also, a Cabinet Office does not exist. The machinery of coordination thus depends on which ministries take the lead and which ministers become included in coordination processes chaired or authorized by the prime minister. The unique Danish tradition marked by absence of party politicization in the civil service deprives the government of a 'B-chain' of state secretaries or junior ministers.

In terms of *vertical* coordination of *positions*, the Danish merit system is a quasi-formal obstacle to party politicization, underpinned by an institutionalized tradition adhered to strongly by the bureaucracy itself. This has been true given that introduction of party political actors at the top would not only disturb a long-standing historical tradition, but also deprive bureaucrats of direct access to the processes of political decision-making. So, the other side of the merit model is that functional politicization (Mayntz and Derlien 1989) is a basic feature, as using civil servants in advice, policy-making, and communication is based on evolving and permissive norms (Grønnegard Christensen 2006a). Parliament has abstained from formal regulation of the matter and has based regulation on issuing codices or norms of appropriate behaviour. The core principles are that press secretaries/special advisers are on contract and civil servants must not assist ministers with party political activities and during elections. Other than that, the concept of '*integrated advice*' is considered the ground rule (Finansministeriet 1998, 2004). Political/tactical advice is provided by the merit bureaucracy, notably the permanent secretaries, and both departments and agencies are increasingly involved in policy analysis and and advice to the ministers (Salomonsen 2004; Grønnegard Christensen 2006a; Finansminis-

Table 10.2
Trends in Central Government Strategies after 2000

Dimension	Horizontal		Vertical		Scope	
Aspect	Political	Functional	Positional	Organizational	Political	Institutional
Policy phase *Agenda discourse narrative*	Contract policy Government program Press secretaries Press conferences Government publications Commissions		Special advisers Government programs		Welfare agenda: defining scope of expectations	The view of professions
Decision-making	Strengthening CC PMO based ad hoc committees Grand reforms			University reform: professional boards, and mergers	Strengthening economic governance Detailing documents of economic agreements Centralizing regional funding Issuing specific policy, e.g., opening hours and food in kindergartens	Bypassing institutional autonomy: e.g., guarantees of treatment in health

Table 10.2
Trends in Central Government Strategies after 2000 (*concluded*)

Dimension	Horizontal	Vertical	Scope
Implementation	Centralization of IT, procurement, administration	Check government program	Contract metamorphosis from efficiency to policy University contracts with ministries, strategic funding Process regulation through efficiency strategies. Private hospital promotion Compulsory outsourcing in welfare delivery, e.g.. elderly care Free choice, e.g., in schools and hospitals Compulsory Danish texts in schools
Evaluation	Publishing results across government	Tick boxes of government programs	Annual reports Performance targets in ministries Monitoring/ benchmarking results through reporting systems New evaluation centres on local government/ regions and regions and education

teriet 2006). Further, the ministers have the competence to hire and fire permanent secretaries and agency heads. There has been an increased tendency for holders of these positions to leave before retirement; some because career patterns have changed but also because of tensions between ministers and civil servants. These, however, can rarely be traced to party politics, while 'chemistry' and 'loyalty' are central explanations, and civil servants may get sacrificed when a scandal hits a ministry. All in all, there are ways for ministers to secure and sanction loyalty without party political recruitment (Grønnegard Christensen 2006a: 1009–11). The introduction of performance payment in contracts adds the opportunity to reward senior civil servants for contributions to the wanted policy development and send signals to career-oriented staff about appropriate behaviour. In terms of *organizational* coordination on the vertical dimension, contract negotiations contain the option of building in political performance targets.

Turning finally to the *scope* dimension, the Constitution grants the national level the opportunity to legislate on *political* matters at the local level in terms of economy and tax, policy substance, and issues regarding service provision and the governance of welfare *institutions*. Outcomes on these dimensions are decided by traditions as well as the relative power of central, regional, and local actors. In the context of these countervailing mechanisms, the centralization strategies after 2000 are summarized in Table 10.2 and subsequently unpacked according to the logic presented above.

Contemporary History of Horizontal Coordination: Centralizing the Architecture of Decision

The 1990s are crucial for understanding government strategy after 2000. On the one hand, a structure of centralized top down decision-making inside government was constructed and consolidated around the Ministry of Finance and the Economic Committee. On the other hand, the policy processes and priorities to which this structure was employed illustrated the crucial dangers to political support embedded in too direct central steering based on economic rationality. These experiences paved the way for a broader and more subtle governance strategy of the centre.

From the late 1980s onwards the Ministry of Finance developed a new organizational strategy based on its bad historical experiences of weak influence on the policy-making process. The strategy profited from the absence of a large PMO or a Cabinet Office, and played on the tradition of coalition decision-making through quasi-formal commit-tees. The core idea was to premise central government decision-making on the agenda of the finance minister – and his ministry – via structural and organizational changes to government decision-making.

When in 1993 the Conservative prime minister had to step down because of a scandal concerning Tamil immigrants, a four-party gov-ernment led by the Social Democrats took office. It was haunted by a historical burden of proof from the 1970s to govern responsibly in fiscal terms. So, the strong man in the Social Democratic Party, the economist Mr Lykketoft, became finance minister. In the Ministry of Finance, both were seen as politically helpful because they served to place economic policy on the top of the political agenda. On his first day at work, the minister got two pieces of advice from his new permanent secretary: (1) To reinvent the Economic Committee, which had been discontin-ued for two years and move the chair to the Ministry of Finance and (2) to enhance it with a permanent preparation group of permanent secretaries from the selected ministries – the so-called Steering Group (STG), chaired by the permanent secretary of the Ministry of Finance. The advice was followed as presented. The Ministry of Finance was transformed into a combined secretariat and think tank for STG and EC. For several years, the ministry had been working on its internal structure, priorities, and processes in order to substitute routine work with broader policy analysis targeting government decision-making via adequately 'dressing up' the finance minister for internal decision processes (Jensen 2003, 2008).

The new structure required that no item enter the Economic Com-mittee's agenda without prior treatment in the Steering Group, and nothing enter the STG agenda without consent of the permanent sec-retary of the Ministry of Finance. The political construction of the EC was a mix of economic ministers and coalition party leaders – except for the prime minister, who headed the CC. In this way decisions reached in the EC were almost impossible to reverse – deliberately so, even for the prime minister. Research shows that over the following eight or nine years, internal government decision-making was prima-rily coordinated through this mechanism, not only in terms of fiscal policy and budgeting (Jensen 2003, 2008). The prime minister and the finance minister seemed to agree on a division of labour, so that the prime minister – increasingly occupied with foreign policy – dealt with only the principal government issues and critical single cases, while leaving economic and structural issues to his finance minister. The definition of 'economic' widened significantly. In effect, all key strategic issues, major reforms, or cross-cutting decisions on structural policy within the labour market, taxation, the environment, welfare, and so on were channeled through the EC pipeline, which served not only as a decision machine, but also as a socialization device. Ministers and ministries learned what it took be taken seriously and how to argue in an economic code to gain legitimacy. The machine was effective and by and large seen as 'the only game in town,' strongly underpinned by the authority of the finance minister and his alliance with the minister of economic affairs (Jensen 2003). The CC – although termed 'the finer committee' in the media – never developed into a decision machine and never developed a policy-preparation structure. If the EC had reached a decision, cases generally were settled and were not renegotiated at CC level. EC decisions were eventually, if not cleared on beforehand, brought to the parliament in the annual budget round, which became the preferred arena and mechanism for reforms and horizontal policy coordination, particularly as the coalition diminished. The finance minister became famous for his 'patchwork deals' shifting between different majorities.

In the course of the 1990s, the Ministry of Finance became aware of the significance of publicity and developed a publication policy of unprecedented breadth and volume: From advanced economic analysis and routine budget documentation – both historical routine products – to analysis of a variety of policy areas and soft debate, publications on public sector efficiency were issued in fancy formats. A basic idea was to gain support in the environment for the necessary primacy of economic discourse through 'lectures' from the centre. The Ministry of Finance cultivated a considerable self-confidence as the government's powerhouse and 'the biggest think tank in Denmark' (Østergaard 1998). The underlying assumption was that 'what is good for the government comes from the MoF' (Jensen 2003: chapter 7).

In sum, horizontal coordination in the 1990s was primarily developed under the auspices and authority of the Ministry of Finance and its minister. It focused on structural economic reforms in the longer term and on capturing the decision structure and defining the premises for decision ex ante. No political key initiative was launched, no central deal struck without the consent of the EC. The system worked with remarkable efficiency and had only feeble competition from other coordination structures. However, this authority and efficiency developed into a deficit of legitimacy by the end of the decade. 1998 is widely considered the 'Annus Horribilis' of government, significantly influencing the strategies of horizontal coordination design after 2001 (Grønnegard Christensen et al. 2009).

Annus Horribilis of 1998: The Lesson Premising Future Coordination

Just after re-election in early summer of 1998, the government quickly made an agreement with the socialist parties to dampen economic activity through a tax reform targeting real estate, savings, and prices on petrol and oil. The government was flogged by the opposition and its own support declined, but economists supported the decision. The rationale in government – and the Ministry of Finance – was that the public did not understand the technicalities, but in the long run government would be rewarded for economic stability – and by the way, there were four years to the next election. The erosion of support for the government was compounded massively by a reform of the early pension scheme during the budget round in the autumn of 1998. Forecasts revealed future expenditure explosions, so the prime minister came under political pressure from the unions to guarantee the program. In August it appeared that expenditures would explode even more than anticipated. Tight preparations and negotiations inside government under the auspices of Ministry of Finance evolved. The budget round was secretly used to strike a deal with the Liberal leader, Mr Fogh Rasmussen, who ideologically supported the adjustment. But he also knew that it was politically lethal. Hence, he let government take the entire credit – that is, the blame – for the ensuing decision, which was seen as breaking its promise. The prime minister had to publicly apologize that he had not communicated clearly enough that the adjustments were carried out to secure the scheme in the long run. Support for the Social Democrats dropped from 36 per cent to 20 per cent (Larsen and Andersen 2004; Jensen and Mouritzen 2009). Although, again, cherished by economists, the reforms came to symbolize the dominance of the Ministry of Finance and the finance minister in government policy-making, in decision coordination, and in the public discourse. The Social Democrats never recovered. The government lost the 2001 election to a well-prepared Liberal leader, who could base his leadership on several lessons learned about central steering.

Horizontal Coordination after the 2000s: From Economy to Welfare and the Governance of Narrative, Agenda, and Evaluation

Incoming Prime Minister Fogh Rasmussen, was known as an ambitious, clever, and control-oriented strategist with good systemic insights after a long career. The past decade had taught this neo-liberal leader that his brand had to be transformed because it had no electoral mileage. Also, he had learned that the whole air of economic technocracy represented by the Ministry of Finance was politically devastating. His closest strategic ally, Minister of Labour Hjort, gave name to the so-called Hjort doctrine (Hardis and Mortensen 2010) according to which no policy initiative offending voters must be presented. Marketization of party politics had come to Denmark. Controlling the new welfare image became a central concern, particularly given the keen criticism from the dethroned Social Democrats. At the same time, the welfare image had to be balanced to accommodate Liberal welfare scepticism, Conservative low tax proponents, and the nationalist immigrant policy of the supporting Danish Peoples Party, who – in return for political influence – supported the tax freeze from 2001 onwards. The freeze was the backbone of the government's high-profile 'contract philosophy.' The diversity of interests highlighted the need for tight political coordination to straddle different preferences as well as for communication of a coherent and consistent government across this diversity. A central tool became government programs of unprecedented detail. It was repeatedly communicated that, in contrast to its predecessors, the government would stick to its defined promises, which voters could tick off in the boxes of the government program. In this way, policy evaluation became a matter of concern and communication.

On the whole, government attention to, and management of, communication changed markedly after 2001. An intense focus on media, framing, narratives, discourses, market analyses, and focus groups inspired by British spin doctor manuals and the techniques of the Blair government followed (Hegelund and Mose 2006: 56ff.). The prime minister used communication offensively and strategically. He introduced weekly press sessions in the Prime Minister's Office, signalling to the press that he set the agenda and decided when he was accessible and to whom. Journalists who wanted interviews on controversial issues could wait for years. Others were invited for coffee and regular briefings. He became known for repeating few, short, and understandable statements. His press adviser worked from the rationale that: 'If it isn't communicated, it does not exist; what cannot be explained cannot be justified and timing is 90% minimum' (Administrativ Debat, 2005). The 1990s communication by the Ministry of Finance through heavy economic lecturing on politically inconvenient times did not meet these criteria. The air around economic publications and forecasts, celebrated by the 1990s government as star publications by the best and the brightest, changed gradually to be treated as specialist publications in the background issued at longer intervals.

Turning to the decision-making phase, horizontal coordination was built into government programs in the sense that they defined the terms for line ministers. A clear hierarchy evolved, comparable to a professional company structure: The CEO (the prime minister) and his deputy (the Conservative coalition partner), the board of directors (3 key Liberal ministers) and the middle-level managers (line ministers with varying significance). Once the program was announced, it was considered central to governing, and ministers and their systems were kept on track (Hegelund and Mose 2006: chapters 5, 8, 10, and 12).

The committee structure changed according to the new power structure in government. The CC was revitalized and held regular meetings, and a preparatory body, similar to the EC-STG construction of the 1990s, was added. The Economic Committee, Steering Group, and Ministry of Finance construction of the 1990s became relegated to a secondary, albeit central, preparatory role (Fuglsang and Jensen 2010). Where in the 1990s, it had been the locus of reforms, strategies, and analysis, a careful leveling took place, which clearly took into account that the Ministry of Finance was a necessary and important machine, but dangerous to publicize. The prime minister supplemented the permanent committee structure with ad hoc committees addressing key reform topics or hot issues: local government structure, welfare sustainability, globalization, labour market reforms, and climate change. Some responded to sudden strategic needs or signaled a special concern; others served to postpone, kill, or mature difficult issues. Some were external expert-committees; others were a mix of politicians, civil servants, and external representatives depending on the need for professional knowledge and legitimacy as well as inclusion/capture of veto players (Grønnegard Christensen et al. 2009).

The decision structure around reforms changed. The more politically sensitive or significant were steered from small ad hoc secretariats in the PMO, recruiting staff from relevant ministries and linking to the rest of the government machinery in a matrix structure as long as it lasted. The Ministry of Finance played a central role in all committees, but it was clearly signaled that economy was only one concern among others and distributive conflicts were not on the menu. This was further underlined when the reports from several of the more controversial committees, addressing the need for economic and labor market reforms entailing possible voter resistance, were dismissed publicly and loudly by the prime minister and subsequently the finance minister shortly after or even *before* they were released because of 'political tone deafness.' This was a strong symbol communicating the ownership and control of the agenda, as well as an indication of the significance the centre paid to its governance narrative: (1) We listen to voters; and (2) we are not dismantling the welfare state. The 1998 reforms had provided the lesson that reforms have to be accepted before a decision rather than explained afterwards. Therefore, the prime minister launched a rationale in which reforms must not come 'as a burglar in the night.' Committees became one tool for maturation – or delaying, even abandoning reforms. Where reforms in the 1990s were referred to the log rolling of the budget round, reforms after 2000 could be decided by a comfortable majority once deals were struck, usually between the government and its supporting party.

Commissions also became a way of extending the governance narratives and discourses beyond the state to substate welfare issues and behind enemy lines on opposition territory and among organized interests. In the run-up to the 2007 election, the prime minister announced a so-called quality reform of the public sector in the areas of childcare, health, and the elderly with the broad rationale to get more quality for money in the future, facing demographic and fiscal problems – and opposition issue ownership. The process built on broad involvement of all conceivable veto players in meetings and events around the country, signaling closeness and bottom up processes, and expressing respect for welfare staff and users. Communication around the process, however, was considerably centralized to press conferences and government pamphlets, and the narrative was well policed. All attempts, for example, from Liberal Party ministers to raise debates on retrenchment, user payment, and other themes echoing the ancient minimal state identity were immediately discontinued by the prime minister, who stressed that this was no cutting exercise. The process was, again, coordinated by a secretariat in the PMO and steered by a group of ministers among whom the finance minister was only one. The process resulted in a successful capture of the unions (and hence a decoupling of the opposition) at the price of massive investments in welfare and supplementary education of staff plus tax relief as political payment to the Conservatives (Grønnegard Christensen 2008). Economists warned that the economy would overheat. The prime minister recommended a revision of economic text books!

The quality reform was the clearest indication of a shift from an economic top down to a political bottom up rationale for decision making and governance narrative as well as of the expansion of scope in narratives and agenda setting beyond the national state. We will return to the implications when looking at the scope dimension. The *functional aspect* of horizontal coordination and the role of Ministry of Finance turned towards identifying funding for the political promises embedded in the government programs and the additional political agreements. As the welfare areas – covering the majority of the budget – were almost politically untouchable, attention turned towards systemic efficiency. We will turn to that when discussing the organizational aspect of vertical coordination below.

Vertical Coordination: Political Accommodation in a Merit System

In terms of *positions* the vertical dimension of coordination is based on a combination of meritocracy and 'integrated advice' regulated softly by committee reports in 1998 and 2004. After 1998 it has been deemed legitimate for ministers to employ press secretaries on contract. Partly, this was considered a necessary professionalization of communication in the ministries. Moreover, defining the need for special advice as 'communication' is a way for the permanent civil service to prevent further politicization of executive advice. In 2001 the prime minister issued an 'allowance' of one special adviser / press secretary per minister. By 2009–10 seventeen special advisers were on contract. Being a new phenomenon, 'spin doctors' and their role in the design of government appearance and policy through priming, framing, and timing has been widely discussed by the media itself and in the literature (Lund and Esbensen 2006). Their impact on the permanent bureaucracy in terms of 'administrative politicization' (Eichbaum and Shaw 2007; Salomonsen 2010) remains under-researched. But special advisers have no formal powers to instruct the civil service, and their inclusion and role in policy and communication hinges on the preferences of the minister. Only seventeen individuals without formal powers hardly change the work of the permanent bureaucracy. However, the introduction of press secretaries/advisers per se does indicate an increase in media sensitivity in the bureaucracy. A larger newspaper calculated that in 2008, about fifty staff members worked with political communication across the government – a significant increase in personnel and in expenditure since 2002 (*Politiken* 2008). Finally, both research (Salomonsen 2004) and official accounts (Finansminsiteriet 2006) show that the involvement in broad policy-making and advice extends beyond the upper echelons of departments. Staff lower down the ranks recognize the political nature of their tasks and are aware of the political realities ('counting to 90'). As shown below, agencies are also increasingly involved in political advice and policy-making.

So, while vertical coordination qua politicization in the sense applied by Dahlström, Pierre, and Peters (this volume) is close to absent, vertical control of the bureaucracy develops more indirectly within the logic of the 'integrated model,' which implies few hard limitations on the ministers' use of staff, and ample career incentives to perform to political wishes unless a change of guard looks plausible.

The introduction of government programs has explicitly been seen as a way of disciplining the bureaucracy, according to one political adviser: 'This government has strengthened the political level more than ever towards the civil service. We got the contract with voters into the government program. To these kinds of written statements, civil servants are 100% loyal. It is a bible for them, whilst they can always kill the ideas a minister otherwise gets. It's easy to draft a memo telling the minister why his idea is not feasible' (Hegelund and Mose 2006: 19). Finally, the participation of civil servants in campaign activities not formally related to elections or referenda has become more accepted. While in 2000 the Social Democratic government received intense scrutiny and criticism from the opposition for alleged politicization using taxpayers' money (Parliamentary Inquiry 22.11.00) when letting civil servants prepare Popular Hearings as a response to accusations of elitist decision-making in the government's reform technology, the Theme Meetings around the country in the 2006 Quality Reform, which consumed extensive bureaucratic manpower, were widely celebrated as a professionalization of the Popular Hearing technology, although perceived as a de facto pre-election campaign.

Vertical coordination also takes the form of political control of bureaucratic organizations. Here, the introduction – and subsequent metamorphosis – of agency contracts is central. In the 1980s agency control was a concern of MoF in order to keep aggregate ceilings. The quid pro quo contracts with agencies focusing on internal efficiency were introduced from 1991 onwards. Longitudinal research (Binderkrantz and Grønne-gard Christensen 2009: 66) shows that the agency model covers most agencies (92%). More importantly, the profile of the performance targets has changed remarkably from introverted efficiency demands towards more extroverted targets directed towards specified target groups. Users and citizens, who are a central concern to ministers, are on top of the list, but also performance targets oriented directly towards ministers and departments have increased from 2 per cent to 10 per cent from 1995 to 2005. The conclusion is that given the strong ministerial autonomy, agency contracts are subject to shifting actor strategies and contexts, rather than a fixed New Public Management device controlled by the Ministry of Finance. Instead of inducing centrally defined efficiency, these contracts have become a tool to ensure vertical policy alignment with the goals of the minister. Accordingly, the Ministry of Finance backed out of its initial involvement.

By 2003, a metamorphosis occurred, as Finance Ministry instructions began to stress external stakeholders rather than internal efficiency targets (Finansministeriet 2003). This can be seen as a joint effect of increasing political awareness of the contract tool as a policy steering instrument in combination with government programs and the declining expectations in the ministry that process regulation would help to realize efficiency potentials. The Ministry of Finance has abandoned the intense process regulation of soft measures and introduced legally stipulated rules for procurement and tendering across ministries and introduced a number of central meta-institutions to organize and drive through cross-cutting efficiency, centralizing information technology (IT), procurement, and administration (Finansministeriet 2010). So, the role of the Ministry of Finance in functional horizontal coordination has moved from overt economic agenda-setting and substantive decision-making to a less externally visible regulation of ministry and agency administration.

Contract steering has also reached beyond agencies to include universities in controversial reforms in 2003 and 2007. Successively, contracts with the ministries and external professional boards, increased political involvement in strategic research funding, and mergers between universities and former sector research institutes have brought universities closer to the government machinery. The reform has come to symbolize a combination of the paradoxical centralism of a Liberal government and the government's strategy to target 'value' institutions such as culture, education, and research. The reform has repeatedly been criticized for undermining the independence of research, necessary for democracy (Grønnegard Christensen 2006b; *Information* 2009).

Scope of Coordination: The Struggle over Substance, Regulation, and Finance in the Welfare Arena

Over the recent decade conflict levels have escalated between state and substate levels. A reform in 2007 changed the map from 245 municipalities to 98 and fourteen counties to five regions, the latter now without the right to tax and entirely devoted to the hospital sector. Reforming the regions is widely seen as centralization, and recurring conflicts between state and regions as well as professions have been played out, over finance, substance, and governance (Christiansen and Klitgaard 2008). Regarding the *political scope*, the government has issued guarantees of treatment in selected areas (e.g., cancer, heart diseases), crowding out other areas, and stimulated a market for private hospitals to which patients can turn with vouchers (Rigsrevisionen 2009). This has expanded the *institutional scope* of coordination, as has a variety of monitoring systems to guarantee specific routines and standards in the implementation phase. In sum, the increasing voter focus on health and the potentially infinite expenditure increases as demography changes, medical care becomes globalized, and patients more assertive, has alerted national politicians to demonstrate action and accommodation to popular concerns as well as fiscal pressure. To this, an ideological preference for privatization has been added to the welfare focus. Intense blame shifting takes place when budgets entail visible choices among services or firing hospital personnel. Looking to the *political* aspect of coordination between state and local government, a dual pattern has emerged: policy and economic conflicts.

On the policy side, the centre continually issues political guarantees or detailed regulation in the welfare areas otherwise decentralized to the local level, for example, earmarked funds for the elderly and guarantees for hot meals in day care. The document specifying the annual agreement over general tax and expenditure levels has become extended to thirty pages, also covering a host of policy initiatives in the welfare area (Lotz 2007; Regeringen and KL 2008). Local government representatives see the maintenance of substantive political autonomy as a significant challenge (*Kommunen* 2010).

On the economic side, the government and its supporting party passed legislation in 2005 that permitted sanctions on overspending municipalities, and in 2008 it was added that municipalities would be sanctioned according to their share of overspending. This has served to increase conflicts, subsequently compounded by the financial crisis (Fabrin 2009). The nodal point in the conflicts between state and sub-state levels is aptly captured by the Liberal head of Local Government Denmark: 'Pay or prioritize!' (Fabrin 2009). From the local perspective, the centre raises ever-increasing expectations, without either paying or telling the voters that other areas will have to finance new prom-ises. The government, on its side, argues that agreements have been reached, in accordance with which local government will be able to finance extended welfare service through debureaucratization.

This finally leads to the *institutional aspect* of the scope dimension. Government policy has challenged individual institutions and profes-sions as well as institutional borders and historically acquired autono-my with a variety of monitoring tools, such as benchmarking, reporting requirements, and compulsory outsourcing. Also, two evaluation insti-tutes have been created to focus on local government and regions' effi-ciency and education, respectively (www.krevi.dk; www.eva.dk).

In the school sector, evaluation of pupils and quality of schools, report-ing systems, and lists of specific compulsory Danish literature (canons) have evolved. The government has recently nominated schools as their new focus area, indicating that central politicians want to be visible in the politics that matters to the everyday lives of their constituencies. In sum, government has significantly expanded its scope of governance both in terms of agenda-setting, decisions, implementation, and evalu-ation. The continual game between central and local about who defines, who decides, who pays the bills, and who gets the blame if voter expec-tations are not met is set to continue.

Steering from the Danish Centre: A Combined Assessment

In the case of Denmark a combined assessment across the dimensions of horizontal, vertical, and scope coordination conveys a more complex picture than responding to the consequences of New Public Manage-ment by 'thickening of government' by an increase in political appoint-ments. The polity is differentiated along institutional paths as much as reforms, and the centralization tendencies we have seen respond to pressures on and opportunities of the centre to demonstrate control as well as to the political and economic situation. This not least the result of the high degree of informality of the political and administrative system, which sensitizes it to the way central actors perceive and handle it strategically.

Horizontal coordination in contemporary history departs from the economic crisis in the 1970s, in the aftermath of which the Ministry of Finance exploited the political tailwind and the loose internal structure of the centre to drive through a structural centralization of the decision structure and processes. The mode of steering was top down based on the rationale: 'it's the economy, stupid!' in the sense that long-term challenges to the economy and short-term political challenges to demonstrate economic responsibility were seen as producing their own authority and legitimacy, premising more substantive policy initiatives. This premise deteriorated. The change of government in 2001 demonstrated a learning process changing both the focus and mode of horizontal governance. Explicit economic governance provokes distributive conflicts and makes government vulnerable to accusations of welfare retrenchment. As such accusations were crucial for government to dismantle, the welfare narrative and the discourse of welfare became the criteria for horizontal policy coordination as well as the mode of decision making became broad inclusion – and lock in – of vested interests far beyond the national government.

The new government narrative and the intense interest of the centre in welfare discourse and agenda-setting fuelled a keen focus on media governance. Also, it expanded the *scope of government coordination*. This increased the level of conflict by creating: welfare expectations at the local level; restrained funding opportunities related to the tax freeze and the option to sanction local overspending; increased pressure to outsource; enforcement of competition from private hospitals and the increasing detail of regulation in service delivery and monitoring. In terms of *vertical coordination*, the absence of party politicization is compensated for by an extensive functional politicization. The 'integrated advice' codex, the permissive and soft regulation by Parliament, and the options of designing incentive structures signaling government wishes to the bureaucracy through contracts and performance payment expand the central government's room for political maneuver much more than a few special advisers do, although some of them in particular have contributed intensively to central control of government narrative and discourse. Agency contracts have metamorphosed from introverted efficiency tools to more extroverted policy tools stressing stakeholder priorities. This rationale has been extended to institutions with historical independence, most notably the universities, as governance boards, funding, and research profiles have been subject to political regulation. This move mirrors that government has sought to gain the 'value territory' of heretofore more-independent institutions regarded as hostile to the national-conservative agenda and market orientation.

Returning to the opening question of the book, it is worth considering the motives and strategies for central government coordination. The underlying assumption of the volume is that governments strive to reach a coordinated outcome avoiding incoherence, lacunae, and overlaps. Complex systems, however, straddle masses of all three as government moves on from one policy situation to the next, sometimes catering to one group, other times to the other, sometimes heralding a principle, other times acting in opposition to the very same one. Claiming that huge public expenditure increases and simultaneous tax reductions implie no economic contradiction might of course be a consistent but extreme interpretation of supply-side economics. But it may also illustrate that the narrative of grand government and consistent governance is more prominent than the actual praxis, but necessary in the age of communication and, hence, an object of steering in its own right.

REFERENCES

Administrativ Debat. (2005). Interview med Michael Kristiansen. *Administrativ Debat* 4: 2.

Andersen, J.G. (2008). Et valg med paradokser. *Tidsskriftet Politik* (3 Nov.).

Binderkrantz, A.S., and J. Grønnegard Christensen. (2009). Governing Danish Agencies by Contract: From Negotiated Freedom to the Shadow of Hierarchy. *International Journal of Public Policy* 29: 55–78.

Blom-Hansen, J., and S. Serritslew. (2008). Budgetlægning i kommuner og regioner. In P.M. Christiansen (ed.), *Budgetlægning og offentlige udgifter.* Gylling: Academica.

Brink Lund, A. (2006). Strategisk offentlighedsarbejde. In B.B. Lund and M.C. Esbensen (eds.), *Samtaler om Spin.* Århus: Haase og Søns Forlag.

Christiansen, P.M., and M.B. Klitgaard. (2008). *Den utænkelige reform: Strukturreformens tilblivelse 2002–2005.* Odense: Syddansk Universitetsforlag.

Constitution (Danmarks Riges Grundlov). Available at www.grundloven.dk/.

Derlien, H., and R. Mayntz. (1989). Party Patronage and Politicization of the

West German Administrative Elite 1970–1987 – Toward Hybridization? *Governance* 2: 384–404.

Eichbaum, C., and R. Shaw. (2007). Ministerial Advisors, Politicization and the Retreat from Westminister: The Case of New Zealand. *Public Administration* 85: 609–40.

Ejersbo, N., and C. Greve. (2005). *Moderniseringen af den offentlige sektor.* Gylling: Børsens Forlag.

Fabrin, E. (2009). *Velfærd skal prioriteres eller finansieres.* Available at http://www. rudersdal.dk.

Finansministeriet. (1998). *Betænkning 1354: Forholdet mellem minister og embedsmænd.* Copenhagen: Finansministeriet.

– (2003). *Effektiv opgavevaretagelse i staten.* Copenhagen: Finansministeriet.

– (2004). *Betænkning 1443. Embedsmænds rådgivning og bistand.* Copenhagen: Finansministeriet.

– (2006). *Centraladministrationens organisering – status og perspektiver.* Copenhagen: Finansministeriet.

– (2010). *Ansvar for styring – vejledning om styring fra koncern til institution.* Copenhagen: Finansministeriet.

Floris, T., and C. Bidsted. (1996). *Brugerbestyrelser på tværs: Erfaringer fra kommuner og amter.* Copenhagen: AKF forlaget.

Fuglsang, N., and L. Jensen. (2010). Magtens mekanismer: Regeringens udvalgsstruktur og koordineringspraksis under Nyrup og Fogh. *Samfundsøkonomen* 2: 17–23.

Green-Pedersen, C. (2002). *The Politics of Justification.* Amsterdam: Amsterdam University Press.

Greve, C. (2006). Public Management Reform in Denmark. *Public Management Review* 8: 616–19.

Greve, C., and N. Ejersbo. (2005). *Moderniseringen af den offentlige sektor.* Gylling: Børsens Forlag.

Grønnegard Christensen, J. (2006a). Ministers and Mandarins under the Danish Parliament. *International Journal of Public Administration* 29: 997–1019.

– (2006b). Sanders betændte metode. *Politiken* (14 Sept.).

– (2008). Korporatismens genkomst. *Administrativ Debat* 4: 10–13.

Grønnegard Christensen, J., and L. Jensen. (2009). The Executive Core and Government Strategy in the Nordic Countries. Paper presented at the ECPR General Conference, Potsdam University, 10–12 September.

Grønnegard Christensen, J., et al. (2007). *Stat og forvaltning.* Gylling: Academica.

Grønnegard Christensen, J., et al. (2009). At regere et uregerligt samfund. In J. Grønnegard Christensen et al. (eds.), *De Store Kommissioner.* Odense: Syddansk Universitetsforlag.

Hardis, A., and H. Mortensen. (2010). Hjort doktrinen. *Weekendavisen* (14 Jan.).

Hegelund, S., and P. Mose. (2006). *Håndbog for statsministre*. Århus: Gyldendal.

Holstein, E. (2003). *Fyrsten: Et portræt af Mogens Lykketoft*. Nørhaven: Aschehoug.

Information. (2009). *Universitetslov undergraver demokratiet: Information* (14 June).

Jensen, L. (2003). *Den store koordinator*. Gylling: DJØF Forlag.

– (2008). *Væk fra afgrunden*. Viborg: Syddansk Universitetsforlag.

Jensen, D., and P.E. Mouritzen. (2009). Pinsepakken og Efterlønsreformen. In J. Grønnegard Christensen et al. (eds.), *De Store Kommissioner*. Odense: Syddansk Universitetsforlag.

Knudsen, T. (1995). *Dansk statsbygning*. Gentofte: DJØD Forlag.

– (2009). Partierne er blevet markedspartier. *Information* (17 July).

Knudsen, T. (ed.). (2000). *Regering og embedsmænd*. Herning: Systime.

Kommunen. (2010). KL spidser bekymrede over overformynderi. *Kommunen* (4 Feb.).

Langer, R. (2006). Mod kanalstyring og effektivitet. In B.B. Lund and M.C. Esbensen (eds.), *Samtaler om Spin*. Århus: Haase og Søns Forlag.

Larsen, C.A., and J.G. Andersen. (2004). *Magten på Borgen*. Gylling: Århus Universitetsforlag.

Lotz, J. (2007). Spillet om kommunernes økonomi. In S. Lundtorp et al. (eds.), *Rigtigt kommunalt: Ledelse i kommuner og amter fra reform til reform*. Gylling: DFØF Forlag.

Lund, A.B. (2006). Strategisk Offentlighedsarbejde. In B.B. Lund and M.C. Esbensen (eds.), *Samtaler om Spin*. Århus: Haase og Søns Forlag.

Lund, B.B., and M.C. Esbensen (eds.). (2006). *Samtaler om spin*. Århus: Haase og Søns Forlag.

Mayntz, R., and H. Derlien. (1989). Party Patronage and Politicization of the West German Administrative Elite 1970–1987: Toward Hybridization? *Governance* 2: 384–404.

Mylenberg, T., and B. Steensbeck. (2009). *Præsidenten*. Århus: Gyldendal.

Østergaard, H.H. (1998). *At tjene og forme den nye tid*. Copenhagen: Finansministeriet.

Parliamentary Inquiry, S 526; Reply 22.11.00. Available at http://webarkiv.ft.dk/?/samling/20001/salen_spor/s526_9.htm.

Pedersen, K.M. (2006). Sandhedens time for regionerne. *Mandat* 6: 1–7.

Peters, B.G. (1998). Managing Horizontal Government: The Politics of Coordination. *Public Administration* 76: 295–311.

Poguntke, T., and P. Webb. (2005). The Presidentialisation of Contemporary Democratic Politics: Evidence, Causes and Consequences. In T. Poguntke and P. Webb, *The Presidentialisation of Politics*. New York: Oxford University Press.

Politiken. (2008). *Fogh sætter rekord i spindoktorer. Politiken* (8 March).

Regeringen and KL. (2008). *Aftale om kommunernes økonomi for 2009. Copenhagen:* Regeringen.

Rigsrevisionen. (2009). *Beretning om pris, kvalitet og adgang på private sygehuse. Copenhagen:* Regeringen.

Ross, F. (2000). Beyond Left and Right: The New Partisan Politics of Welfare. *Governance* 13: 155–84.

Salomonsen, H. (2004). *Embedsmænds fornemmelse for politik: Institutionalisering af danske embedsmænds politiske rådgivning af ministeren.* Doctoral dissertation, Ålborg University.

– (2010). Formal, Functional or Administrative Politicisation? Special Advisers and the Civil Service in Denmark. Paper for Seminar on the Executive Core, Department of Political Science, Aarhus University, 20 Jan.

Schick, A. (1998). *A Contemporary Approach to Public Expenditure Management.* Washington, DC: World Bank Institute.

Wolf, A. (1997): Policy-making and Decision-making in a Coalition System: The Case of Denmark. Paper presented at the 2nd SIGMA meeting, Warsaw, 27–28 Feb.

11 Towards Stronger Political Steering: Program Management Reform in the Finnish Government

SIRPA KEKKONEN and TAPIO RAUNIO

The Finnish political system is normally categorized as semi-presidential, with the executive functions divided between an elected president and a government that is accountable to the Eduskunta, the unicameral national parliament. However, recent constitutional reforms have transformed Finnish politics through strengthening parliamentary democracy. The new Constitution of Finland (731/1999), proclaimed 11 June 1999 and which entered into force in 2000, completed a period of far-reaching constitutional change that curtailed presidential powers and brought the Finnish political system closer to normal parliamentary democracy. Government formation is now based on partisan negotiations, and the president is almost completely excluded from the policy process in domestic matters.

Foreign policy leadership has also been parliamentarized. Under the old constitution, foreign policy was the exclusive domain of the president. But according to section 93 of the new Constitution 'the foreign policy of Finland is directed by the President of the Republic in co-operation with the Government.' Significantly, with the partial exception of treaty amendments and foreign and security policy, European Union (EU) matters belong to the jurisdiction of the government. This means that also in foreign relations the government is the main actor, with the president clearly subordinate to the prime minister (PM) and his cabinet (Raunio 2008). Overall, leadership by presidents has been replaced with leadership by strong majority governments. Indeed, free from presidential interference, the making of public policy and the passage of legislation are now more controlled by the government and governing parties than at any time since the declaration of independence; on the period of constitutional reform and its consequences, see Jyränki and

Nousiainen (2006), Nousiainen (2001), Paloheimo (2001), Raunio (2004), and Raunio and Wiberg (2008). It is thus fair to argue that since the early 1990s Finland has become a strongly government-dominated polity.

The dominant position of the government in making and implementing public policy raises also questions about coordinating the work of the executive and the relationship between directly elected politicians (MPs and ministers) and the bureaucrats. This chapter examines how the Finnish government has coped with these challenges, with the main emphasis on horizontal coordination inside the executive branch. In the next section we present briefly the main features of Finnish governments, focusing on both their internal division of labour and partisan composition. This is necessary as the multiparty coalitions, normally containing parties from both the left and the right, create particular challenges in terms of policy coordination and strategic management. The empirical analysis in the third section of the chapter is divided into two parts. First, we examine the increasing role of the government program in setting ex ante constraints and guidelines on government action. Then we analyse horizontal and vertical coordination through the new process of monitoring the implementation of the government program and the government's intersectoral policy programs. In the final section of the chapter we summarize the main arguments and evaluate the effectiveness of the coordination mechanisms.

Main Features of Finnish Governments

Internal Division of Labour

Although recent constitutional developments have undoubtedly strengthened the position of the prime minister, the collegiate style of Finnish governments and the bargaining involved in forming coalition cabinets and keeping them together act as significant constraints on the executive powers of the prime minister (Paloheimo 2002, 2003, 2005). This concerns particularly her ability to hire and fire line ministers. Apart from ministers from her own party, and with the possible exception of the two most important sectoral portfolios (the finance minister and foreign minister), the prime minister has hardly any influence on the selection of ministers, the coalition partners being responsible for choosing them. The same applies to dismissal powers. Since 1991 the prime minister has had the right to ask the president to fire an individual minister. However, although the prime minister can certainly put pressure on coalition partners, she cannot in practice appoint or dismiss individual ministers without the consent of the government parties. In case the prime minister resigns, the whole cabinet is dissolved. The Prime Minister's Office (PMO) has risen in stature in recent decades. It coordinates governmental decision-making and operates as a broker in the case of disputes within or between ministries. In 1970 the PMO had a staff of 70, in 1980 of 192, in 1990 of 124, in 2000 of 227 (Paloheimo 2002: 213), and 243 people worked for the PM in late 2007.

There are two kinds of government plenary meeting, those chaired by the prime minister and those chaired by the president. In the latter there is no voting, as the president alone takes the decision. In plenaries chaired by the prime minister, however, voting is used (the decision rule being a simple majority), but decisions are taken collegially (Paloheimo 2003: 226). Besides plenary meetings, the work of the cabinet is coordinated through four statutory ministerial committees chaired by the prime minister: the Cabinet Committee on Foreign and Security Policy, the Cabinet Finance Committee, the Cabinet Committee on Economic Policy and, since 1995, the Cabinet Committee on European Union Affairs. The full plenary is seldom the place where decisions are in reality taken, and hence the work carried out in ministerial committees or at the level of individual ministers has become increasingly relevant in terms of understanding where power lies within the cabinet. However, the most important decisions are taken in discussions between the leaders of the coalition parties. The same applies to planning the government's agenda (Paloheimo 2002, 2003; Tiili 2003, 2008).

Individual ministers have become more autonomous actors in recent decades, wielding stronger influence in their fields of competence than before. The number of ministers has stayed fairly constant since the Second World War, but there has been a slight increase, with recent governments having eighteen ministers. The government appointed after the 2007 elections has an all-time high of twenty ministers, twelve of whom are women. The number of ministries has likewise stayed about the same, with the current number being twelve. Since 1970, all ministers have had their own special political advisers, distinct from the civil servants in the ministries. As of 2005, ministers can also have their own state secretaries. In the cabinet appointed after the 2007 elections, just over half of the ministers have such a state secretary. This decentralization of authority from the prime minister and the cabinet to the individual ministers is primarily explained by the increasing workload of the government, and the resulting need to divide labour and delegate power to the line ministers (Nousiainen 2000: 89–92; Paloheimo 2002: 211–14; Paloheimo 2003). Nevertheless, individual action by ministers is strongly constrained by the government program and the agreements between the leaders of the coalition parties – even to the extent that, at least in politically significant matters, the autonomy of Finnish line ministers has been argued to be minimal in comparison with those in other European countries (Nousiainen 2000: 270).

Decentralization applies also to the role of civil servants. Finland is one of the countries where the role of civil servants has arguably become more accentuated in the policy process. However, it must be emphasized that there are very little data on the accountability or control of civil servants. The only real exception is the Nordic study on political coordination in EU matters, according to which in 1998 Finnish civil servants received fewer guidelines or instructions from government than their colleagues in the other Nordic countries (Jacobsson et al. 2004; Lægreid et al. 2004: 355–61). Ministers control the agencies under their jurisdiction, but their steering authority is constrained by the lack of effective appointment and dismissal powers and the legalistic tradition of the Finnish bureaucracy. Particularly noteworthy is that the top civil servants in the ministries, the permanent secretaries, are not appointed by the ministers but by the president. In terms of agenda-setting, legislation and public policy reforms have traditionally been prepared within ministries in committees where both politicians and civil servants are represented. However, the number of such committees has dwindled since their heyday in the 1970s, and they have been replaced by reports produced by non-partisan policy advisers or working groups consisting primarily of civil servants appointed by the ministries (Temmes 2001). The developments indicate a decline in the connection between government members and their political parties and policy formulation and have strengthened the technocratic and legalistic nature of the administration. These changes are part of broader reforms introduced in line with the New Public Management (NPM) doctrine. They have been carried out since the early 1990s, and aim to promote more managerial and cost-effective organization of the central state bureaucracy, including ministries, public agencies, and state-owned companies (Salminen 2001; Temmes 1998, 2003; Temmes and Kiviniemi 1997; Tiihonen 2006).

Partisan Composition

When compared with those of other European countries, Finnish governments are outliers in three respects: their parliamentary support, level of fragmentation, and ideological diversity. Finland used to be characterized by short-lived and unstable governments living under the shadow of the president. Among the former 'Western' European countries, only Italy had more cabinets between 1945 and 2000 than did Finland (Nousiainen 2000). Constitutional reforms have had an impact also on cabinet termination. Now cabinet stability and termination are explained by disputes between the government parties, not by relations between the government and the president. Indeed, it was customary for the government to resign when a presidential election was held, but the last time this happened was in 1982.

In his excellent analysis of the development of Finnish parliamentarism, Nousiainen (2006) divides the post-1945 era into three phases: the period of adjustment following the Second World War (1945–61), parliamentarism in the shadow of the president and corporatism (1962–81), and stable majority parliamentarism (1982–). Table 11.1 contains basic information about Finnish governments formed after the 1983 elections – the first elections held after the long presidency of Urho Kekkonen. The oversized coalitions have controlled safe majorities in the Eduskunta. The centre-right cabinet led by Esko Aho had the narrowest majority, with 57.5 per cent of the seats (53.5% after the Christian Democrats left the government in 1994), while the first 'rainbow' coalition led by Paavo Lipponen controlled as many as 72.5 per cent of the seats. The current government controls nearly two-thirds (63%) of Eduskunta seats. Not surprisingly, the oversized coalitions have ruled without much effective opposition; for an informative analysis of the role of opposition in Finland, see Arter (2006: 177–237).

Measured by the number of effective parties, the Finnish party system is the most fragmented among the 'West' European countries, with an average of 5.1 effective parties between 1945 and 2000 (Mattila and Raunio 2004: 269). No party has at any point since the declaration of independence (1917) come even close to winning a majority of the seats in the parliament, and the lack of a clearly dominant party (such as the Social Democrats in Sweden) has necessitated cooperation between the main parties. Thus, the overwhelming majority of Finnish governments have been cross-bloc coalitions, bringing together parties from the left and the right. Reflecting the fragmentation of the party system and the tradition of forming majority governments, the mean number of parties represented in cabinet between 1945 and 2000 was 3.5, the highest figure among 'Western' European countries (Mattila and Raunio 2004: 269). Despite their size and ideological heterogeneity, the gov-

Table 11.1
Finnish Governments, 1983–2009

Government	Government parties	Appointed	Share of seats controlled by the government (%)	Length of the government program (in words)	Reason for cabinet termination
Sorsa VI	SDP, KESK, SMP, RKP	06.05.1983	61.5	1,788	Elections
Holkeri a	KOK, SDP, SMP, RKP	30.04.1987	65.5	2,861	Dispute about state budget
Holkeri b	KOK, SDP, RKP	28.08.1990	61	2,861	Elections
Aho a	KESK, KOK, RKP, KD	26.04.1991	57.5	2,697	Pro-EU stance of the government
Aho b	KESK, KOK, RKP	28.06.1994	53.5	2,697	Elections
Lipponen	SDP, KOK, VAS, VIHR, RKP	13.04.1995	72.5	4,541	Elections
Lipponen II a	SDP, KOK, VAS, VIHR, RKP	15.04.1999	70	6,711	Government decision to build a fifth nuclear reactor
Lipponen II b	SDP, KOK, VAS, RKP	31.05.2002	64.5	6,711	Elections
Jäätteenmäki	KESK, SDP, RKP	17.04.2003	58.5	12,187	Personal dispute between the PM and SDP about the conduct of the election campaign
Vanhanen I	KESK, SDP, RKP	24.06.2003	58.5	12,024	Elections
Vanhanen II	KESK, KOK, VIHR, RKP	19.04.2007	63	15,304	Elections

Source: updated from Nousiainen (2000: 276–7). The letters 'a' and 'b' in the first column indicate a change in the party composition of the government. For example, 'Aho a' became 'Aho b' when the KD left the cabinet because of the pro-EU stance of the government. KD = Christian Democrats; KESK = Centre Party; KOK = National Coalition; RKP = Swedish People's Party; SDP = Social Democratic Party; SMP = Rural Party; VAS = Left Alliance; VIHR = Green League.

ernments formed since 1983 have been surprisingly stable. The only exception was the short-lived coalition between the Centre Party, the Social Democrats, and the Swedish People's Party that took office after the elections held in March 2003. Prime Minister Anneli Jäätteenmäki was forced to resign in June of that year after allegations concerning her use of secret Foreign Ministry documents during the election campaign. The same three parties formed a new cabinet immediately after Jäätteenmäki had resigned. In addition, three small coalition partners have left governments: the Rural Party in 1990 over budgetary disagreements, the Christian Democrats in 1994 owing to the government's pro-EU stance, and the Green League in 2002 because of the decision to build a fifth nuclear reactor. These defections did not threaten the overall stability of the cabinets.

These governments have as a rule included two of the three main parties, the Social Democrats, the Centre Party, and the National Coalition. Between 1995 and 2003 Finland was ruled by a rainbow government, which brought together the Social Democrats, the National Coalition, the Left Alliance, the Swedish People's Party, and the Green League (Jungar 2002). According to Nousiainen (2000: 270), the formation of that coalition indicated that 'the traditional bloc boundary of the party system has lost much of its importance.' Since the 2007 elections, Finland has been governed by a centrist coalition bringing together the Centre Party, the National Coalition, the Green League, and the Swedish People's Party.

Having introduced the main features of Finnish governments, we shall next analyse how the government has responded to the challenges posed by decentralization and the delegation of authority to both individual ministers and the bureaucracy.

Providing Central Direction to Governance in Finland

Governments have a variety of strategies and instruments available for providing central direction to policy-making. In Finland the most important policy coordination tools can be divided into the two following categories.

Forums for political and administrative coordination
- Mandatory cabinet committees
- Various groups of ministers
- Meeting of the permanent secretaries

- Meeting of the leaders of the government parties
- Meeting of the political advisers of the leaders of the government parties

Coordinating processes
- The government program monitoring process (GSD)
- Government intersectoral policy programs
- Other strategies and programs with a more limited focus
- Frame budget and annual budget process
- Preparation of the government's reports to the Eduskunta in various policy areas

In this section we shall primarily focus on two interrelated mechanisms that are of particular importance in Finland: the role of the government program, and the new process of monitoring its implementation and horizontal coordination through the government's intersectoral policy programs. (The roles of the cabinet ministerial committees and the meetings of the leaders of the government parties have already been explored in the previous section.) The rationale for first discussing the increasing role of the government program is that the coordination mechanisms and strategies serve mainly to oversee the implementation of the program.

Government Program

Prior to a constitutional amendment in 1991, the cabinet was not obliged to present its program in the Eduskunta. A new vote of investiture was first used in 1995, when the rainbow coalition headed by Paavo Lipponen took office. Under the new constitution, the government shall without delay submit its program to the parliament in the form of a statement, which is then followed by a debate and a mandatory confidence vote, in which the government must obtain a simple majority. By approving the program, the government parties commit themselves to abiding by it. However, one can also argue that the introduction of the investiture vote strengthens the parliament, as it enables the individual government parties to at least set certain ex ante limits or guidelines for government behaviour (Paloheimo 2003: 232; Aula 2003: 103–4).

The programs of Finnish governments are in international comparison long and detailed, outlining the priorities and policy objectives of the cabinet for the various policy areas. This does not necessarily apply to all policy sectors contained in the program or say that the program would be a coherent document; while the programs contain detailed and specific objectives for some policy areas, they have been vaguer on other matters, with much depending on the ability of the coalition partners to find agreement on specific questions (Tiili 2008). The length of the programs is primarily explained by the high number of parties forming the government and the need to commit them (and their party groups) to established rules and policies. The programs have become much longer and more detailed over the decades, particularly since the early 1980s. Whereas the program of the Sorsa VI government, appointed in 1983, contained 1,788 words, the program of the Vanhanen cabinet from 2007 contained 15,304 words (Table 11.1). There was a major leap at the turn of the millennium: the program of the Lipponen II government from 1999 (and 2002 as the program was not rewritten when the Greens left the cabinet) had 6,711 words, but the governments appointed since the turn of the century have drafted programs in excess of 12,000 words. This very recent increase in program size explains why in the leading book on coalition governance the Finnish government programs are in comparative terms described as short (Müller and Strøm 2008).

It is commonly accepted that the program forms the backbone of the cabinet and that it is binding on all the coalition parties (Nousiainen 2000: 278–80; Paloheimo 2003: 228–9). The binding nature of the program and the resulting lack of discussion inside the government have attracted criticism from some leading politicians. Current Minister for Foreign Trade and Development Paavo Väyrynen, who has served in the government during every decade since the 1970s, commented in an interview that 'the most important change concerns the detailed nature of the government program. The real bargaining occurs during the government formation process. When the Cabinet begins its work on the basis of the program, there is not much room for discussion' (Hautamäki 2007; see also Tiili 2004, 2008). Coalition partners invest a lot of resources in bargaining over the program, and the government parties also monitor that their party groups support the agreed program. Bargaining is not only restricted to the coalition partners; representatives from the various ministries and interest groups are heard during the process, with particularly the leading civil servants from the ministries leaving their imprint on the final program (Paloheimo 2003: 228). The cooperation rules between the governing parties' parliamentary groups that have been in use since the early 1980s effectively prevent any disagreements or public conflicts between the government and their party groups. The only exceptions are matters that are clearly 'local' by nature and certain questions of conscience (Nousiainen 2006: 308–10; Wiberg 2006: 191–3).

We shall next turn to the new coordination mechanisms that operate ex post, that is, after the government has been appointed to office. But before that it is necessary to explain the background of the reforms.

Government Strategy Document Process and Government Intersectoral Policy Programs

Background of the Reform

The reforms implemented in 2003 were the outcome of extensive and careful analysis and preparatory work undertaken by Prime Minister Lipponen's second government (1999–2003) which put reforming the central government on its agenda. The present changes stem back to the analysis commissioned by the government from three foreign high-level experts who were asked to identify the most urgent needs for change (Bouckaert et al. 2000). According to these international experts the most important aspect to be changed in the Finnish central government was the sectorized way of managing central government (see also Tiili 2008). The experts pointed out that central government needed to overcome ministerial stovepipes, both politically and managerially. They also advocated, among other things, the primacy of politics in the functioning of central government. As the lack of horizontality was identified and criticised by the evaluators, the government took it as the main target of central government reform.

Thorough background work was done in many working groups and reports analysed the true nature of the problems and identified the proper tools and content for the reform; see, for example, Kekkonen (2001) and VM (2002). Lipponen's government had a group of ministers to deal with the reform. Thus, from the very beginning, there was a strong political impetus. Problems and solutions came under a lively political discussion. Also, a critical number of civil servants from various ministries participated in defining the new working method, and a series of training and development sessions were organized where the proposed model was discussed.

The reason the reform was undertaken is explained by high political interest in the question. What made this reform politically motivated, what were the political interests involved? At least two things can be observed. First, there was the question of citizens' trust in politicians and the administrative machinery. One part of the background work was an extensive study on the trust of the citizens in Finnish ministries. The results were not very encouraging. It was perceived that the government does not necessarily meet the real needs of the citizens when it has to operate with the help of sectorized administrative machinery. The way problems were identified and how they were dealt with within the government were structured by the competencies of the ministries, not the actual needs of the citizens. It was thought that the problem of horizontality was not so much a question of the ministries overlapping and fighting for power. Rather, there were numerous issues that were not taken care of effectively because they fell between sectoral accountabilities. Typical examples were drugs policy and policies concerning children and young people.

Another assumption was that citizens are nowadays much more demanding and better equipped to analyse the real outcomes of political decisions than they used to be. There is a better awareness of the connection between decisions and their impact on people's everyday lives. Politicians are required to show real results and progress in issues they have talked about in the electoral campaign, using language citizens can understand. There is more pressure for politicians to show their own pro-activeness instead of following the advice of sectorized and specialized administrative experts.

As a result of these discussions and analyses, the government ended up in 2002 with a package of recommendations related to enhancing horizontal and more coherent policy-making. The set of actions started to be called Program Management. The main objective was to improve horizontality within central government in order to enhance the implementation of the government program. Instead of trying to solve problems by structural changes, 'box management,' the decision was to go for a much more ambitious objective of reforming the working methods of the government. The strategic objectives of the reform were both political and managerial: to strengthen political steering and to increase horizontality. This overall objective of strengthening policy coordination can be broken down into more specified objectives, which can be summarized as follows:

- To improve the prime minister's possibilities to manage and assess horizontal government action

- To strengthen individual ministers' possibilities to participate in the collective work of the government to enhance effective and well-functioning coordination and networking within central administration
- To profit from modern management tools, based on networking, both administratively and politically

The main concerns around the reform can thus be divided into political as well as administrative and managerial concerns. For the first time in Finland, the borderline between politics and management was overcome in designing public management reforms.

Government Strategy Document (GSD)

As part of the wide reform package called the introduction of Program Management, Prime Minister Matti Vanhanen's first government adopted in 2003 a new method for monitoring the implementation of the government program, the Government Strategy Document (GSD); for more details on the objectives and implementation of the program management reform and on the four policy programs of the Vanhanen I government, see PMO (2007). Earlier the main tool had been a document called the Government Portfolio. The government program used to be specified in the portfolio document by pointing out individual projects, legislative measures, etc., which were then followed up quite technically. The information the government got through this process twice a year mainly concerned what had been done and hardly at all the outcomes and effects of the policies.

As a result, it is understandable that the portfolio document did not raise political interest or discussion. It was far too technical for political debates and was usually handled within the government in a routine way. Significant political debates and solutions took place in different arenas and on different occasions. The ambition of the program management reform was to change this. The idea was that the government would obtain really relevant information about developments within society related to its own operation and decisions. The intention was also to develop strategic tools for the government so that it could more flexibly and legitimately redirect its policies without ruining the basic structure of the government and the division of labour between the various ministers and political parties. The Government Strategy Document is supposed to:

- Be horizontal, which in practice means that it focuses on the particular government intersectoral policy programs, but also on 'other horizontal policies' of the government
- Identify clear effectiveness targets for programs and policies with an indication as to the way of measuring them
- Define sets of indicators for identifying trends in the policy fields most important to the government
- Offer added value to the government program by specifying target-setting in the form of tangible acts needed
- Be consistent with the financial prerequisites, that is, the government's frame budget as well as the annual budgets

With the new horizontally oriented and indicator-based GSD process the role of the PMO has been strengthened, including resources for policy analysis and monitoring of the government's horizontal objectives. The connection between the GSD process and the budgetary process is very important because of the evolving roles of the various actors. From the very beginning, the idea of a strengthened political role of the government program monitoring process was built on the assumption that no formal changes in authority or power between organizations were needed. Therefore the way the roles of the PMO (with responsibility for the evaluation of government program implementation) and the Ministry of Finance (MOF) Budget Office will develop in practice is crucial.

The GSD evaluation process is characteristically a self-evaluation tool of the government aimed at strengthening the knowledge base on which the prime minister and the government as a whole can redirect policies if needed. In the GSD process, the development of various policy sectors is analysed and evaluated systematically to form a picture of the most urgent challenges that the government faces, as well as the effects and sufficiency of government activities. This is supposed to lead to the necessary conclusions for policy decisions, for example, budgetary decisions and other decision-making processes.

The main actor in the preparation of the government strategy evaluation is the PMO's Policy-Analysis Unit under the leadership of the PM's secretary of state. Most of the work related to preparing the evaluation reports to the prime minister and the government, as well as the overall guidance of the process, is conducted by the PMO. Cooperation between the PMO's non-partisan officials and the prime minister's special political advisers is also highly important. In practice, the collection of relevant information and the assessment of the success of the policies are carried out in close collaboration between the PMO, the government intersectoral policy programs, and the ministries. For example, the set of indicators to be used in the evaluation is negotiated and discussed by experts from the PMO, the ministries, and the policy programs. In every ministry there is a special network of officials responsible for coordinating data collection and preparing the positions that the policy programs and the ministries represent in GSD evaluation.

In 2005, for the first time, two special afternoon sessions, so-called government mid-term review sessions (policy forums), were organized. Similarly, in spring 2009 Prime Minister Vanhanen's second government had mid-term review sessions, this time for two whole days. In these sessions ministers had an opportunity to concentrate on major policy developments and to discuss them freely without having to make concrete decisions in that particular situation. The idea was not only to evaluate the effectiveness of the policies, but also to form an overall picture of major developments in society by the middle of the government's term and to draw policy conclusions for the remaining period. This was a part of the program management reform that had not been foreseen or planned, but which emerged spontaneously based on political will.

The evaluation data collected by PMO were available to the ministers before the mid-term review sessions, and were presented in a very concise form on paper. But the most important thing was that the data were presented orally by the ministers with their own analyses. These government mid-term policy-review sessions have been estimated quite unanimously to have been successes. Certain new political initiatives can also be identified to be consequences of these political discussions. For instance, as a consequence of the 2005 review session a reform of the municipal structures providing the major welfare services was started – a highly political and sensitive subject whose implementation will take many years. The timing of the government mid-term review sessions was planned so that they took place close to, but well before, the government's annual frame budget meeting. It was important that there was some time for political negotiations after the review sessions but before final decisions had to be made at the frame budget meeting. It was also important that enough time was reserved for analytical political discussions between government members.

Government's Intersectoral Policy Programs

In order to strengthen horizontality in government operations, the first Vanhanen Cabinet also adopted in 2003 another new working method and way to organize its work, the intersectoral policy programs. The most important horizontal priorities of the government were organized as policy programs dealing with all the political questions and decisions related to the program area. Prime Minister Vanhanen's first government identified four policy programs in its government program: employment policy, entrepreneurship policy, information society, and citizen participation. Vanhanen's second government in its turn launched three policy programs with the themes of employment, entrepreneurship, and work life; health promotion; and the well-being of children, youth, and families (http://www.vn.fi/toiminta/politiikkaohjelmat/en.jsp).

When the government starts its term with new policy programs, it names the ministers designated as coordinating ministers, sometimes also called program ministers. This means a minister who, in addition to her own portfolio, carries political responsibility for the horizontal policy program in question. It is worth noting that these are not ministers without portfolio. No formal ministerial powers have been changed, but the coordinating minister can make, for example, budget proposals in the areas of responsibility of other ministers in the name of the program. The coordinating ministers can come from any sector, but in reality they have been chosen from areas quite evidently related to the program in question; for example, the minister of labour coordinated the employment policy program in 2003–07. In the first Vanhanen government there was an interesting case, the information society program, which was chaired by Vanhanen himself. A coordinating group of ministers has also been set up for all of the policy programs. This is important because all political decisions related to the programs are coordinated in these groups.

On the managerial side, the success of the full time program director is critical. Program directors do not have any formal powers. Their challenge is to succeed in running a network of representatives from various ministries participating in the program work, getting them to make new initiatives in order to achieve common goals. The policy programs are run within the traditionally structured state budget with fairly small financial resources directly allotted to the program The role of a program director has been described as 'not having formal power but influence.' This is also true in reality. One of the program directors has described this new management style as 'management by asking.' Program directors have often appeared in the media and have made new openings and initiatives, which 'normal' civil servants would not necessarily have done. Program directors are located in the ministries of the coordinating ministers.

It is worth noting that at least so far the government intersectoral policy programs have not been given any formal powers, either administrative or budgetary. Their influence is based on political support. The difference between these new types of policy programs and the traditional interministerial working groups is that the former have been dedicated a special status in the government program. It is underlined that intersectoral policy programs are *programs of the government* as a collective, whereas the other horizontal constructions are usually initiated by sectoral ministers/ministries and are from the beginning identified with a certain ministerial sector, even if they involve other sectors too. However, lack of formal powers has been considered as a weakness of the present form of intersectoral policy programs.

Conclusion

Achieving efficient central coordination within the government is no easy task. In Finland the ideologically heterogeneous multiparty coalitions create further challenges for both horizontal and vertical coordination inside the executive branch. But in the evaluation report on Finnish program management, including the new GSD process and the intersectoral policy programs, it was concluded that the experiences of the program management system were to a large extent positive (VNK 2005).

There was a common and shared view that the reform had taken major steps forward in terms of the main objectives set, that is, strengthened political steering of central government and increased effectiveness in managing horizontal policy issues within the government. The policy programs have provided a better opportunity to place on the political agenda questions that require painful solutions. The strength of the policy programs seems to lie in their effectiveness in initiating new political undertakings and underlining the importance of these policy areas. Policy programs have also stimulated the handling of horizontal issues within ministries. They inspire civil servants to participate in new combinations in the handling of policy issues. Program directors have also succeeded in bringing new dynamics into administration. But according to the evaluation report there were nonetheless still elements that needed to be either changed or strengthened in the system if it was to serve horizontality in the government in the most appropriate way. It was stated that the government had not yet profited enough from the opportunities for coordination offered by the new system.

Comparing the achievements and the two main objectives of the reform, the results of the evaluation report were somewhat surprising. There was a presumption that if there were some weaknesses or difficulties in the new system, the problems would be more on the administrative than the political side. But the evaluation indicated the opposite. Civil servants considered that the reform had strengthened political steering in horizontal policy areas. In contrast, in the eyes of ministers and in the everyday life of the government, the policy programs did not yet occupy a very important position. Program management has not changed political preparation to a remarkable extent, but cooperation and coordination in the preparatory work by civil servants seems to have improved significantly. However, it can also be argued that the system of government program monitoring reduces political fragmentation within the coalition governments, by putting a lot of weight on the collective self-assessment of government policies.

The program management system in Finland seems to evolve continuously. The present government, in office since 2007, has adjusted the original model mainly regarding the monitoring of the government program. There is now an even stronger emphasis on indicator-based analysis, with the government clearly underlining the importance of evidence-based policy-making. This means that the indicator data offered by expert civil servants and research community are growing in importance. The functioning and effectiveness of the present three intergovernmental policy programs have not yet been systematically evaluated. It seems, though, that the characteristics of the objectives of any such program are vital to the way they operate and what they can achieve. For example, two of the present programs, the one to promote health and the one concentrating in the problems of the children and youth, deal with policies that are mainly implemented by municipalities. As a consequence, the tools available for the intersectoral programs are to a large extent those of communicating and promoting 'the good message' of the government. These intersectoral programs necessarily also raise very profound questions related to the alternative ways to influence effective public service delivery from the centre, for example, the choice between information or binding norms as steering mechanisms. At this stage, it seems that the existence of intersectoral policy programs challenges the present situation in Finland, where much binding legislation has been replaced by soft steering with the introduction of NPM in the early 1990s. An interesting question for the future is whether there is the political will to give these intersectoral programs a stronger role in coordinating hard political conflicts. This would obviously require giving them more formal and budgetary powers vis-à-vis sectoral ministries. And this in turn would further challenge the fragmentation of the Finnish governance system.

Recent efforts in Finland have undoubtedly improved central coordination of government decision-making. Yet, it is very difficult to evaluate the extent to which the prime minister and sectoral ministers are effectively in control of the policy processes. After all, the establishment of these formal institutional steering mechanisms was mainly a response to observed weaknesses in ensuring central coordination of public policy-making. With information and policy expertise in an increasingly influential role at all stages of the policy process, the success of even carefully designed coordination structures depends a lot on the commitment of the cabinet ministers, not least on the commitment and 'ownership' of the prime minister of these new mechanisms.

REFERENCES

Arter, D. (2006). *Democracy in Scandinavia: Consensual, Majoritarian or Mixed?* Manchester: Manchester University Press.

Aula, M.K. (2003). Eduskunta Suomen poliittisessa järjestelmässä. In P. Saukkonen (ed.), *Paikkana politiikka: Tietoa ja tulkintoja Suomen poliittisesta järjestelmästä.* Helsinki: Acta Politica 26, Yleisen valtio-opin laitos, Helsingin yliopisto, 93–126.

Bouckaert, G., D. Ormond, and B.G. Peters. (2000). *A Potential Governance Agenda for Finland.* Helsinki: Ministry of Finance.

Hautamäki, Jaakko. (2007). Paavo Väyrynen: Hallitus käy varsin vähän sisäisiä keskusteluja. *Helsingin Sanomat* (11 June).

Jacobsson, B., P. Lægreid, and O.K. Pedersen. (2004). *Europeanization and Transnational States: Comparing Nordic Central Governments.* London: Routledge.

Jungar, A.-C. (2002). A Case of Surplus Majority Government: The Finnish Rainbow Coalition. *Scandinavian Political Studies* 25/1: 57–83.

Jyränki, A., and J. Nousiainen. (2006). *Eduskunnan muuttuva asema: Suomen eduskunta 100 vuotta, osa 2.* Helsinki: Edita.

Kekkonen, S. (2001). *Hallituksen yhteisen poliittisen johtamisen vahvistaminen. Keinona ohjelmajohtaminen.* Helsinki: Valtiovarainministeriö.

Lægreid, P., R.S. Steinthorsson, and B. Thorhallsson. (2004). Europeanization of Central Government Administration in the Nordic States. *Journal of Common Market Studies* 42/2: 347–69.

Mattila, M., and T. Raunio. (2004). Does Winning Pay? Electoral Success and Government Formation in 15 West European Countries. *European Journal of Political Research* 43/2: 263–85.

Müller, W.C., and K. Strøm. (2008). Coalition Agreements and Cabinet Governance. In K. Strøm, W.C. Müller, and T. Bergman (eds.), *Cabinets and Coalition Bargaining: The Democratic Life Cycle in Western Europe.* Oxford: Oxford University Press, 159–99.

Nousiainen, J. (2000). Finland: The Consolidation of Parliamentary Governance. In W.C. Müller and K. Strøm (eds.), *Coalition Governments in Western Europe.* Oxford: Oxford University Press, 264–99.

– (2001). From Semi-presidentialism to Parliamentary Government: Political and Constitutional Developments in Finland. *Scandinavian Political Studies* 24/2: 95–109.

– (2006). Suomalainen parlamentarismi. In *Eduskunnan muuttuva asema. Suomen eduskunta 100 vuotta, osa 2.* Helsinki: Edita, 179–335.

Paloheimo, H. (2001). Divided Government in Finland: From a Semi-presidential to a Parliamentary Democracy. In Robert Elgie (ed.), *Divided Government in Comparative Perspective.* Oxford: Oxford University Press, 86–105.

– (2002). Pääministerin vallan kasvu Suomessa. *Politiikka* 44/3: 203–21.

– (2003). The Rising Power of the Prime Minister in Finland. *Scandinavian Political Studies* 26/3: 219–43.

– (2005). Finland: Let the Force Be with the Leader – But Who Is the Leader? In T. Poguntke and P. Webb (eds.), *The Presidentialization of Politics: A Comparative Study of Modern Democracies.* Oxford: Oxford University Press, 244–66.

PMO. (2007). *Program Management within the Finnish Government.* Helsinki: Prime Minister's Office Publications.

Raunio, T. (2004). The Changing Finnish Democracy: Stronger Parliamentary Accountability, Coalescing Political Parties and Weaker External Constraints. *Scandinavian Political Studies* 27/2: 133–52.

– (2008): Parlamentaarinen vastuu ulkopolitiikkaan: Suomen ulkopolitiikan johtajuus uuden perustuslain aikana. *Politiikka* 50/4: 250–65.

Raunio, T., and M. Wiberg. (2008). The Eduskunta and the Parliamentarisation of Finnish Politics: Formally Stronger, Politically Still Weak? *West European Politics* 31/3: 581–99.

Salminen, A. (2001). The Reform 'Industry' in the Finnish Government: Towards the New Welfare Idea through the Central and Local Administrative Reforms of the 1980s and 1990s. In B.G. Peters and J. Pierre (eds.), *Politicians, Bureaucrats and Administrative Reform*. London: Routledge, 142–53.

Temmes, M. (1998). Finland and New Public Management. *International Review of Administrative Sciences* 64/3: 441–56.

– (2001). *Määräaikaisen valmistelun kehittäminen*. Helsinki: Valtiovarainministeriö, Hallinnon kehittämisosasto, Tutkimukset ja selvitykset 6.

– (2003). Valtionhallinto: Jatkuvuutta ja muutosta. In P. Saukkonen (ed.), *Paikkana politiikka: Tietoa ja tulkintoja Suomen poliittisesta järjestelmästä*. Helsinki: Acta Politica 26, Yleisen valtio-opin laitos, Helsingin yliopisto, 187–212.

Temmes, M., and M. Kiviniemi. (1997). *Suomen hallinnon muuttuminen 1987–1995*. Helsinki: Edita.

Tiihonen, S. (2006). *Ministeriön johtaminen: Poliittisen ja ammatillisen osaamisen liitto*. Tampere: Tampere University Press.

Tiili, M. (2003). *Ministerit strategisina johtajina: Tutkimushankkeen loppuraportti*. Helsingin yliopiston yleisen valtio-opin laitos ja Valtiovarainministeriön hallinnon kehittämisosasto. Helsinki: Edita.

– (2004). Hallituksen keskustelukulttuuri: Kurkistus kollektiivisen ja kollegiaalisen ulkokuoren alle. *Politiikka* 46/2: 137–42.

– (2008). *Strategic Political Steering after NPM Reforms in Finland*. Helsinki: Acta Politica 34, Department of Political Science, University of Helsinki.

VM. (2002). *Ohjelmajohtaminen valtioneuvostossa: Uusi menettely ja uudet asiakirjat*. Valtioneuvoston ohjelmajohtamisen simulointihankkeen raportti 15.10.2002. Helsinki: Valtiovarainministeriö.

VNK. (2005). *Verkostojohtamisen mahdollisuudet valtioneuvostossa: Politiikkaohjelmien ja hallituksen strategia-asiakirjamenettelyn toimivuus hallitusohjelman toteuttamisessa*. Helsinki: Valtioneuvoston kanslian julkaisusarja.

Wiberg, M. (2006). *Politiikka Suomessa*. Helsinki: WSOY.

PART FIVE

Conclusion

12 Steering Strategies in Western Democracies

CARL DAHLSTRÖM, B. GUY PETERS, and JON PIERRE

Since the 1980s we have seen numerous public sector reforms in Western democracies (Peters and Pierre 2001; Pollitt and Bouckaert 2004). Several of the reform initiatives, most notably New Public Management (NPM) reform, have contributed to a decentring of government. The basic idea of NPM was to boost the efficiency of the public sector by separating policy from the service delivery operations of government, and also specializing and fragmenting government. Thus, by default or design, these reforms have deprived the centre of significant steering capabilities (Peters 2004). However, many scholars have recently noted systematic patterns of the centre's reclaiming some of those steering capabilities. This pattern is referred to as presidentialization (Poguntke and Webb 2005), rebureaucratization (Olsen 2005, 2008), neo-Weberianism (Pollitt and Bouckaert 2004), or post-NPM reforms (Christensen and Lægreid 2008). It is, however, still unclear how widespread these recentring reforms are, and if they have a common rationale.

This volume describes decentring and recentring tendencies in ten Western democracies and places those tendencies in comparative context. As explained in the introduction to this volume several countries first reacted to decentring challenges by continuing to devolve control from the core government, a strategy that we have referred to as the *letting go* strategy. We believe that it is fair to say that the latest years' recentring processes at least to some extent were also reactions to the decentring processes, and thus represent a shift of strategy in the countries that had earlier relied on the strategy of letting go. Therefore, in this concluding chapter we will mostly focus on the recentring processes and the strategies employed to strengthen the executive. In the introduction we pointed out two broad categories of recentring strategies; the *holding on* and the *restoring of the centre* strategy. We will try to identify the commonalities among the ten countries in this volume with regard to the tendencies towards recentring and, more specifically, the evolving holding on and restoring strategies in these different countries.

We agree with Pollitt and Bouckaert (2004) that public sector reform paints a different picture in different jurisdictions (see also, Pollitt 2002), perhaps – given the accounts of globalization as a standardizing and converging force – surprisingly different pictures. Therefore, we believe that, by the same token, the recentring tendencies are not uniform either but follow different paths that are defined by their national context. To capture such differences, we will cluster the countries according to their administrative tradition. Within these traditions there are enough similarities to make it meaningful to speak of a common tradition, but there are sometimes also marked differences within a cluster of countries that we will try to acknowledge. The countries in this volume fall into four categories: Continental Europe (both the Napoleonic and the Germanic countries), the Anglo-American countries, and the Scandinavian countries.

We can observe three different ways of holding on and restoring the centre in the chapters in this volume. Very generally, it is our contention that these recentring strategies are strongest in the Anglo-American countries, which also were the countries that initially most used the letting-go strategy, not so strong in the Scandinavian countries, and even weaker in the Napoleonic and Germanic countries.

The rest of this chapter is divided in four sections. We start by discussing the recentring strategies mentioned in the introduction of this book and to what extent these strategies are used in different types of jurisdictions. Then we discuss what seems to have caused different countries to use different strategies. In this section we also discuses to what extent the recentring process might be seen as a reaction to a previous strategy of letting go. The third section is devoted to a discussion on the consequences of these patterns. Then we summarize and present conclusions and suggestions for further research.

The Use of Holding On and Restoring Strategies in Practice

The chapters in this volume show a variety of challenges facing the centre of government in modern societies. Albeit to a varying extent, all West European countries have been affected by NPM reform and the decentring processes that are integral to these ideas. This is especially true in the Anglo-American countries, not the least in Great Britain (Pollitt and Bouckaert 2004). Martin Smith describes the reactions from the actors in the British government on decentring reforms; the decentring has created a growing frustration in the British Prime Minister's Office (PMO), and as a result the PMO has tried to increase its policy capacity, which can be seen as an example of a shift from a letting go to a restoring strategy.

However, the chapters also show how traditional tensions both within central government and between the central and the local levels of government produce new reform initiatives. Within central government there is an ongoing struggle between line departments and the core executive, often represented by the PMO, creating demands for horizontal coordination (Peters, Rhodes, and Wright 2000). For instance, this pattern is found in the multiparty systems of Finland and Denmark (see chapters by Kekkonen and Runio and by Jensen, this volume).

Sirpa Kekkonen and Tapio Runio show that 'program management,' introduced by Finish Prime Minister Matti Vanhanen in 2003, has been implemented in order to increase horizontal policy coordination on the central level. Program management is a new, intersectional method of organizing policies, which is supposed to strengthen cooperation between different ministries. Although not neutralizing the power struggle between its two strongest actors – the Finance Ministry and the PMO – the Coordination and Economic committees seem to play a similar role in the Danish government.

The French case provides an example of how decentralization challenges the central government. Philippe Bezes and Patrick Le Lidec (this volume) describe how the decentralizing processes in France in the 1980s, 1990s, and 2000s put strain on the strong French central state. Bezes and Le Lidec do, however, strongly emphasize the survival of the hierarchic Napoleonic steering model.

The steering strategies created by these challenges can be divided into three broad groups which relate to the recentring strategies in the following way: (1) holding on by politicization of the core executive, (2) restoring the centre by horizontal coordination of government, and (3) restoring the centre by vertical coordination. We will address these strategies in that order.

Holding On by Politicization of the Core Executive

At the heart of the holding on strategies we find the tighter political control of the state apparatus, which has been observed by many scholars.

In this volume the move towards a more politicized centre is represented foremost by countries that have traditionally had a relatively non-politicized centre. These countries belong primarily to the Scandinavian and the Anglo-American administrative tradition. Sweden, as an example from the Scandinavian group, shows a clear growth of political appointees at the political centre. Carl Dahlström and Jon Pierre (this volume) argue that this development has been driven by a need for more political coordination rather then by mistrust in the professional bureaucracy. In Great Britain a similar development has occurred. Politically appointed special advisers have grown in numbers as well as in importance since New Labour came to power. Political advisers are today a significant source of advice, not the least for the prime minister (Heffernan and Webb 2005).

It is important to underline that the development towards a more politicized centre tends to occur in countries with traditionally low levels of political appointees, such as Sweden and Great Britain. In the Napoleonic and Germanic countries, with higher initial levels of politicization (in this volume represented by France and Germany, respectively), the same growth cannot be identified. In both France and Germany the central power seems to use the relatively high levels of political appointees to steer from the centre (in the French case) or for coordination (in the German case), but at the same time no growth seems to occur.

It should however also be noted that in Denmark – the country in this book with the least influence from political appointees in the executive – no growth is observed (Jensen, this volume). Italy provides another counter-example to the observation that increasing politicization occurs only in the countries with the lowest levels of politicization in terms of political appointees in the executive. Italy belongs to the Napoleonic tradition and has for a long time had a relatively highly politicized centre (Cassese 1999). Francesco Stolfi (this volume) describes how the Italian reforms from the 1990s and onwards have been aimed at increasing vertical coordination by introducing more political appointees, from already high levels. Stolfi does, however, argue that this strategy has failed and instead developed into a clientelistic tool, 'breaking down the very separation of politics and administration' (Stolfi in this volume).

Restoring the Centre by Horizontal Coordination

We referred to the second recentring strategy identified in the introduction as *restoring the centre*. The primary instrument of this strategy is horizontal coordination. There are tendencies to strengthen horizontal coordination on the central level in several of the countries covered in this volume. There is a power struggle between the PMO (or the president's office), on the one hand, and line departments, on the other, in all of the countries covered in this volume; indeed, this tension seems to be endemic to almost any system of government (see Peters, Rhodes, and Wright 2000). This tension has no definite solution and is handled in a variety of ways across time and between different countries. It does, however, seem like the last years of decentring have provoked a reaction of strengthening coordination capacities at the centre. This is probably most spelled out in countries belonging to the Anglo-American tradition, where the British 'joined-up government,' or 'whole of government' as it is sometimes called, approach set the tone. In the late 1990s, the Labour government in Great Britain believed that the government had lost its capacity to act as a coordinated, single actor, and joined-up government was the answer to this challenge (Richards and Smith 2006). It was an attempt to strengthen the policy capacity of the centre that spread to other Anglo-American countries, such as Canada and Australia. In this volume John Halligan reports how this strategy has been carried out in three different ways in Australia: first, at the political level where the prime minister committed himself to a series of political priorities that cut across departmental lines. Second, a range of new processes for increased coordination, including committee and task force initiatives, have been launched. Third, the joined-up government agenda was strengthened by a report indicating how cross-cutting issues should be addressed.

Initiatives for strengthening horizontal coordination have, however, not only occurred in the Anglo-American countries, but also in Italy, where the institutional reform of the 1990s strengthened the prime minister, and in Finland where the program management introduced in the early 2000s was aimed at improving horizontal coordination. Finland provides a very interesting example of central government reform aiming precisely at integrating different line departments. One of the more innovative ways of creating horizontal coordination in the Finish government after the reform is through the 'intersectoral policy programs.' This means that the government assigns ministers who are responsible, not only for their own ministry, but also for coordinating policy programs that cut across different ministries (Kekkonen and Raunio, this volume).

As shown in the chapters on the United States and on Denmark chapters, horizontal coordination is not only a consequence of recent decentring reforms. In both the United States (belonging to the Anglo-

American tradition) and in Denmark (belonging to the Scandinavian tradition) the government steering structure has been complex and rather decentralized since long before the reform wave of New Public Management. As Peters (this volume) points out, governing from the centre in the United States is and always has been a challenge, largely because there is no single centre in the U.S. government. Therefore there is constant pressure for more coordination, but also, as Peters puts it, barriers hindering efficient coordination. Several instruments, such as the operational units within the Executive Office and appointments are available for strengthening the coordination capacity of the President, but these are not new features of governing in the United States. Governments in Denmark fight the same kind of battle, but with very different means. The coordination process is much more informal and works mainly through the committee structure. Here the balance of power between the Coordination Committee, chaired by the prime minister, and the Economic Committee changed in 2000. However, more importantly for the themes of this volume is Jensen's observation (this volume) that the roots of this struggle in Denmark do not come from a New Public Management experience but rather from economic experiences and party political realities.

Restoring the Centre by Vertical Coordination

The restoring strategy also involves more vertical coordination. Most importantly, this strategy concerns growing audit capabilities in the centre of government. This development fits in the general pattern of a more important role for auditing in governing, observed by scholars for more then a decade (Hood et al. 1999; Power 1997). There are reports of reforms strengthening the auditing competence at the centre from almost all of the countries included in this volume. Again this development seems to be led by the Anglo-American countries. In Great Britain, as Smith reports (this volume), the creation of the Prime Minister's Delivery Unit (PMDU) is the most important reform of the PMO. The PMDU creates a government body, close to the prime minister, that has the capability to directly follow up on the prime minister's priorities. It is a forceful tool for focusing the state apparatus on the delivery on one specific policy issue. In Canada the mere growth of analytical capacity in the centre has created a demand for information from line departments. As Savoie notes (in his chapter), 'if one removes prescribed rules and attaches more importance to horizontal government and less to hierarchy, then one has to identify other means to ensure accountability.' In both Great Britain and Canada policy targets and other types of output evaluations have been the most important means used to 'ensure accountability.'

In the Scandinavian countries, and especially in Finland, something similar is happening. One part of the program management reform package is a new form of monitoring implementation, called the Government Strategy Document (GSD). The main actor in the GSD process is the policy analysis unit in the PMO, which has strengthened the role of the PMO not only vertically but also horizontally in the policy-making process.

Politicization and Coordination

We have implied that the tension created both by NPM reforms and more traditional power struggles within government and between the central and local levels of government seem to have created a frustration at the centre, a frustration most clearly spelled out in the Anglo-American countries. The same tensions exist in the other systems, albeit not so overtly.

The politicization response appears especially important for the Anglo-American democracies, perhaps in part because of their majoritarian character (Lijphart 1984). The swings back and forth between control by one party or another, and the need for those parties to produce effective governance while in office has been associated with using more political appointments in government. Multiparty consensual governments, on the other hand, tend to rely more on the permanent civil service with some capacity to serve a range of parties.

Decentring and Recentring Processes

We have now identified three strategic responses used by the centre of government: letting go, on the one hand, and holding on and restoring the centre, on the other hand. But are these decentring and recentring processes causally connected? The accounts presented in this volume suggest that decentring (letting go) and recentring (holding on and restoring) strategies are indeed linked. The recentring strategies identified in the last section are most evolved in the countries where decentring reforms, particularly NPM reforms, have had the most impact. This also represents a shift in strategy in these countries from a letting go strategy to a restoring strategy. The Anglo-American countries, including the countries that Pollitt and Bouckaert (2004: 98) call 'the core NPM group,' are leading the way (back) towards a stronger political centre (probably in the United Kingdom, Canada, and Australia more than in the United States).

The Anglo-American group is followed by the Scandinavian countries, where Sweden seems to be a forerunner when it comes to the holding on strategy and Finland when it comes to the restoring strategy. The countries in the Scandinavian group are often portrayed as reluctant NPM reformers, as the NPM rhetoric has not dominated the public administration discourse as much there as in the Anglo-American countries (Christensen and Lægreid 1998; Grønnegaard Christensen 2001; Pierre 2001; Salminen 2001). Cross-country comparisons show, however, that managerial reforms such as management by objectives (MBO) and performance-related pay (PRP) have been introduced to a large extent in Scandinavia (OECD 2005; Christensen and Laegreid 1998). Among the Scandinavian countries Sweden is probably the country where both MBO and PRP reforms have had the most impact (Dahlström and Lapuente 2008; Sundström 2006). In comparison with the other Scandinavian countries Swedish agencies are also the most independent. This is, however, not a product of agencification, but rather a historically rooted Swedish system of governing (Jacobsson and Sundström 2009).

The continental European countries, belonging to either the Germanic or the Napoleonic administrative traditions, are the countries with the weakest tendencies towards restrengthening the political centre. It is well known that, for example, Germany and France have not embraced the NPM reforms of recent decades to any large extent. Germany is often considered an NPM reform 'laggard' (Thompson 2007: 53–4), and has been referred to as a 'solid rock in rough seas' (Schröter 2001: 61). France, as Bezes and Le Lidec note in their chapter (this volume), has not lost its Napoleonic structure, and compared with the Anglo-American countries France is relatively unaffected by NPM reforms.

Taken together these reform patterns seem to suggest that recentring processes are first and foremost a reaction on earlier decentring. Martin Smith describes the reasons for recentring in Britain thus: 'Public sector reform has fragmented the processes of governance frustrating government concerned to implement policy goals. Consequently, New Labour has put considerable effort into institutionalizing the power of the Prime Minister and increasing the policy and delivery capability of the centre' (Smith 2009: 23). Similar observations are made in the chapters on Australia and Canada, and to some extent also in the one on Sweden.

The observations made here support Pollitt and Bouckaert's analysis regarding a particular neo-Weberian reform pattern of central and northern Europe. As Pollitt and Bouckaert (2004: 99) note, countries outside the Anglo-American hemisphere have often been portrayed as NPM laggards. Pollitt and Bouckaert offer an alternative, and more positive, interpretation of the development in central and northern Europe. In their analysis, countries in central and northern Europe are not NPM laggards; they have simply chosen another way of modernizing the public sector, and they call this the neo-Weberian state (Pollitt and Bouckaert 2004: 99).

The reform patterns disclosed in this volume are compatible with the neo-Weberian-state analysis. Furthermore, looking at the decentring and recentring cycles it does seem like the neo-Weberian-state model is the more stable model, modernizing government without creating a contra-movement, while the NPM model is more disruptive. The German case is perhaps the clearest example of the reassertion, or indeed the persistence, of the neo-Weberian style of governing with the professional public service continuing to play a dominant role in governing.

Is the Restoring Strategy and Media Attention Creating Disruptive Governance?

Theory predicts that a stronger centre leads to stable steering from the centre and long-term strategies of reform. The chapters in this volume do, however, tell a partly different story. A stronger centre allows policy-makers to respond more swiftly to policy challenges and to focus on specific issues, but it does not in and of itself provide the tenacity to follow the same policy issues for any longer stretch of time. This is especially true if the centre is forced to play a reactive role, something that ministerial accountability and media attention might force even a strong centre to. Such a reactive rather than a proactive policy role can lead to non-deliberate behaviour of the political centre, where short-term objectives trump long-term policy goals.

Again, the tendency towards what might be called 'disruptive steering' seems to be most viable in the Anglo-American countries. In Canada, the media to a large extent indirectly choose what policy issues the political centre will be involved in. As Donald Savoie suggests in his chapter, 'media attention can, on very short notice, turn an issue, however trivial, into an important file.'

The British situation is quite similar, particularly after the creation of the Prime Minister's Delivery Unit (PMDU). Smith describes the creation of PMDU as the 'most important development in terms of strengthening the centre' in Britain. The PMDU has given the prime minister in Britain a forceful tool for policy intervention. Comparable with Canada the reason for intervention has nor, however, been to ensure long-term policy goals, but rather 'a mechanism that quickly responds to the aspects of public service that are annoying voters and therefore are electorally problematic' (Smith, this volume). The presidency in the United States has not required new structures to have that capacity to govern, but during the administration of George W. Bush the increasing degree of political control over appointments and decisions reflected a comparable move towards more political control (Lewis 2008).

It is probably true that the media affect the policy agenda in a similar manner in all Western democracies. We have certainly no reason to believe that the media are affecting public discourse more strongly in the Anglo-American countries than in other countries. The strengthening of the centre and the possibilities this gives to the PMO for direct involvement in policy issues do, however, seem to improve the effect of media influence on policy priorities. Here the German Chancellery can provide a counter-example. Julia Fleischer (this volume) underlines the Chancellery's coordinating role. She describes how it is more involved in creating coherent policy than in enforcing policy initiatives of its own. Another example, but this time from the Scandinavian group, can be found in Sweden. There, Cabinet ministers are notoriously careful not to intervene in agencies' deliberation of specific matters, something that could trigger parliamentary scrutiny and critique for 'ministerial steering,' which is prohibited by law in Sweden (Jacobsson and Sundström 2009). Of course, if you cannot intervene in specific cases the media effect is hampered.

Conclusion

Faced with the need to provide some central direction to governance, central government offices have a range of alternative strategies and instruments available. This volume has identified three instruments increasingly used by governments. One way of *holding on* to increase political control has been to increase the number of political advisers and other politically appointed staff in the executive, a strategy that has been referred to as the 'presidentialization of politics' or a 'thickening of government' or simply 'politicization' (Poguntke and Webb 2005; Light 1995; Peters and Pierre 2004). Another strategy, used by some governments, has been to restore central control by implementing institutional and procedural measures that increase horizontal coordination, as in the case of the Blair government's joined-up strategy. Finally, a third strategy to reassert central government control has been to emphasize strategic management and coordination in an attempt to provide more vertical coordination with less overt political involvement; governments have therefore strengthened their auditing capabilities.

These three strategies seem to be most used in the countries belonging to the Anglo-American administrative tradition, suggesting that recentring is indeed a reaction of the last decade's tendencies to decentring created by NPM reforms. That said, however, a number of the other political systems also displayed some of the same tendencies towards restoring more power to the centre. This tendency has been more apparent for the coordination strategies, for example, in Finland and Denmark, but it still represents an important movement to empower the centre. The observations made in this volume thus point out that administrative experiences give some explanation to why different strategies are used in different countries. This is, however, probably only a fragment of the story and further research is indeed needed to more fully understand the dynamics of decentring and recentring tendencies.

Another observation from this volume is that recentring does not necessarily mean more stability. Several of the chapters in this book provide examples pointing in the opposite direction. The reason for this is that no centre can be strong enough to steer all policy areas in detail. A strong centre can, however, be strong enough to focus on one policy area at a time, crowding out a stable leadership on agency, or at local level. This becomes especially problematic when the centre is reactive to media, which fairly often seems to be the case. Paradoxically, a stronger centre might then create an unstable and inconsistent government that is less effective in governing.

This movement back towards the centre may also simply be one more movement in the continuing attempts to find the right format for governing. This search is difficult, as it involves matching changing environmental conditions with changing political practices and governance requirements. The centralization that is to some extent being created at present may soon be seen as too centralized, and then yet another round of reform may begin.

REFERENCES

Cassese, S. (1999). Italy's Senior Civil Service: An Ossified World. In E.C. Page and V. Wright (eds.), *Bureaucratic Elites in Western European States*. Oxford: Oxford University Press.

Christensen, T., and P. Lægreid. (1998). Administrative Reform Policy: The Case of Norway. *International Review of Administrative Sciences* 64: 457–75.
– (2008). NPM and Beyond: Structure, Culture and Demography. *International Review of Administrative Sciences* 74: 7–23.
Dahlström, C., and V. Lapuente. (2008). *Do You Believe Me? Public Sector Incentive Systems in Japan, Korea, Spain, and Sweden*. QoG Working Paper Series 2008: 25. Gothenburg: Quality of Government Institute, University of Gothenburg.
Grønnegard Christensen, J. (2001). Bureaucratic Autonomy as a Political Asset. In B.G. Peters and J. Pierre (eds.), *Politicians, Bureaucrats and Administrative Reform*. London: Routledge.
Heffernan, R., and P. Webb. (2005). The British Prime Minister: Much More than 'First among Equals.' In T. Poguntke and P.D. Webb (eds.), *The Presidentialization of Politics: A Comparative Study of Modern Democracies*. Oxford: Oxford University Press.
Hood, C., C. Scott, O. James, G. Jones, and T. Travers. (1999). *Regulation Inside Government: Waste-Watchers, Quality Police, and Sleaze-Busters*. Oxford: Oxford University Press.
Jacobsson, B., and G. Sundström. (2009). Between Autonomy and Control: Transformation of the Swedish Administrative Model. In P.G. Roness and H. Stætren (eds.), *Change and Continuity in Public Sector Organizations*. Bergen: Fagbokforlaget.
Lewis, D.E. (2008). *The Politics of Presidential Appointments*. Princeton: Princeton University Press.
Light, P. (1995). *Thickening Government: Federal Hierarchy and the Diffusion of Accountability*. Washington, DC: Brookings Institution.
Lijphart, A. (1984). *Democracies: Patterns of Majoritarian and Consensus Government in Twenty-One Countries*. New Haven: Yale University Press.
OECD. (2005). *Performance-Related Pay Policies for Government Employees*. Paris: Athor.
Olsen, J.P. (2005). Maybe It Is Time to Rediscover Bureaucracy. *Journal of Public Administration Research and Theory* 16: 1–24.
– (2008). The Ups and Downs of Bureaucratic Organization. *Annual Review of Political Science* 11: 13–37.
Painter, M., and B.G. Peters. (2010). Administrative Traditions in Comparative Perspective. In M. Painter and B.G. Peters (eds.), *Tradition and Public Administration*. New York: Palgrave Macmillan.
Peters, B.G. (2004). Back to the Centre? Rebuilding the State. In A. Gamble and T. Wright (eds.), *Restating the State?* Oxford: Blackwell.
Peters, B.G., and J. Pierre. (2001). Civil Servants and Politicians: The Changing

Balance. In B.G. Peters and J. Pierre (eds.), *Politicians, Bureaucrats and Administrative Reform*. London: Routledge.
– (2004). Introduction. In B.G. Peters and Jon Pierre (eds.), *Politicization of the Civil Service in Comparative Perspective*. London: Routledge.
Peters, B.G., R.A.W. Rhodes, and V. Wright. (eds.). (2000). *Administering the Summit: Administration of the Core Executive in Developed Countries*. London: Macmillian.
Pierre, J. (2001). Parallel paths? Administrative Reform, Public Policy and Politico-Bureaucratic Relationships in Sweden. In B.G. Peters and J. Pierre (eds.), *Politicians, Bureaucrats and Administrative Reform*. London: Routledge.
Poguntke, T., and P.D. Webb (eds.). (2005). *The Presidentialization of Politics: A Comparative Study of Modern Democracies*. Oxford: Oxford University Press.
Pollitt, C. (2002). Clarifying Convergence. *Public Management Review* 4: 471–92.
Pollitt, C., and G. Bouckaert. (2004). *Public Management Reform*. Oxford: Oxford University Press.
Power, M. (1997). *Audit Society: Rituals of Verification*. Oxford: Oxford University Press.
Richards, D., and M. Smith. (2006). The Tensions of Political Control and Administrative Autonomy: From NPM to a Reconstituted Westminster Model. In T. Christensen and P. Lægreid (eds.), *Autonomy and Regulation*. London: Edward Elgar.
Salminen, A. (2001). The Reform 'Industry' in the Finnish Government: Towards the New Welfare Idea through the Central and Local Administrative Reforms of the 1980s and 1990s. In B.G. Peters and J. Pierre (eds.), *Politicians, Bureaucrats and Administrative Reform*. London: Routledge.
Schröter, E. (2001). A Solid Rock in Rough Seas? Institutional Change and Continuity in the German Federal Bureaucracy. In B.G. Peters and J. Pierre (eds.), *Politicians, Bureaucrats and Administrative Reform*. London: Routledge.
Smith, M.J. (2009). *Power and the State*. London: Palgrave.
Sundström, G. (2006). Management by Results: Its Origin and Development in the Case of the Swedish State. *International Public Management Journal* 9: 399–427.
Thompson, J.R. (2007). Labor-Management Relations and Partnerships: Were They Reinvented? In B.G. Peters and J. Pierre (eds.), *The Handbook of Public Administration*. London: Sage.

Contributors

Philippe Bezes is senior research fellow at the National Centre for Scientific Research (CNRS) and member of the Centre d'Etudes et de Recherches de Sciences Administratives et Politiques (CERSA, Université of Paris 2, France). He is also lecturer in public policy and public administration at Sciences-Po in Paris. His academic interests are administrative reforms, comparative public administration, institutional change, and public policy. He recently published the book *Réinventer l'Etat: Les réformes de l'administration française (1962–2008)* (Presses Universitaires de France, 2009), and he has published several articles in English in edited books and journals.

Carl Dahlström is associate professor at the Quality of Government Institute and Department of Political Science, University of Gothenburg. His research is concerned with comparative and historical perspectives on public administration and public policy-making. His papers have appeared or are due to appear in international academic journals, such as *Journal of Public Administration Research and Theory, Governance, Journal of European Public Policy, Journal of Public Policy,* and *Scandinavian Political Studies.*

Julia Fleischer is a senior research fellow at the Faculty of Economics and Social Sciences at the University of Potsdam. Her research interests include comparative public administration, executive politics, and risk governance. Currently, she is working on a comparative research project analysing the organizational and policy responses of Western European governments to climate change and georisks.

John Halligan is professor of public administration, University of

Canberra. Recent co-authored books are *Performance Management in the Public Sector* (Routledge, 2010); *The Centrelink Experiment: Innovation in Service Delivery* (Australian National University Press, 2008); *Managing Performance: International Comparisons* (Routledge, 2008). His research interests are comparative public management and governance, specifically public sector reform, with a focus on Australia and other Anglophone countries.

Lotte Jensen is professor of core executive governance at the Department of Management, Politics and Philosophy, Copenhagen Business School. She has published widely on core executive governance in Denmark and in a comparative perspective, focusing particularly on the role of finance ministries and institutional design of core executive coordination, expenditure politics, and budgeting.

Sirpa Kekkonen works in the Finnish Prime Minister's Office as head of government program monitoring in the Policy-Analysis Unit. She has wide experience in reforming steering mechanisms of the central government and is specialized in horizontal governance and evidence-based policy-making. She has been the key actor in designing the program management system in Finland and is a frequently used speaker both domestically and internationally on her fields of expertise.

Patrick Le Lidec is senior research fellow at the National Centre for Scientific Research (CNRS) and member of the Centre d'Etudes et de Recherches de Sciences Administratives et Politiques (CERSA, Université of Paris 2, France). He is also lecturer in public administration at Sciences-Po and at the University of Paris 1. His academic interests are administrative reforms, federalism and decentralization, local government reforms, and comparative public administration. He won the CNRS/GRALE prize for his doctoral dissertation.   .

B. Guy Peters holds a PhD degree from Michigan State University (1970) and honorary doctorates from two European universities. He is currently Maurice Falk Professor of American Government at the University of Pittsburgh, and also professor of comparative governance at Zeppelin University in Germany. He also has honorary professorships in Hong Kong, Belgium, and Denmark. He has published 40 books and over 300 articles, including *The Handbook of Public Administration, Institutional Theory in Political Science*, and *Debating Institutionalism*. The first two were co-edited with Jon Pierre, and the last with Jon Pierre and Gerry Stoker. He was founding co-editor of *Governance* (now rated as the number one international journal in policy and administration), and is now founding co-editor of the *European Political Science Review*. He is also an associate editor of the *International Encyclopedia of Political Science*.

Jon Pierre is professor of political science at the University of Gothenburg. He is also adjunct professor at the University of Pittsburgh and 'Professor 2' at the University College in Bodö. He has published extensively on public administration and governance.

Tapio Raunio is professor in political science at the University of Tampere. His research interests include the role of national legislatures and parties in European integration, the European Parliament and Europarties, and the Finnish political system. He has published articles in journals such as the *Comparative European Politics*, *European Journal of Political Research*, *European Union Politics*, *Journal of Common Market Studies*, *Party Politics*, *Scandinavian Political Studies*, and *West European Politics*. He has also, together with John O'Brennan recently co-edited the volume *National Parliaments within the Enlarged European Union: From 'Victims' of Integration to Competitive Actors*.

Donald J. Savoie holds the Canada Research Chair in Public Administration and Governance at the Université de Moncton. He has published numerous books on public policy, public administration, and governance, and his work has won prizes in Canada, the United States and Europe. He was elected fellow of Canada's National Academy and awarded several honorary degrees from Canadian universities.

Martin Smith is professor of politics at the University of Sheffield. He has published widely on British politics, public policy, and the changing nature of the state. His latest book is *Power and the State* (Palgrave Macmillan, 2009). He is also editor of the journal *Political Studies*.

Francesco Stolfi teaches at the University of Exeter. His research interests focus on Europeanization, public sector and budget reform, the role of political and bureaucratic actors in public sector reform, and the relative explanatory power of institutional and ideational factors in policy change.